Date Due

Challenging Images of Women in the Media

Challenging Images of Women in the Media

Reinventing Women's Lives

Edited by Theresa Carilli and Jane Campbell

LEXINGTON BOOKS
Lanham • Boulder • New York • Toronto • Plymouth, UK

Published by Lexington Books
A wholly owned subsidiary of The Rowman & Littlefield Publishing Group, Inc.
4501 Forbes Boulevard, Suite 200, Lanham, Maryland 20706
www.rowman.com

10 Thornbury Road, Plymouth PL6 7PP, United Kingdom

British Library Cataloguing in Publication Information Available

Library of Congress Cataloging-in-Publication Data
Challenging images of women in the media : reinventing women's lives / edited by Theresa Carilli and Jane Campbell.
p. cm.
Includes bibliographical references and index.
ISBN 978-0-7391-7698-6 (cloth : alk. paper)—ISBN 978-0-7391-7699-3 (electronic)
1. Women in mass media. I. Carilli, Theresa. II. Campbell, Jane.
P94.5.W65C465 2012
305.4—dc23
2012017611

☺™ The paper used in this publication meets the minimum requirements of American National Standard for Information Sciences Permanence of Paper for Printed Library Materials, ANSI/NISO Z39.48-1992.

Printed in the United States of America

We dedicate this book to cancer survivors like us who have crossed a threshold but still have a vision.

Contents

Acknowledgments

We would like to thank our department heads, Dr. Dennis Barbour and Dr. Daniel Punday from the Department of English and Philosophy, and Dr.Yahya Kamalipour from the Department of Communication and Creative Arts for their support on this project. Also, we would like to thank Erin Okamoto Protsman and Ami Kleminski for their help preparing this manuscript. We are excited to share this provocative selection of chapters with our readers.

Introduction to *Challenging Images of Women in the Media: Reinventing Women's Lives*

Theresa Carilli and Jane Campbell

While working at a television station in San Francisco in the 1980s, I learned of a brave African American anchorwoman named Valerie Coleman. Coleman, who was quite a celebrity at the time, was frustrated because she was not allowed to begin the 5 p.m. news report. That task was given only to her male coanchor. Eventually, Coleman resigned in protest. That protest sent shock waves throughout the television market because Coleman was taking a stand for the marginalization of women in the media. Today, female anchors are "allowed" to report on the lead story and can coanchor with another woman. While such progress continues, many gender-related media issues need examination. —Theresa Carilli

For women and the media, the message is anything but clear. While more women contribute to the media as successful news anchors or talk show hosts, depictions of women on reality television shows or in music videos present an entirely different scenario. Like a cake ad followed by a diet commercial, media messages confuse women. While witnessing the success of Oprah as a businesswoman and entertainer who has used her celebrity to pitch political candidates, the likes of Snooki from the reality television show *Jersey Shore* can overshadow the progress of such a powerful woman and institution. The mixed messages that women receive from the media muddle attempts at breaking through the "glass screen," keeping women in a state of constantly questioning their role in global culture.

In our first book, *Women and the Media: Diverse Perspectives* (2005), we demonstrated how global media images of women are problematic. For example, Hello Kitty's absent mouth encourages a silence among Japanese girls and women, all in the name of cuteness. As Kimiko Akita observes in her chapter, "Cuteness: The Sexual Commodification of Women in the Japanese Media," "when I was a woman's junior college teacher in Japan, what struck me most were my observations of supposedly mature students (ages nineteen to twenty-one) wearing "cute" childish outfits, various Hello Kitty items, speaking in "cute" baby-like voices, and behaving with "cute" infantile manners . . . (p. 45). According to Catherine Gillotti in her chapter, "Lesbians in Film: An Examination of Intimate Danger," an authentic lesbian relationship threatens both heteronormativity and male fantasy. Adopting Theresa Carilli's 1998 definition of intimate danger, whereby "the behavior that validates the worldview of one group's existence ultimately threatens the other group" (p. 36), Gillotti demonstrates the marginalization of lesbian relationships through four films. Gloria Gadsden in her chapter "Safety and Restriction: The Construction of Black Women's Sexuality in *Essence* Magazine" explores how oversexualized images of black women render them as societal deviants. Gadsden writes, "categorizing Black women's sexuality as deviant potentially prohibits Black women from creating their own images and re-defining their position as the surveyed group" (p. 120). Orly Shachar in "The Israeli Womb: Images of Gendered Nationalism in the Israeli Press" describes how women's bodies were targeted by a campaign to promote reproduction. Shachar concludes, "when women are defined by their wombs, their entire existence is validated by that one bodily part and its function" (p. 30).

As we reexamined the status of women in the media, we realized that the images have changed, but the messages have remained static or gotten worse. For example, according to Media Report to Women, 2009–2010 statistics for women in the media workforce or women who contribute to the media show small gains but troubling declines, particularly among women in the film industry. According to the most recent report by Martha Lauzen, "in 2009, women comprised 16 percent of all directors, executive producers, producers, writers, cinematographers, and editors working on the top 250 domestic grossing films. This represents a decline of 3 percentage points from 2001 and is even with 2008 figures."

Our first book identified female pioneers like photojournalist Francis Benjamin Johnston, who photographed President McKinley, and Joan Ganz Cooney, who revolutionized television programming for children. Work by women like Cooney and Johnston has far-reaching political implications. Through their work and their lives, these women, like many other media pioneers including journalists Martha Gellhorn and Barbara Walters, introduced a female sensibility which enriched our knowledge of women's experiences.

In a global market which values product and profit over message, women's primary value appears to be as commodities. We offer this book as a journey into what has been termed "post-feminism," an era in which women supposedly no longer need to strive for equality. Yet, in the United States, *Roe vs. Wade* faces the threat of being overturned. Globally, the sex trade industry proliferates, women earn 17 percent less than their male counterparts, and 70 percent of women live in poverty (www.Unifem.org). With these observations in mind, here is a glimpse into this book.

The first section of *Challenging Images of Women in the Media: Reinventing Women's Lives* is entitled "Reinscribing Women's Roles." In this section writers demonstrate that the strides women have made are being erased, reinforcing their powerlessness. In their chapter "'Feeling Good Never Looked Better': Examining Stereotypical Representations of Women in Special K Advertisements," Vanessa Reimer and Rukhsana Ahmed analyze how the cereal's ten-year advertising campaign has become detrimental to women's sense of self. Special K's "feeling good never looked better" slogan, according to the authors, "has been accompanied by advertisements which arguably perpetuate harmful stereotypes about women's bodies and behavior." Kimiko Akita's "Tales from *Ooku*: The Shogun's Inner Palace and the Outer (Mediated) World" describes how Japanese film and television have represented women who were tied to key military leaders from 1600 to 1868 as "shallow, jealous, bullying, vengeful, vicious, violent, untrustworthy, emotional, materialistic, promiscuous, and inferior to men." Akita maintains that the Japanese media, dominated by men, "do not depict authentic Japanese women ancestors, but rather idealized women created from male fantasies." Saman Talib and Zara Idrees demonstrate how the Pakistani media relies on traditional cultural narratives in their chapter, "Pakistani Media and Disempowerment of Women." These authors explore, for example, how the media equate marriage with womanhood and insist on women's frailty and need for rescue by men. And, finally, in this section, Lisa French's "Women in Film: Treading Water but Fit for the Marathon" examines the participation of women in film in several Western industrialized countries, concluding that "the gains women made and the momentum they once achieved have not been sustained."

The second section, "Political Issues," comprises three chapters, maintaining that media agenda-setting still operates in relation to women's issues. In "Mass Media Explain the Global Sex Trade," Anne Johnston, Barbara Friedman, and Autumn Shafer examine the media in its coverage of sex trafficking, noting that even though the mass media contribute to global discourse on sex trafficking, "news organizations are blamed for underre-

porting the problem, misrepresenting the problem, promoting ineffective solutions, and worse." Nicole Defenbaugh and Kimberly Kline argue in "Gendered Construction of HPV: A Post-Structuralist Critique of Gardasil" that
Merck, the pharmaceutical giant which manufactures Gardasil, frames HPV
as a women's issue. Even though Merck has created ads targeting males, this
original framing of HPV contributes to assumptions about illness, disease,
and responsibility. The authors analyze the way in which Gardasil ads oper-
ate as "commodity feminism," targeted at "a seemingly empowered group of
young women." With "Who's Afraid of the Pink *Chaddi*? New Media, Hindutva, and Feminist Agency in India," Saayan Chattopadhyay introduces
readers to a political movement created by a female journalist responding to
a mob attack on a group of women at a pub in India. The journalist, Nisha
Susan, created a Facebook group known as the "Consortium of Pub-going,
Loose, and Forward Women," which attracted forty thousand members. This
group evolved into a formidable Internet movement which gave voice to
women.

Section three, "Westernizing Women," explores how images of the
"sexy" Westernized woman are valued in two Eastern cultures. Wei Luo's
chapter, "*Women of China* Magazine: The 'Modern' Woman in a Discourse
of Consumerism," studies how the images of a women's magazine in China
has changed since the 1990s. Through extensive textual analysis, Luo concludes that *Women of China* presents post-feminist media representations
which privilege "meritocracy and elitism." Elza Ibroscheva's piece, "From
'*Babushki*' to 'Sexy Babes': The Sexing-Up of Bulgarian Women in Advertising," explains that previous portrayals of Soviet women as matronly,
shapeless, asexual, and unattractive have been replaced with a Westernized
notion of the sexy woman. Simultaneously, Bulgarian women, who once had
access to maternity leave, state-sponsored childcare, and abortion, are experiencing diminishing rights.

With section four, "Political Individuals," the authors focus on women
who have contributed to a discourse on media visibility. Steven Carl Smith's
chapter, "For and About Women: Dorothy Jurney and 'The Women's Network,'" lauds the accomplishments of newspaper journalist Dorothy Jurney,
who created "The Women's Network" to help other women locate jobs as
journalists at a time when newspapers did not offer women the same opportunities as men. In "Angela Merkel Has More to Offer: Satirical Images of
Germany's First Female Chancellor," author Lynn Kutch exposes how the
German media struggled with its presentation of Chancellor Merkel. Elizabeth Johnson's chapter, "All Hail the Queen: The Metamorphosis or Selling
Out of Queen Latifah," argues that Queen Latifah often has been cast in a
Mammy role but has debunked this stereotype of Mammy with some of her
films. In "18,000,000 Cracks or How Hillary Almost Became President,"
Lori Montalbano examines Clinton's balancing act as she attempted to build

a palatable image during the 2008 presidential campaign. Finally, section five offers two provocative reflective pieces, one on depictions of full-figured black women by Deatra Sullivan-Morgan, and the other by Theresa Carilli on contributions made by lesbian comics to mainstream television.

About twenty years ago, we developed a course at our university called "Women in the Media." At the time, we didn't know how the class would be received. In an attempt to locate an appropriate text for our course, we found several different books, but none that provided both a feminist vision and a media critique. The dialogue we began in our classroom twenty years ago continues in *Challenging Images of Women in the Media: Reinventing Women's Lives*. The fifteen chapters in this collection address some of the continued challenges faced by women who work in the media and challenges depictions of women in the media. We offer this volume of essays as an assertion that feminist critiques are essential to changing the status quo for women.

With this book, we hope to continue our dialogue about media representations of women, posing the question of whether life has improved for women globally and how the media plays a significant role in answering this question.

Theresa Carilli and Jane Campbell
Purdue University Calumet

I

Reinscribing Women's Roles

Chapter One

"Feeling Good Never Looked Better"

Examining Stereotypical Representations of Women in Special K Advertisements

Vanessa Reimer and Rukhsana Ahmed

Somehow, somewhere, someone must have figured out that [women] will buy more things if they are kept in the self-hating, ever-failing, hungry and sexually insecure state of being aspiring "beauties." —Naomi Wolf (1990); *The Beauty Myth*, p. 49

Advertising is successful, not only because of its audiences' largely dismissive attitudes toward the industry's effectiveness, but also because it relies upon cultural stereotypes that its audiences associate with lived reality as they encounter and enact them in their day-to-day lives. As Kilbourne (1999) aptly notes, advertising is a multi-billion dollar industry that is as effective as it is lucrative. Advertisements that interpolate (creating a binding obligation derived from what is more or less a cultural law) women in accordance with culturally constructed body image norms are of course no exception.

Kellogg's Special K has always taken an arguably innovative approach to its advertisement campaigns, ever since its "Time to get back into things" and "Pinch more than an inch" television marketing campaigns throughout the 1970s and 1980s. Simply put, Special K is a breakfast cereal that has always been marketed as a weight loss aid and has always been marketed almost exclusively to women. However, even within this marketing realm, the company's advertising approach has taken a new direction in the past ten years that is arguably more detrimental in terms of how it represents women and communicates the centrality of slimness to desirable femininity. For instance, in the late 1990s Special K's advertising took an interesting and constructive approach with its progressive "Look good on your own terms"

3

campaign, which manipulated and challenged the very gender norms that it had used to sell its product in the past. Goodman (1998) describes the witty advertisements, where men are shown to complain about having their "mother's thighs," and the voiceover suggests to the female audience that "men don't obsess about these things [so] why do we?" (p. 8).

Recently, however, a product line expansion (including new cereal varieties, snack bars, and even protein water), in accordance with the "Special K Challenge" and the "Feeling good never looked better" campaign, has been accompanied by advertisements which arguably perpetuate harmful stereotypes about women's bodies and behaviors. The question thus arises as to whether Special K advertisements actually represent healthy behaviors for their female audience to emulate, or if they simply necessitate cultural stereotypes of women's bodily fears and anxieties as they encourage women to attain the socially entrenched thin ideal. In what follows, this chapter reviews literature that examines the socially embedded issues of gender inequality, particularly pertaining to cultural bodily expectations which are enacted through gender normative behavior. The chapter then examines and evaluates the representations of women's health in Special K television advertisements through an ethnographic content analysis. Using the lens of feminist theory, the chapter deconstructs the manifest and latent cultural meanings embedded in Special K advertisements' images and messages, focusing specifically on how they present women to relate to food and to their own bodies in pursuit of the healthy lifestyle that Special K promotes through the consumption of its products. The chapter concludes with suggestions for future change that can help remedy the problems that have been identified to reside within the representations and discourses conveyed by the reviewed Special K advertisements, followed by a brief discussion of the limitations of this study.

LITERATURE REVIEW

The appropriate feminine appearance in white North American culture is currently defined by the thin ideal, which is an overarching cultural value that women are expected to demonstrate through perpetual self-control and self-negation; in this respect, a good woman is a thin woman (Arnold & Doran, 2007). As such, a woman's weight is a reflection of her self-control, which is why women are often made to feel guilty; their appearance and weight are completely their responsibility and their appetites in this sense become a social embodiment of shame (Wolf, 1990). This historical issue of physical self-control in all respects is inextricably linked to sexual acts, and this remains a prevalent metaphor in today's advertising realm. Particularly within Catholic religious doctrine, it is acceptable for people to engage in sex for procreation, while sex for pleasure is a sin; the same distinction is made today for women who eat to sustain life and women who eat for pleasure. This double standard that gives men sexual license, but still renders a sexually liberated woman to be a "slut," has created the double standard in which men also have greater oral license than women; a sexually unchaste woman is seen as "fallen," just as women fall from their dieting regimens. This also explains why overweight women are held with greater social contempt than overweight men (Kilbourne, 1999).

Friedan (1963) identifies a lack of private image as the heart of North American women's problems, both currently and historically. They can no longer access a private image to forge an identity; rather they must rely on the hyperbeautified and hypersexualized female enigmas that mass media advertisements perpetuate:

> Public images that defy reason and have very little to do with women themselves have had the power to shape too much of their lives. These images would not have such power if women were not suffering a crisis of identity. (p. 63)

Germov and Williams (1999) identify this trend to correspond with the economic and cultural rise of mass production and consumption, which led the body image industries to develop a definitive formula for success: Promote a thin ideal of beauty that the majority of women can never attain, which will initiate consumption. Faludi (1991) also attests to this phenomenon, stating that the "feminine" traits that the beauty industry celebrates are grossly unnatural and achieved with increasingly harsh, unhealthy, and punitive measures; the beauty industry ultimately relies upon low self-esteem and high anxiety about a "feminine" appearance in order to be profitable. Most critical is the fact that these culturally constructed ideals are marketed as *attainable* to women in beauty and health magazines and advertisements, thus holding women responsible when they do not meet these often impossible standards (Germov & Williams, 1999).

Friedan (1963) explains the oppression that accompanies predetermined bodily ideals for women to meet, which stand in blatant opposition to what nature allots. In the 1950s, bra manufacturers began marketing brassieres with fake foam bosoms to girls as young as ten years old; three out of ten women dyed their hair blonde; women ate a type of chalk called Metrecal instead of food to shrink their bodies to the new thin ideal which, according to American department stores, had shrunk by three to four sizes since 1939. Similarly, Faludi (1991) describes the 1980s trends that women submitted to in the name of beauty: Anti-wrinkle treatments exposed women to carcinogens, acid face peels burned their skin, silicone injections left painful deformities, and liposuction caused complications and infections. Of course, the consequences of such procedures are perceived as women's personal ills, a result of vanity and the futility of pursuing a perfected image that nature did not bestow upon them. The larger entendre, of course, lies in the fact that in order to meet the standards of the cultural beauty ideal most women *must* physically change themselves, yet they are simultaneously scrutinized for doing so.

Faludi (1991) specifically explores the thin ideal of the 1980s: A prominent mannequin sculptor, Robert Filoso, sculpted his idealized "New Generation Woman" mannequin as shorter, with an additional three inches on her breasts and an inch less from her waist, ultimately establishing the ideal female measurements of 34–23–36. Such a thin ideal is indeed unnatural given the body shapes and sizes of most women, and the only way to attain such measurements would be through bodily modifications that ultimately begin with dieting. The diet industry, like the larger beauty industry, thrives on its product failures, all the while encouraging obsessive and anxious attitudes toward food consumption; the unsuccessful nature of dieting can lead to "yo-yo dieting" and "weight cycling" that can result in a lifelong tug of war with food, and female food consumption can become wrought with guilt, anxiety, and deprivation (Germov & Williams, 1999). In this respect, the dieter, even more than the addict, is the ideal consumer, as she will compulsively spend money on food and weight loss products in pursuit of the thin ideal. The fact that dieting is a biologically unnatural behavior means that dieting products cannot offer long-term solutions to weight issues and compulsive eating, thereby resulting in a profitable consumption cycle (Kilbourne, 1999). These compulsive dieting behaviors are also at the root of the self-objectification that so many women regularly engage in.

According to objectification theory, women are trained to see themselves as objects, whose only bodily value is based on the pleasure that it gives to others (Stevens-Aubrey, 2007). Self-objectifying women, then, are constantly aware that their bodies are on display, and are thereby constantly monitoring their bodily appearance. As Berger (1972) so eloquently states it, "Men look at women. Women watch themselves being looked at. This determines not only the relations between men and women, but also the relation of women to themselves" (p. 41). And this self-objectification is indeed perpetual; once a woman has lost excessive weight, she must continue to monitor her weight to ensure that her bodily appearance remains acceptable within the cultural definition of femininity. Unfortunately, this sort of compulsive behavior is exactly what the diet industry encourages, which includes advertising for products like Special K.

METHODOLOGY AND RESEARCH DESIGN

Developed by Altheide (1987), ethnographic content analysis is rooted in the principles of qualitative research, where both numeric and narrative data can be collected for the purpose of analyzing various media such as film and television, among others. Unlike a quantitative content analysis, the role of the researchers is central to ethnographic content analysis, who seek meaning rather than theoretical verification through their research. The methodology involved in ethnographic content analysis is systematic and analytic, but not rigid; the ability to understand messages is rooted in the constant discovery and constant comparison of relevant styles, meanings, settings, and images presented by various media.

The media documents analyzed for this study are Special K television advertisements, aired since 2000, that are available on the YouTube website. In order to qualify for this study the advertisements had to meet the following criteria: a) be broadcast in English, b) have decipherable audio content, and c) be aired after 2000. As a result, sixteen Special K advertisements which satisfied all three criteria were chosen.

Next, the selected Special K advertisements were transcribed. Over the course of one week, each advertisement was viewed a minimum of five times in its entirety throughout the transcription process. The transcriptions account for four main elements of the media documents: a) aesthetic visuals (for example, describing what the featured actors in the commercials look like, what they are doing, how the setting appears, shot composition), b) print visuals (for example, the content of any fine print, logos, or copyrights), c) diegetic sound (any speech performed by the actors in the context of the commercial), and d) non-diegetic sound (for example, voiceover narration and music). All of these elements were broken down on a shot-by-shot basis, requiring multiple viewings of each selected Special K advertisement. After the transcriptions were completed, it was decided that the infamously obligatory "fine print" would not be considered during the coding process because any individual viewing these commercials on television would likely be unable to adequately decipher this text, both due to the text's size and the inadequate amount of time that the text appears on-screen. Therefore, this content is essentially irrelevant when considering the grander narrative that Special K television advertisements try to convey.

Next a coding protocol was developed, whose categories remained in flux as the coding and organization of data proceeded. This protocol was not designed to fit data into preexisting categories, but to guide the systematic coding of the Special K advertisements' content. The coding categories, developed in accordance with the reviewed literature, were developed to identify the major thematic units perpetuated by the selected advertisements, drawing from their narrative, visual, and audio elements. Repeated readings of the selected advertisements allowed for the development of more specific sub-themes thereafter. In this case, the major thematic units refer to stereo-typically unhealthy behaviors represented within the context of the examined advertisements, identified as self-monitoring and self-objectifying behaviors by Wolf (1990) and Stevens-Aubrey (2007), respectively.

RESULTS AND ANALYSIS

The following stereotypical, unhealthy behaviors were identified in the re-viewed Special K advertisements:

Self-Fulfillment through Slimming the Body

The fact that Special K products are largely marketed as dieting aids trans-lates into a single goal that women are encouraged to reach through their consumption: slimming the body. The manner in which Special K advertise-ments encourage women to pursue the thin ideal is especially troubling be-cause the women that are featured are already slim, yet they are shown still to be in pursuit of the thin ideal. It should be noted that slim in this context does not refer to bodies that are excessively thin: Slim in this case applies to women who maintain a culturally acceptable body size without being over-weight or excessively thin. The fact that these women straddle a middle ground of acceptable bodily appearance puts them into a precarious position because they must, in the context of the selected Special K advertisements, engage in perpetual self-monitoring and self-objectification in order to en-sure that they maintain their acceptable body size. The inherent message of this campaign, then, becomes clear: Thinner is *always* better, and a woman can *never* be comfortable with her weight because the possibility of becom-ing overweight will (and should) perpetually haunt her.

For instance, in an advertisement for original Special K cereal, the cultu-ral preference for thinness is illustrated without any featured women. In this advertisement a box of Special K cereal is turned 45 degrees around so that the side panel is facing the camera, declaring this to be the "after" stage, and inevitably the preferable one as the advertisement encourages its audience to "turn your life around." Similarly, in an advertisement for the Special K Challenge, the featured woman is shown to be happy and confident after she apprehensively slips into a pair of jeans that would have presumably been too small for her before she began her diet of substituting a Special K product for two meals a day over the course of two weeks.

Perhaps even more disconcerting than the paradigm of slimness as the uncompromising bodily preference for women is the emphasis in the selected Special K advertisements on the dangerous psychological aspects of dieting identified by Orbach (1978). Orbach critiques the perpetual, cyclical nature of dieting, epitomized by the fact that once a particular weight loss goal has been reached (especially if it has been attained through the unnatural state of dieting) women must work tirelessly and endlessly to ensure that the thin ideal is *maintained*. Therefore, even though women may already be slim, it is important for them to continuously engage in a low calorie diet in order to ensure that their bodies remain slim and, ultimately, culturally acceptable and desirable.

For instance, in another advertisement for original Special K cereal, a number of already slim women are shown to avoid eating breakfast for fear of gaining weight. In the end Special K encourages women to eat breakfast but manages to naturalize the fact that women do and perhaps should skip breakfast for fear of compromising their slimness, since a number of different slim women are shown to engage in the same behavior (and seem oddly pleased with themselves once they have successfully evaded the waiter who would otherwise serve them breakfast). Special K does encourage women to eat breakfast, but only presents Special K as a breakfast option *because* it is low in fat, and encourages women to eat Special K because "people who eat a low fat breakfast, like Special K, are more likely to be slimmer than those who skip breakfast all together." Therefore women are not encouraged to eat breakfast because of the benefits that it provides for their bodies, but because the Special K breakfast option does not compromise their slimness. At no point does this advertisement debunk the belief that preserving slimness is more important than eating breakfast.

Self-Fulfillment through "Resisting Temptation" or Denying the Desire to Eat for Pleasure

The selected Special K advertisements convey to women time and again that the desire to eat for pleasure is undesirable because it compromises their ability to attain the thin ideal. For instance, in an advertisement for Special K Crispy Bites, the featured women are able to feel good by looking good, which is achieved through opting for low calorie Special K snacks instead of the sweet desserts that they actually desire to eat. It is clear in all of these advertisements that the desire to eat for pleasure, which is collectively equated with "temptation," is undesirable for women, no matter their size, if they are to maintain the ever important thin ideal. In accordance with Wolf's (1990) definition of self-monitoring and Stevens-Aubrey's (2007) definition of self-objectification, these advertisements arguably encourage women to find satisfaction in *denying* their bodily desires in order to maintain a male-defined standard of beauty, finding value not in the enjoyment that women derive from their own bodies but from the enjoyment that their bodies provide for others.

A similar approach is incorporated in two advertisements for Special K Chocolatey Delight cereal. In these advertisements the featured product is presented as a low calorie snack alternative to the chocolate "temptations" that the featured women actually desire to eat. Interestingly, Special K in this instance is actually declared to be an indulgence, as the omniscient voiceover in one of the advertisements interpolates the viewer, "what's the difference between indulging and overindulging?" Again in this instance Special K is presented as a redemptive entity that allows women to satisfy their snack cravings (as opposed to actual hunger). It could be seen as constructive that these Special K advertisements acknowledge the featured women's desires to eat for pleasure, and even provide them with an outlet to do so. However, it is ever implicit that it is *only* acceptable to eat for pleasure if the snack is low calorie, thus not compromising the women's ability to maintain the thin ideal; eating anything else would qualify as "overindulging." The fact that both featured women in these advertisements are slim has troubling implications, especially when the second advertisement implies it to be inappropriate for its featured woman to lick a dime-sized amount of chocolate icing off her finger (regardless of the fact that it arguably has fewer calories and would be more satisfying than a bowl of Special K). This advertisement epitomizes the naturalization of self-monitoring as it becomes clear that *any* indulgence is inappropriate for women who wish to maintain the thin ideal. The fact that the slogan for Special K Chocolatey Delight cereal promises that the product "won't undo your whole day" implicitly states that a meticulous diet with a special care not to eat for pleasure is (and should be) a natural and central part of women's day-to-day lives.

The use of "temptation" in these Special K advertisements is particularly important when considered in the context of the religious subtext that is often applied to dieting discourses. As Wolf (1990) explains, like religious texts, dieting discourses revolve around cycles of temptation, sin, and redemption for women. Similarly, in the context of these Special K advertisements, eating for pleasure is prohibited for women. This prohibition can be likened to sex that is pursued outside of marriage for an enjoyable experience (also prohibited for women in Christian paradigms). According to the selected Special K advertisements, then, women should learn to resist temptation and deny themselves pleasurable experiences that are not required for bodily sustenance.

Fear of Body Size

A woman's fear of her body size relates directly to her ability to attain and maintain the thin ideal in accordance with culturally defined standards of feminine beauty (Arnold & Doran, 2007). Because a woman's slimness is perceived as an explicit indicator of her ability to exercise self-negation and self-control over her body and appetite, it is obvious why body size will evoke anxiety among women. However, this cultural expectation does not make the self-monitoring behavior healthy or justifiable, and, yet, the selected Special K advertisements work to naturalize women's bodily anxieties on several levels.

In an advertisement for original Special K cereal, for instance, a slim woman is shown to be mortified at her weight as she steps onto a scale. This Special K advertisement is meant to be humorous as the woman removes her clothing, jewelry and eyeglasses in a vain attempt to change her weight, but in actuality this advertisement works to perpetuate the belief that all women, no matter how slim they are, are (and should be) anxious and unsatisfied (and even a bit neurotic) about their weight. The fact that the omniscient voice-over in this advertisement addresses the featured woman's plight by advising the audience to "relax, exercise gently and, of course, eat sensibly" implies that a healthy, balanced lifestyle is the ultimate solution to an unsatisfactory bodily weight. Although seemingly constructive, when this advice is imparted, the images in the advertisement simultaneously naturalize the notion that this woman is terrified of her weight and body size, in spite of the fact that she is obviously slim. Any constructive advice is unfortunately obscured by the fact that this advertisement emphasizes that no women, not even slim women, should be satisfied with their weights.

Similarly, in an advertisement for the Special K Challenge, another humorous advertisement, a woman becomes disconcerted when her child mistakes her for Santa Claus while she bends over to tend the fireplace, dressed in a red and white robe. The omniscient voiceover lends no consolation, as it states that "now is when you regret all those holiday cookies." Once again, even though the featured woman is slim, the advertisement implies that she should rightfully be anxious and fearful about her weight because she failed to exercise the proper self-control and self-negation over her eating behaviors over the holidays. Luckily, Special K's product line allows women to redeem themselves by losing "up to six pounds in two weeks" by substituting meals with Special K. In this advertisement it is apparent that women who lose sight of the thin ideal *deserve* to be anxious and fearful about their weight, and should remedy the situation by immediately subjecting themselves to a strict diet of low calorie meals that promote slimness above anything else.

Fear of Food/Hunger

The naturalization of women's fear of food and hunger has already been touched upon in the discussion of women's fear of body size, and this tendency is heightened in an advertisement for Special K Chocolatey Delight cereal, where the concept of fear is simultaneously explicit and metaphoric. In this advertisement, a woman is watching a horror film on television, obviously frightened by what she is seeing. The omniscient voiceover then proclaims it to be that "dangerous time of night where you fall victim to chocolate temptations lurking in the kitchen." The very use of words like "dangerous," "victim," and "lurking" make it obvious enough that a woman's craving for chocolate and chocolate itself are somehow sinister, in addition to the fact that it is up to women not to allow themselves to fall "victim" to their desires. This paradigm coincides with other reviewed Special K advertisements which collectively imply that a woman's desire to eat for pleasure is not only destructive to her ability to maintain the thin ideal, but it is downright dangerous because of the cultural ramifications that could accompany a woman's inability to maintain a slim body. It is an indicator of self-objectification and the fact that women must perpetually control their appearance, desires, and appetites in order to maintain a body that is pleasing to others, since that is women's principal role in life (de Beauvoir, 1971). As Germov and Williams (1999) contend, the discourses that encompass dieting, which are aptly applied in this advertisement, encourage women to engage in a lifelong tug of war with food that results in guilt, anxiety, and deprivation. Lucky for women that "lower calorie" Special K Chocolatey Delight is a nighttime snack that they "don't have to be afraid of."

Serve Others Rather Than Self

The fact that women are culturally encouraged to be self-sacrificing creatures who suppress their own desires while acting as servants to others, especially in a maternal context, is explored by Arnold and Doran (2007). The maternal context of this tendency is also evident in the selected Special K advertisements. For instance, in an advertisement for Special K Chocolatey Delight cereal, a woman resists her desire to lick some chocolate icing off her finger while her young son playfully spreads chocolate icing all over a cake on the kitchen table. It is true that the boy is not eating the icing or the cake, but the implication exists that this woman is preparing a cake that she has no intention of partaking in (since she is so self-controlled that a single lick of icing off her finger is unacceptable). In this instance it is insinuated that the featured woman desires the treat that she will be serving to her child (who is, incidentally, a boy) but is able to suppress her cravings due to her admirable self-control and obligation to maintain the thin ideal.

Collectively, these stereotypical self-monitoring behaviors situate women so that their own needs and desires are dismissed, and the pleasure that their bodies can provide to others becomes the priority (Wolf, 1990). It is true that these represented unhealthy behaviors are not so much directly encouraged through the discourses offered by the reviewed Special K advertisements as much as they are *naturalized* by them; they are perpetuated to be behaviors that all women engage in rather than being problematized by the advertisements. This is the underlying issue that needs addressing in the broader question of the implications that Special K advertisements have for the representations and reality of women's health.

DISCUSSION AND CONCLUSION

On the whole, the selected Special K television advertisements represent the healthy behaviors of women to consist of stereotypical self-monitoring behaviors defined in the reviewed literature as largely *unhealthy*. In the context of the reviewed Special K advertisements, health becomes equated with slimness for women, and healthy foods are defined solely as those that have minimal calorie and fat contents—being defined by what they *withhold* from women's bodies, rather than what they offer to them.

Orbach (1978) states that a healthy woman allows her body to be a self-regulating system, alerting the mind when it is hungry and letting it know exactly what it wants to eat. The reviewed Special K advertisements naturalize the fact that women regularly deny their physical appetites and cravings, allowing hunger pangs to be a sacrifice in the name of the thin ideal. This represented self-denial inherently implies self-objectification on behalf of the featured women, who prioritize the way that their bodies appear to others as more important than how their bodies feel and function for themselves (Calogero, Davis & Thompson, 2005; Hill & Tylka, 2004).

Orbach (1978) states that women should eat a balanced diet that consists of a variety of foods, not all of which will be low in fat and calories. The selected Special K advertisements only encourage women to eat a variety of Special K products, especially in the context of the Special K Challenge since substituting a bowl of Special K cereal or a Special K snack bar for two meals a day does *not* provide the range of vitamins and other nutrients required by the World Health Organization (2009) to sustain a healthy, balanced lifestyle and body.

It is the conclusion of this study that, even if Special K products were to be marketed as part of a weight loss regimen, it is important that they be overtly suggested as part of a larger balanced lifestyle where health, not just slimness, is the principal emphasis. It is not enough for health disclaimers to materialize in an advertisement's fine print; they must be the central focus in order for the foundations of these feminist criticisms to be erased.

It is the stereotypical cultural foundation holding women's bodies (and the ability of these bodies to emulate a culturally and historically contextual, hegemonically imposed standard of beauty) as the key indicators of their social worth that needs to be decisively overhauled. Slimness is only one aspect of this conundrum and because a woman's slimness has become culturally indicative of her willingness to submit herself to external cultural control, it is a relevant if not crucial paradigm to start with because it is the necessity for this control that needs to be painstakingly questioned and, eventually, thoroughly addressed and remedied.

Finally, this study of representations of women's health in Special K television advertisements is limited in making generalizations by the lack of reliability provided by numerical data and predefined coding categories, which are central to the principles of quantitative research (Altheide, 1987). It cannot be said that the results of this study are definitive or unarguable; rather, they are the outcome of cultural experiences that have been channeled into the observation and analysis of a specific selection of data. As such, individuals with different cultural experiences may observe the very same selection of cultural artifacts and draw a very different analysis. Future studies, then, could address the implications that arise for the women of races and classes who are not granted representation in media venues such as the selected Special K advertisements. Or, from a marketing standpoint, subsequent studies could consider *why* these women are not featured since slimness, as explored by Bordo (1993), may not be as much of a cultural priority for these women as it is for white, middle-class women.

REFERENCES

Altheide, D. L. (1987). Reflections: Ethnographic content analysis. *Qualitative Sociology*, *10*(1), 65–77.

Arnold, L. B., & Doran, E. (2007). Stop before you hurt the kids: Communicating self-control and self-negation in femininity, mothering and eating disorders. *Women's Studies in Communication, 30*(3), 309–39.

Berger, J. (1972). *Ways of seeing: Based on the BBC television series*. England: Penguin.

BMI classification. (2009). *World Health Organization*. Retrieved October 15, 2009, from apps.who.int/bmi/index.jsp?introPage=intro_3.html.

Bordo, S. (1993). Hunger as ideology. In D. B. Holt & J.B. Schor (Eds.), *The consumer society reader* (pp. 99–114). New York: The New York Press.

Calogero, R. M., Davis, W. N., & Thompson, K. J. (2005). The role of self-objectification in the experience of women with eating disorders. *Sex roles, 52*(1/2), 43–50.

De Beauvoir, S. (1971). *The second sex*. New York: Borzoi.

Faludi, S. (1991). *Backlash: The undeclared war against American women*. New York: Crown.

Friedan, B. (1963). *The feminine mystique*. New York: Dell.

Germov, J., & Williams, L. (1999). The thin ideal: Women, food, and dieting. In J. Germov & L. Williams (Eds.), *A sociology of food and nutrition: The social appetite* (pp. 337–67). Australia: Oxford Press.

Goodman, D. (1998). Special K drops thin models for health theme. *Marketing news, 32*(5), 8.

Hill, M. S., & Tylka, T. L. (2004). Objectification theory as it relates to disordered eating among college women. *Sex roles, 51*(11/12), 719–30.

Kilbourne, J. (1999). *Deadly persuasion: Why women and girls must fight the addictive power of advertising.* New York: The Free Press.

Orbach, S. (1978). *Fat is a feminist issue: The anti-diet guide for women.* New York: Galahad Books.

Stevens-Aubrey, J. (2007). The impact of sexually objectifying media exposure on negative body emotions and self-perceptions: Investigating the mediating role of body self-consciousness. *Mass Communication & Society, 10*(1), 1–23.

Wolf, N. (1990). *The beauty myth.* Toronto: Random House.

Chapter Two

Tales from *Ooku*

The Shogun's Inner Palace and the Outer (Mediated) World

Kimiko Akita

Japanese TV shows and movies have long dramatized *Ooku* (pronounced "*Oh-uh-koo*," usually translated as "Great Interior"), the secluded inner palace of the Tokugawa *shoguns*, or military leaders, which from 1600 to 1868 quartered up to three thousand women at a time: the shogun's wife, concubines, previous shoguns and their concubines, the wife of the shogunal heir, and female servants—none of whom was ever permitted to leave or to speak about Ooku. No man except the shogun was ever allowed to enter there. Every evening, Ooku provided the shogun with his choice of women since they existed mainly for procreation to maintain succession; it was also where male heirs were reared until their ninth birthday (Hata, 2009). A strict hierarchy existed in Ooku, with the shogun at the top. Its other inhabitants competed for attention, promotions, power, and survival. Any woman who bore a son for a Shogun achieved great power, for a woman.

Contemporary Japanese mass media have represented the women of Ooku as shallow, jealous, bullying, vengeful, vicious, violent, untrustworthy, emotional, materialistic, promiscuous, and inferior to men. Ooku women are treated as commodities, offered to the shogun as a reproductive, sexual, or political toy. Mediated tales from Ooku have included melodramatic scenes of rape by the shogun as female bodyguards eavesdropped; mysterious deaths of shogun wives and sons; fights between concubines and wives; and suicides.

As in other Japanese historical dramas, the concept of *ie* (pronounced "*ee-eh*," the patriarchal Japanese social family system) features prominently in Ooku stories. *Ie*, in both fiction and reality, governs the behaviors of individuals—especially women. It represses them and forces them to sacrifice self for the sake of family name and social face. *Ie* "virtues," such as perseverance, male superiority, repression of women, and continuation of primogeniture consanguinity family succession, are epitomized and glorified for the outer world through mediated tales from Ooku. But until the end of World War II, *ie* had been rigidly preserved and practiced, in fact, only among the upper class; until then, most Japanese were farmers or peasants who could not afford *ie* traditions (Akita, 2009). Yet, Ooku dramas aim to convince Japanese audiences that they are being treated to factual, historical glimpses of their ancestors' lifestyles and cultural traditions over time. The rigid *ie* practices depicted in Ooku dramas provide the Japanese, most of whom do not descend from the upper class, with an imagined collective memory, manufacturing false pride, adoration, and an affinity with this mediated Japanese culture and tradition. I argue in this chapter that mediated tales from Ooku induce audiences to believe that they share a collective memory—but one that is false.

Several Ooku TV series, each titled *Ooku*, have been broadcast periodically from 1968 through 2008. Movie versions have been released: *Ooku Emaki* (1968), *Ooku* (2006), and *Ooku* (2010). A theatrical performance titled *Ooku* was staged in 2007. Most of the TV dramas consisted of fifty to fifty-two episodes, programmed for broadcast over a single year, except for the 2003 and the 2004 versions, with eleven episodes each. The 2008 TV series was titled *Atsuhime* but was centered on Ooku life during Princess Atsu's reign (1856–1867).

In this chapter, I examine Ooku dramas produced since 2003 to analyze their mediated representations to modern Japanese audiences. I discuss how fictions of Ooku were created and re-created by men who depict not authentic Japanese women ancestors, but rather, idealized women created from male fantasies arising from *ie*. I argue that, for almost a half century, mass-mediated Ooku dramas have served as a patriarchal device to expand, perpetuate, and reinforce the idealized *ie* woman across classes and to institutionalize a no-longer legitimate *ie* as ideology in postwar Japan. This revisionist history of Ooku has resulted in the reinforcement of a hegemony of servitude and inferiority of women in modern Japan.

OOKU WOMEN AND *IE* SINCE EDO ERA

The Tokugawa Shogunate controlled Japan during the Edo era (1603–1868). Continuation of the shogun's *ie* meant continuity for the nation. Although women in Ooku did not participate in politics, they played an important role in preserving the shogun's *ie* lineage and helping the nation through procreation of and rearing of an heir. The Edo government legitimized *ie* and enforced it to ensure control (Inoue, 2000; Koyama, 1961). The government designated a hierarchy of four social classes: *samurai* (warriors), the highest class; *hyakusho* (farmers), the second class; *shokunin* (artisans), the third class; and *shonin* (merchants), the lowest class (Hane, 1982; Kitche, 1995). The government defined farmers as second rank merely to appease them, but the majority of Japanese belonged to the farmer class and most of them were peasants. The *ie* concept was adopted and practiced by *samurai* (the upper class) first, then trickled down to the lower class. Warrior class, top farmer (landowner) class, and top merchant class practiced *ie* rigidly. The true lower classes, artisans and peasants, could not afford to practice *ie*.

In the *ie* system, not only Confucian values of obedience and endurance, but also Confucian etiquette and deportment were required of women (Robertson, 1991). A wealthy woman with refined *ie* deportment, wearing a beautiful kimono, earned respect and status. Both the social-class system and *ie* created gender hierarchy among women. Women in Ooku were the most respected and idealized (Walthall, 2001). Women of the Edo era aspired to work in Ooku before marrying. Ooku was considered a bridal training school. Unless chosen by the shogun to become his concubine or an attendant for his wife, servants were allowed to leave Ooku after some time. Women who went to work there gained experience, not wealth, and became more marketable for marriage (p. 56).

The new Meiji era (1868–1912) government abolished feudalism but legalized *ie*. Suddenly, everyone appeared as social equals; however, an *ie* class competition arose in its place immediately, in which families sought to outdo others in education, occupation, and wealth (Akita, 2009). All Japanese endeavored to project a good *ie* image according to this new status system. Women participated by demonstrating appropriate manners and domestic skills. Men inherited family property. Under *ie*, a woman was conditioned to become "a good wife and wise mother" to care for her family, to maintain her home, her own *ooku* (inner quarter), without participating in outer politics. The gender hierarchy—men superior to women—became more distinct. A woman was to submit to men (husbands, fathers, sons), to endure, and to sacrifice self. A wife belonged to the patriarch, the "father" of her husband, the head of *ie* (Koyama, 1961). To help the nation become stronger, women were encouraged to produce more children. Women were alienated from their own sexuality by being treated as "borrowed wombs" whose primary function was to extend the husband's lineage (Mihalopoulos, 2009, p. 20).

Until the end of World War II, therefore, *ie* legally controlled women; Ooku women continued to be the ideal. The legality of *ie* was abolished in 1948 by the post-war constitution (Kano, 1983, p. 6), but its ideology has remained dominant, and competition for status has continued. Ooku women of mass-mediated dramas—perseverate and servile—now teach audiences a woman's presumably appropriate *ie* manners, deportment, and duties. Ooku women demonstrate that they achieve happiness and find love by performing as the male fantasy of the *ie* woman.

OOKU CREATED AND RECREATED BY MEN

No one was ever permitted to talk to outsiders about what she or he saw and experienced in Ooku (Hata, 2009). Japanese men, however, were eager to know what was going on inside. During the Edo era (1600–1868), fantastic fictions about Ooku were being written by men for men, asserting male superiority, with women mere objects to be tamed and watched, commodified and sexualized (Walthall, 2001, pp. 44–45). Men were doers and heroes; women were passive, with no autonomy or power. Among scholars who have studied Ooku, Cecilia Segawa Seigle, a native Japanese and now Professor Emerita of Japanese Studies at the University of Pennsylvania, researched the real histories of Ooku and discovered historical discrepancies. She found, for instance, that *Gokoku onna taihei ki* and *Gokkoku onna-taiheiki*, two popular novels published during the Edo era, merit little credibility today, including the false rumor that the fifth shogun, Tsunayoshi (1680–1709), had an affair with *Osome*—the concubine of his right-hand man, Yanagisawa—who bore him an heir (Seigle, 1999, p. 504).

During the later Meiji era (1868–1912), interviews with fourteen former shogunate officials and servants were conducted January 1891–November 1892 by Kyuji Shimonkai, or the Society for Inquiring into Bygone Days (Beerens, 2008). Transcripts of the collected work, *Kyuji shimonroku* (Record of Inquiries into Bygone Days), were published, then not reprinted until 1954; the first widely available versions were not published until 1964 ('68). Male newspaper reporters of the Meiji era also published interviews   ᴧen and women who had worked in Ooku in a serial account called   ᛁ*o ooku* (The Great Interior of Chiyoda Castle) in the newspaper   *ʰun* in 1892 (p. 271). In 1930, Engyo Mitamura published *Goten-* of the Palace), for which he interviewed a former Ooku servant

(p. 271). Both *Chiyodajo ooku* and *Gotenjochu* provided an enormous amount of credible information about customs, manners, dress, and lifestyle in Ooku (p. 272).

In 1920, Kaneyoshi Takayanagi wrote and published *Ooku no seikatsu* (Lifestyle of Ooku), a novel about Ooku based on a semi-fictive history of Tokugawa shoguns (the fifth, sixth, and ninth shoguns) written by Yashi Tobu in 1880 (Seigle, 1999). Takayanagi described Hiroko, the wife of the sixth shogun, Ienobu, as "an unfortunate woman who had lost a daughter and a son soon after their birth, and lost her husband's love to her competitors" (Seigle, 1999, p. 486). Seigle asserted, however, that Takayanagi distorted accounts from Hiroko's father's journal. Takayanagi described Hiroko as a sad, neglected wife, jealous of her husband's concubines, and falsely portrayed Ienobu as cold toward his wife (p. 495). In fact, Seigle's historical research found that Ienobu and Hiroko were close and deeply cared for each other (p. 487). Both Takayanagi and Mitamura, fiction writers of the 1920s and 1930s, repeated the falsehood that Ienobu favored a concubine over Hiroko, but in fact, the shogun did not show any favor toward his concubine until her son became his sole heir (pp. 506–11). These early fictions, however, became the primary source of early twentieth-century understanding of Ooku—and have been perpetuated in modern dramas.

During the Allied Occupation, however, all such feudalistic topics temporarily disappeared in Japan, censored by the Supreme Command (Beerens, 2008, p. 269). By the mid-1950s, tales from Ooku began reappearing. Soon, TV became the most popular medium for their retelling. The first Ooku drama was broadcast in 1968; it and the 1983 version were written by a man (Furuzaki, 2008a; 2008b). In 2003, a woman was involved in the writing (Asano & Sogou, 2003), and the Ooku story in 2006 was written by a woman (Asano, 2006). All of these stories, however, derived from fictions written by men of the Edo and Meiji eras.

For instance, the 2005 TV series was based on Edo-era fictions about Shogun Tsunayoshi and his right-hand man, Yanagisawa. In the 2005 TV drama, when Yanagisawa learns that Tsunayoshi cannot father an heir, Yanagisawa offers him his wife, already pregnant. Yanagisawa first arranges for Tsunayoshi to have an affair with her, then asks her to become the shogun's concubine. Yanagisawa explains that it would be good for her and for him since their child would become the shogun's heir, whom Yanagisawa, in his high position, could then care for. For Yanagisawa, the act is not one of kindness, but rather one of purely political ambition; he seeks a promotion and to serve both the shogun and his heir. Yanagisawa's wife agrees to help and eventually bears a son in Ooku. Although knowing that Yanagisawa is the real father, the shogun claims the baby as his heir. Yanagisawa's wife eventually commits suicide when she can no longer stand living a lie.

OOKU CREATED AND RECREATED BY WOMEN

The 2008 Ooku TV series, *Atsuhime* (the title refers to Princess Atsu, wife of the thirteenth shogun) reflects a feminist perspective, having been written by a woman, Kumiko Tabuchi, based on the fiction written by Tomiko Miyao (Miyao, 1987). The series was broadcast for fifty weeks, consistently earning a 25 percent share. The highest-rated episode (29.2 percent) was the forty-eighth, when the Edo castle was handed over to the new Meiji government (*Telebi shichoritsu nippou*, 2008). This episode focused on Princess Atsu, not Ooku, but all the episodes took place in Ooku depicting it in detail. Unlike the 2003 Ooku version, in which Princess Atsu was commodified and sacrificed without any political power, the 2008 version portrayed her as a charismatic leader making crucial political decisions, with interests in history and politics, playing *go* (Japanese chess), acting like a tomboy, and attending school—which was only for boys then—disguised as a boy. Atsu agrees to marry the shogun for political purposes: to help her hometown lord, a future national leader, who is about to drastically change Japan.

The 2008 story of *Atsuhime*, however, has commonalities with previous Ooku stories in terms of characters preserving and following *ie* rules. In *Atsuhime*, Princess Atsu goes through stringent bridal training to acquire the proper *ie* mannerisms and speech. She must learn to walk slowly and femininely, move elegantly, speak calmly and gently using the most refined honorifics and humble expressions and employing women's language, listen to others demurely, take tiny bites of food without finishing the entire meal, and never turn down Shogun's demands for sex. She is not allowed to ask any questions about Shogun but is instructed only to please Shogun and bear his son. Due to weak health, Shogun dies naturally two years after their marriage. Atsu refuses to return to her maiden home, saying that she has married into the Tokugawa family and is determined to remain in Ooku, pray for the late Shogun's dead spirits, preserve Ooku culture and tradition, and protect the women of the inner palace for the rest of her life.

IDEOLOGICAL IMPACT OF *IE* THROUGH MASS-MEDIATED OOKU

Mass-mediated tales from Ooku are fictions created by men out of their rich fantasies over centuries. Although Ooku's inhabitants were mostly women, their stories have been misappropriated and falsely told. Historical facts have been distorted, misrepresented, replaced, sexualized, exoticized, and turned into stories that oppress women. Knowing that Ooku actually existed and that Ooku dramas are produced by other Japanese, audiences for Ooku dramas cannot be fully faulted for assuming that the stories are true and that they accurately represent the lives of their ancestors. This lack of verisimilitude represents a dehistoricization and Orientalism, in Said's (1978) term, of Japanese women. Although tales of Ooku women have been created by men, women have collusively supported and accepted these stories without questioning their veracity. Colonization is not just a one-way domination of the colonized: "Domination even at its most violent can still be permeated with ambiguity, uncertainty, and peculiar mixtures of fantasy and reality; resistance can occur simultaneously with collusion" (Sider, 1987, p. 3).

Male and female viewers want to imagine that their ancestors were the ideal *ie* role models they see in Ooku stories. Male viewers are excited to see that Ooku women serve men, cater to men, and sacrifice their lives for men. Female viewers are excited to see that Ooku women manifest the ideal *ie* deportment and speech style, make selfless decisions for the sake of *ie* (family, Tokugawa, and nation) and for their men, and achieve happiness and love through procreation, thus continuing *ie*. Silently and passively accepting *ie* ideas and tales from Ooku as historical fact contributes to the creation of a *public secret* (Taussig, 1999): something generally known, but never articulated—the "configuration of repression in which depth becomes surface so as to remain depth" (Taussig, 1999, p. 5). Talking about it is taboo. Collectively protecting this secret through *defacement*, Taussig noted, strengthens a bond among Japanese women. I believe the collusive act has taken place because of the public secret, which male and female viewers want to protect without talking about it.

Ooku dramas have played a crucial role in diffusing an imagined *ie* ideal image. When *ie* was enforceable by law, it was repressive. It was what Althusser (1971) called a *state apparatus* (SA): an institution, such as law and politics, sanctioned by a repressive state to control by implied force (pp. 92–94). By contrast, there is a second structure of power: *ideological state apparatuses* (ISAs). ISAs provide unstated objectives, unlike SAs. These are institutions that have an "overt function other than political and administrative" (Allison, 2000). Mass-mediated portrayals of Ooku, as an ISA, exert power not through repression but through ideology. The ideology of *ie* provided through Ooku dramas influences audiences, leading them to idealize themselves by seeing the world in a certain way, and having them accept certain identities as their own within that world (Althusser, 1971/2001). In modern capitalistic societies, Althusser pointed out, ideology has gradually replaced repression as the prime mechanism for behavior enforcement (p. 96). Thus, the *ie* ideology communicated by Ooku dramas has replaced the legitimated *ie* Ooku women of mass-mediated dramas—perseverate and servile—now teach audiences a woman's presumably appropriate *ie* manners, deportment, and duties. Ooku women demonstrate that they achieve happiness and find love by performing as the male fantasy of the *ie* woman.

As a result, viewers are bonded by the false belief that they share a collective memory. They may feel proud and patriotic protecting the tradition of rigid *ie* practices that they wrongly believe all of their ancestors practiced. This represents a *banal nationalism*, which Billig (1995) defined as ideological consciousness of nationhood (p. 4). This idea connects with Anderson's (1983) concept of the *imagined community*, where people "are saturated with ghostly *national* imaginings" (p. 9). Ooku viewers believe that all Japanese have always sought to practice a rigid *ie*; they are proud of their assumed collective memories and want to protect them because they create "sacred communities" (p. 22) and confirm solidarity and security. The repeated production and reproduction of tales from Ooku work as *flagging*, a reminder of national identity and nationhood (Billig, 1995), remembering the ideal image of *ie* and the *ie*-centered world, persuading viewers to believe in their sharing of collective memories. "National identity is not only something which is thought to be natural to possess, but also something natural to remember" (p. 37). The remembering involves a forgetting. Flagging, in this case, signals to viewers to remember that they have lived in Japan, an imagined community where everyone practiced *ie*; that they share proud ancestors; and that they are the descendents of ideal *ie* people.

Audiences do not question whether *ie* rules they see depicted in Ooku stories are correct. They want to preserve the *ie* tradition they now can believe in. The repeated re-creation and flagging of Ooku perpetuate *ie*. One cannot deny that it may be due to Ooku dramas that, in Japan, a mother (who procreates) is respected more than a single successful career woman; or, that a wife often gets blamed for her husband's having a mistress; or, that a man with a mistress is not judged negatively, as in the West; or, that a woman is often judged by her demeanor and deportment instead of by her intelligence; or, that single and divorced women are stigmatized more than are single and divorced men.

REFERENCES

Akita, K. (2009, Autumn). A story of *tansu*, a chest of drawers: Japanese women's love, hope, and despair. *The Journal of Public and Private in Contemporary History*, (4), 17–33.

Allison, A. (2000). Japanese mothers and *obentos:* The lunch box as ideological state apparatus. *Permitted and prohibited desires: Mothers, comics, and censorship in Japan* (pp. 81–103). Berkeley, CA: University of California Press.

Althusser, L. (2001). Ideology and ideological state apparatuses (Notes toward an investigation). In *Lenin and philosophy and other essays* (pp. 85–126). (B. Brewster, Trans.). New York: Monthly Review. (Original work published 1971).

Anderson, B. (1983). *Imagined communities: Reflections on the origin and spread of nationalism*. NY: Verson.

Asano, T., & Sogou, M. (2003). *Ooku*. Tokyo: Kadokawa Shoten.

Asano, T. (2006). *Oh-oku*. Tokyo: Kadokawa Shoten.

Beerens, A. (2008). Interview with two ladies of the *Ooku*: A translation from *Kyuji Shimonro-ku. Monumenta Nipponica, 63*(1), 265–324.

Billig, M. (1995). *Banal Nationalism*. Thousand Oaks, CA: Sage.

Furuzaki, Y. (2008a). Talent schedule: Ooku (1). Available at talent-schedule.tpm.jp/Drama_10865.

Furuzaki, Y. (2008b). Talent schedule: Ooku (3). Available at talent-schedule.tpm.jp/Drama_20163.

Hane, M. (1982). *Peasants, rebels, & outcastes: The underside of modern Japan*, Pantheon Books, New York.

Hata, N. (2009). *Shiranakatta!? O-oku no himitsu* [No one knew before!? Secrets of O-oku]. Tokyo: PHP.

Inoue, H. (2000). *Hakao meguru kazoku ron: Dareto hairuka, darega mamoruka* [Family dispute over grave: Who wants to be buried with? Who has to maintain the grave?]. Tokyo: Heibonsha.

Kano, M. (1983). *Senzen Ie no Shisou* [Ideology of Ie before WWII], Sobunsha, Tokyo, Sobunsha.

Kitche, S. (1995). Antecedents of the Japanese distribution system: Formative agents in Tokugawa Japan. *Japan & The World Economy, 7*(2), 199–210.

Koyama, T. (1961). *The changing social position of women in Japan*. Switzerland: Unesco.

Kubo, T. (1993). *Buke shakai ni ikita kuge josei. Nihon no kinsei* [Women of samurai and royal families] 15 (pp. 71–96). Tokyo: Chuo koronsha.

Mihalopoulos, B. (2009). Mediating the good life: Prostitution and the Japanese woman's Christian Temperance Union, 1880s–1920s. *Gender & History, 21*(1), 19–38.

Mitamura, E. (1976). *Mitamura engyo zenshuu* [A collection of Mitamura Engyo], No. 1 (pp. 120–21). Tokyo: Chuo koronsha.

Miyao, T. (1987). *Tenshoin Atsuhime* [Princess Atsu]. Tokyo: Kodansha.

Robertson, J. (1991). The Shingaku woman: Straight from the heart. In G. L. Bernstein (Ed.), *Recreating Japanese women, 1600–1945* (pp. 88–107). Berkeley, CA: University of California Press.

Said, E. (1978). *Orientalism*. NY: Vintage Books.

Seigle, C. S. (1999). The Shogun's consort: Konoe Hiroko and Tokugawa Ienobu. *Harvard Journal of Asiatic Studies, 59*(2), 485–522.

Sider, G. (1987). Why parrots learn to talk, and why they can't: Domination, deception, and self-deception in Indian-White relations. *Comparative Study of Society and History, 29*(1), 3–23.

Takayanagi, K. (1920/1969). *Ooku no seikatsu*. Tokyo: Yuzankaku.

Taussig, M. (1999). *Defacement: Public secrecy and the labor of the negative*. Stanford, CA: Stanford University Press.

Telebi shichoritsu nippou [Daily TV viewers' rating]. (2008). Tokyo: Video Research, Ltd.

Walthall, A. (2001). The Shogun's domestic quarters in Japanese popular culture. *The Journal of Gender Studies, 4*, 43–64.

Chapter Three

Pakistani Media and Disempowerment of Women

Saman Talib and Zara Idrees

The empowerment of Pakistani women has become part of a significant agenda for the international community as it focuses on combating terrorism. The modern media in Pakistan, particularly due to the explosive growth of the past few years, plays a key role in this drive toward empowerment. Obstacles faced by such an endeavor include a deeply embedded patriarchy that challenges empowerment efforts, as well as media images and narratives which reinforce patriarchal values. This chapter analyzes how media reinforces the cultural mores presented to women. One of the major characteristics of current broadcast and print media is its reliance on traditional cultural narratives. This chapter will focus on the validation of womanhood through matrimony, rescuing the frail maiden, and denigrating women who violate chaddar and chaardiwaari as examples of traditional cultural narratives. Running counter to these traditional narratives are professional female role models who are attempting to change the traditional narratives through shows like *The First Blast* on Dawn News Television. The organization South Asian Women in Media, SAWM, is also trying to extend and enhance opportunities for women in the media through its campaign against harassment in the work place.

The parochial, discriminatory form of Islam imposed on Pakistani culture, with special focus on limiting female agency during military dictator Zia-ul-Haq's reign, proved debilitating for the indigenous women. The process of Islamization and affliction of Shari'a law on the Pakistani legal and constitutional system had the desired effect of pushing women further back into anonymity and segregation (Kothari, 2005). The hegemonic and patriarchal Islamic agenda of Zia's "chaddar and chaardiwaari" portray women as evil

27

protagonists who corrupt the minds of men with their insatiable desire for material accumulations (Mumtaz & Shaheed, 1987). The retention of this image in the collective memory of the nation is challenged by feminists who observe its allusions in current media discourse and seek an alternative method of expression.

Forced into the confinement of their domestic space, Pakistani women find solace in the constructed world of the soap opera. This special intimacy shared with the medium of television has translated into a feeling of deep trust and popular appeal for its narrative (Kothari, 2005). For women, Barbara Easton theorizes that soaps allay real anxieties, satisfy real needs and desires, even while distorting them (Easton, 1978).

Realizing the power of the media and the influence they generate, governments have decided to use television programming for disseminating state agenda and development programs. The "Committee on the Status of Women," which worked for developing nations like India, recommended that mass media could promote women's awareness of their "rights, problems, opportunities and obligations," and pointed out that television could be used as a tool for social transformation (1974). Consequently, in Pakistan soaps form an alternate women's culture within society and are viewed as important vehicles for empowerment. Shuchi Kothari comments that Urdu drama serials, written mostly by women, negotiate the thorny ground of women's lives in all their complexities, trials, tribulations, and pleasures, while seldom discussing resistance to Islamist patriarchy (2005).

VALIDATION THROUGH MATRIMONY

In developing countries such as Pakistan, which has deep social and cultural roots in patriarchy, girls are not given an equal place with their male siblings. Marriage was often seen by young women as a means to "escape" their position at home and enter comfortable settings with their husbands. Increased literacy, changing social dynamics, and the effects of globalization have led to a shift in this perception. More and more young women are excelling in academics and careers while media depiction and narratives, mostly through soap operas, continue to reflect and emphasize that the traditional way for a woman to achieve selfhood and prosperity is through marriage.

As Laura Mulvey explains, it is not mere coincidence that this form of nineteenth century melodrama continues to appeal to women. Unlike film, which empowers its audience, soaps reinforce women's powerlessness (1977). Current Pakistani soap operas demonstrate this disempowerment through the themes of married life and divorce. Specifically, three stories are continuously recycled when examining marriage. In the first story, a young girl is rescued from poverty by a benevolent suitor, and she achieves the reward of marriage for her virtuous behavior. In the second story, a middle-aged woman beset with the difficulties of being single locates a man to give her shelter. A strong, independent woman "seeing the light" and entering into blissful matrimony serves as the third story.

For many of the shows, the significance of marriage does not end with the actual ceremony. Some shows extend this dominant narrative into the married life of the heroine. Now the heroine must maintain her marriage. If the soap opera continues after the marriage, the story begins to revolve around the betrayals and agendas of in-laws (usually women) that lead to misunderstandings between the married couple. Often the heroine is able to prove her righteousness and devotion to her husband and save her marriage. In some cases, however, she loses this battle and ends up divorced. The story then continues with her struggles as a divorcee, leading to her rescue through another marriage.

In addition to soap operas, daytime talk shows promote a patriarchal vision. These shows target women through content and narratives that reveal a preoccupation with marriage and married life. Two of the most popular shows are *Meena Bazaar* and *The Nadia Khan Show*.

Meena Bazaar presents different segments focusing on beauty, interviews, and cooking. The show is geared toward the homemaker. Often, a makeup artist will prepare a bride. Later in the show, the host and the artist will discuss the choices made in decorating the bride. *The Nadia Khan Show*, focused on talk, revolves around married life and marriage. Through the discussion, Nadia Khan, the host, will interject examples from her married life. The show hosts a variety of personalities, including designers, models, and actresses, but with female guests the conversation always turns to marriage.

RESCUING THE FRAIL MAIDEN

Along with the emphasis on marriage, women appear as frail maidens in need of rescue. This theme exists for married and unmarried women. Television abounds with references to and depictions of women suffering and waiting for someone to save them from difficulties. Often the rescue comes in the form of marriage. A woman rarely leaves an abusive situation to create a better life.

Confessional texts, like novels and soap operas, provide female consumers a site for validation and interpretation of social roles and relationships. Usually ending with "resignation and self-suffering or patriarchal expectations," these narratives serve as "a hegemonic force in stabilizing consensus around women's traditional roles and deflecting critique away from systemic causes to internal struggle" (Mandziuk, 2001). Inquiry into the decoding of women's interaction with popular culture by feminist and cultural studies scholars recognizes that such cultural forms are paradoxical as they function both as entertainment and social control mechanisms (Christian-Smith, 1990; Modleski, 1980; Radway, 1984; Scanlon, 1995 & Simonds, 1988). While decoding text, women identify with female characters but also construct a comparison between themselves and the text (Christian-Smith, 1990; Flint, 1993; Honey, 1984; Kunzel, 1995; Radway, 1980 & Simonds, 1988). Modleski concludes that, despite criticism by feminists, perhaps "narrative pleasure" holds divergent meanings for men and women (1979). She adds that the reader is wiser than the character because she is detached and intellectually distanced from the heroine's confusion. This creates both a "submersion and transcendence" from women's own circumstances (Modleski, 1980).

The introduction of satellite television in Pakistan demonstrates the frantic process of globalization. The recent modernity assigned to women has reinforced rather than challenged hegemonic gender roles (Das 1994; Puri 1999 & Rajeshwari 1993, 1999). Scholarship by the Centre for Advocacy and Research revealed that women have been placed by satellite television in the dual role of *the protagonist* and *the consumer* of media. Current media does not act as the agenda setter for women's issues, but rather the facilitator of traditional narratives where women serve the traditional roles of mother, wife, and daughter (2003). Gardezi posits that in Pakistan, patriarchy, within or divorced from the Islamic ideological framework, is integral to the dominant culture and therefore cannot be challenged (1996).

To be in need of rescue, a woman must be abused. To facilitate and actualize the narrative of the frail maiden, growing depictions of women in abusive situations are portrayed. While candid depictions of the abuse facing women could be instructive, media abuse is sensationalized and exaggerated as a dramatic device that creates anxiety rather than offering support or solutions. In addition to depicting disadvantaged women, many soaps will focus on women who are not only financially advantaged but also educated and professional. These stories focus on the emotional and personal helplessness of these women. Often they are mistreated by their husbands or face harassment in the workplace. In *Nur Pur Ki Rani* (Queen of Nur Pur), the audience witnesses the juxtaposition of two women: Rania, the princess of Nur Pur, and Noori, an orphan child. The drama revolves around the struggle for Rania to win the love of her husband, who detests her arrogant and paranoid nature. Eventually, Rania loses this battle, and her husband falls in love with Noori and marries the orphan girl. Rania eventually goes mad and dies.

Talk shows reinforce the narrative of women's frailty and need for protection. Often the emphasis on marriage in the aforementioned talk shows starts with the assertion that a woman is weak on her own and needs the support of a man. Highlighting the struggles of different sorts of women would be a welcome addition to these women-focused talk shows. When these topics merely serve as platforms to reify the patriarchal narrative, the society becomes hostile rather than constructive toward women.

CHADDAR AND CHAARDIWAARI

As further elaboration of the aforementioned stories, emphasis is placed on the safety of chaddar and chaardiwaari. Under chaddar and chaardiwaari, women are only safe when they are veiled and/or within the confines of their own homes. The traditional narrative, from both religious and cultural perspectives, has emphasized the necessity for a woman to stay within the confines of her own house and to eschew any ambitions beyond that realm. The emphasis on the veil has been a constant in the Pakistani woman's heritage. In addition to this emphasis, and as a layer of additional security, women have been severely limited in their mobility and confined to their homes.

Misra and Roychowdhury assert that the introduction of new technologies in media and satellite television might suggest that Indian women have successfully transitioned from their traditional role inside their homes to a more contemporary one in the workplace. Unfortunately, this has not been the case, either for Indian or Pakistani women. Women are still portrayed with a layer of patriarchy motivated by cultural norms. The emancipated woman is viewed with inherent suspicion. She can succeed only by succumbing to her traditional role within the family. The colonial discourse of separating the material from the spiritual resonates. Women are expected to carry the burden of tradition while their issues and concerns remain unresolved (1997).

Commodification and representation of women as "targets and vehicles" of consumerism is criticized by Ganguly-Scrase (2003). The negative stereotype of the "Westernized woman" as a "willful-rights-seeking individual" has been deliberately constructed to give credence to the narrative of the "traditional" virtuous woman as the "privileged national female subject." However, feminist activists challenge this characterization enforcing the "pure Muslim girl" (Jamal, 2006). The traditional narrative asserts that female students or professional women are at risk for abduction and rape. While this rarely occurs, soaps and talk shows exploit such dangers. For example, in the drama *Chehray*, Nadeem, a prominent married politician and professor, develops a fixation on one of his female students, Vaneeza. In the course of the drama, Nadeem kidnaps Vaneeza, forces her to marry him, and abuses her.

Also, strong professional women are often cast as villains. While the submissive housewife saves her family by her virtue and sacrifice, the strong and/or financially secure woman instigates drama and mayhem in her own life as well as the lives of those around her. Often, this strong woman ends up isolated or ostracized as a result of her selfish and unethical behavior, reinforcing the idea that a good woman makes the domestic domain her sole priority and achieves triumph by displaying self-sacrifice and forbearance.

The talk shows also emphasize submissive qualities. The narrative is reinforced through the implicit agenda and framing of discussion topics. Any counter narrative is subjected to disruption. An example of this occurred when Asma Jehangir, a renowned lawyer and women's rights activist, appeared on the show *Meena Bazaar*. As Jehangir discussed women's rights, she was interrupted by a female caller wanting to know why Jehangir was not wearing a chaddar on television. Ms. Jehangir was forced to defend her choice of clothing and profession.

COUNTER NARRATIVES

While the popular media may be steeped in the patriarchal narrative, efforts are being made to introduce counter narratives into the public sphere. Two prominent examples are the talk show, *The First Blast*, on Dawn News channel and the nonprofit organization South Asian Women in Media (SAWM). Jennifer Hayward emphasizes the need for a reexamination of Muslim women's position within society to assert their identities as daughters and citizens (1992). Kothari explains that the discussion on the acculturation and redemption of South Asian women has been historically under male jurisdiction. She insists that women do not succumb to these biased, gender-driven narratives because liberalized media technologies offer a platform to "deconstruct and contest dominant conceptualizations" and "offer alternate representation" (2005). Women's ingenuity finds ways to evade patriarchal scrutiny by "speaking through their silence" to negotiate their independent identity.

Pakistani women historically enjoyed a collective social environment with other female members of their community. Such lively social encounters served the dual task of entertainment and catharsis for the female population. Television created substitutes for these shared collective experiences and offered soap operas as a medium of expression (Kothari, 2005). The patriarchal directives of "chaddar and chaardiwaari" were contested by women in Pakistan when actress Sahira Kazmi walked off the set of her dramatic serial refusing to cover her head with a veil. She stated, "my honor lies in my convictions, not on my head!" (Saleha, 1990; Ahmed, 1983 & Kothari, 2005).

The *First Blast* is described by the channel as focusing "on topics which affect your daily life and provides an empowering, enlightening forum for women to talk, to share, to discuss, to laugh, and to retake control of their lives" (Dawn News). True to its mission, the show has been a pioneer in broadening the agenda and framing women's issues. Topics for the show have included career counseling, osteoporosis, entrepreneurship, mental health, and marital dynamics. The show has even hosted episodes on the harmful side effects of smoking. The hosts and guests emphasize that smoking is indeed a widely practiced habit by women in this society.

SAWM is an organization which seeks to "highlight women's issues and perspectives, in general, and act as a platform where women . . . can identify and find solutions to their problems, in particular" (2009). The organization has been hosting annual conferences each year since 2008 to raise awareness about the challenges confronting women working in media as well as to critique the narratives and depictions of women in media. These conferences have attracted some of the best known and most respected media practitioners in South Asia, garnering attention from prominent politicians and media outlets in countries that hosted the conferences. Such programs and activist organizations are working to illuminate women's issues. Naturally, they face an uphill task as they seek to counter entrenched cultural narratives and agendas, and recast women's roles in society beyond chaddar and chaardiwaari.

REFERENCES

Ahmed, D-S. (1983). *Television in Pakistan: An ethnographic study.* (Unpublished doctoral dissertation). Columbia University, New York.

Barthes, R. (1974). *S/Z,* trans. Richard Miller. (p. 76). New York: Hill and Wang.

Centre for Advocacy and Research. (2003). Contemporary woman in television fiction: Deconstructing role of "commerce" and "tradition." *Economic and Political Weekly, 38*(17), 1684–90.

Christian-Smith, L. K. (1990). *Becoming a woman through romance.* New York: Routledge.

Committee on the Status of Women in India. (1974). *Towards Equality.* New Delhi: Ministry of Education and Social Welfare, 359.

Das, V. (1994). Modernity and biography: Women's lives in contemporary India. *Thesis Eleven, 39*(52), 62.

Dawn News. (2010). *The first blast.* Retrieved from news.dawn.com/wps/wcm/connect/dawnnews/dawnnews-test/lifestyle/firstblast.

Easton, B. (1978). Feminism and the contemporary family, *Socialist Review,* May–June 1978, 34.

Flint, K. (1993). *The woman reader, 1837–1914.* New York: Clarendon.

Ganguly-Scrase, R. (2003). Paradoxes of globalization, liberalization, and gender equality: The worldviews of the lower middle class in West Bengal, India, *Gender and Society*. *17*(4), 544–66.

Gardezi, F. (1996). Islam, feminism and the women's movement, other voices from Pakistan, 61. *Pakistan–India People's Forum for Peace and Democracy*, New Delhi: New Age International.

Hayward, J. (1992). Day after tomorrow: Audience interaction and soap opera production, *Cultural Critique*, (23), 83–109, University of Minnesota Press.

Honey, M. (1984). The confession formula and fantasies of empowerment. *Women's Studies*, *10*, 303–20.

Jamal, A. (2006). Gender, citizenship, and the nation-state in Pakistan: Willful daughters or free citizens? *Signs: Journal of Women in Culture and Society*, *31*(2).

Kothari, S. (2005). From genre to zanaana: Urdu television drama serials and women's culture in Pakistan, *Contemporary South Asia*, *14*(3), 289–305.

Kunzel, R. (1995). Pulp fictions and problem girls: Reading and rewriting single pregnancy in the postwar United States. *American Historical Review*, *100*, 1465–87.

Mandziuk, R. (2001). Confessional discourse and modern desires: Power and please in *True Story* magazine, *Critical Studies in Media Communication*, *18*(2), 174–93.

Misra, K. & Roychowdhury, D. (1997). Vigilantes, virgins, and long-suffering wives: The limitations of contemporary Indian television's reconstructions of femininity, *Contemporary South Asia*, *6*(3), 247–58.

Modleski, T. (1979). The search for tomorrow in today's soap operas: Notes on a feminine narrative. *Film Quarterly*, *33*(1), 12–21.

Modleski, T. (1980). The disappearing act: A study of harlequin romances. *Signs*, *5*, 435–48.

Mulvey, L. (1977). Visual pleasure and narrative cinema. In K. Kay & G. Peary (Eds.), Women and the Cinema. New York: E. P. Dutton.

Mumtaz, K., & Shaheed, F. (1987). *Women of Pakistan: Two steps forward, one step backwards?* Lahore: Vanguard Books.

Porter, D. (1977). Soap time: Thoughts on a commodity art form. *College English*, *38*(8), 783.

Puri, J. (1999). *Woman, body, desire in post-colonial India: Narratives of gender and sexuality*. New York: Routledge.

Radway, J. (1984). *Reading the romance: Women, patriarchy, and popular literature*. Chapel Hill: University of North Carolina Press.

Rajeshwari, S. R. (1993). *Real and imagined women: Gender, culture, and post colonialism*. London: Routledge.

Rajeshwari, S. R. (1999). *Signposts: Gender issues in post-independence India*. New Delhi, India: Kali for Women.

Saleha, S. (1990). *Representations of gender in prime-time television: A textual analysis of drama series of Pakistan television*. (Unpublished doctoral dissertation). University of Wisconsin, Madison.

SAWM. (2009). South Asian Women in Media . Retrieved from www.facebook.com/group.php?v=wall&gid=16984763306.

Scanlon, J. (1995). *Inarticulate longings: The Ladies' Home Journal, gender, and the promises of consumer culture*. New York: Routledge.

Simonds, W. (1988). Confessions of loss: Maternal grief in *True Story*, 1920–1985. *Gender & Society*, *2*, 149–71.

Chapter Four

Women in Film

Treading Water but Fit for the Marathon

Lisa French

As a woman you have a unique and different vision. It's good that these voices are heard in the world. —Jane Campion (in Andrews, 2003)

Affected by a whole host of experiences and perspectives, including class, race, and ethnic origin, female social identity is complex. While women do not constitute a single, homogenous group, and have a diverse range of experiences, perspectives, aesthetic approaches, and interests, what women share collectively is the knowledge of gendered experience, that of being women in a world that is deeply patriarchal. As Judith Mayne has observed, although it might be tenuous, fractured, or complicated, "there is a connection between the writer's gender, her personhood, and her texts; and . . . "there exists a female tradition . . . whether defined in terms of models of mutual influence, shared themes or common distances from the dominant culture" (Mayne, 1990, p. 90). The understanding of being a woman is central to female experience, and it follows that women filmmakers might find gestures, enactments, and significations to explore that experience. Thus, what women represent in their films, and the modes of representation, may well differ from that constructed by men (and vice versa). If women are not given access to, or find it difficult to produce films, female aesthetic approaches and worldviews will have significantly fewer outlets for expression.

In the current climate this is a real possibility, given that the participation of women in key creative filmmaking roles in Western industrialized countries has generally declined or remained static over the past decade. Where they do participate, they do so with considerable success, but numerically progress appears to have stalled, and in some areas there are fewer women. The gains women made and the momentum they once achieved have not been sustained.

Equity and social inclusion are fundamental to civil rights, but there is also a myriad of other reasons underscoring their importance: business, ethical, social, cultural, and legal reasons that make it vital for global Western industrialized film industries to ensure women achieve equal participation. As Cutler and Company (2008) has observed, high quality human capital is critical to productivity and innovation. In order to achieve productive, diverse, and innovative industries, equitable participation is essential because as Bell has found, persistent patterns of gender inequality impact "negatively on men as well as women by narrowing choice and reinforcing historic workforce patterns" (Bell, 2009, p. 10).

This chapter examines the current status of Western women in film, beginning with a perspective on the participation of women in film industries in a selection of Western industrialized countries (the United States, Australia, United Kingdom, Canada, Denmark, and New Zealand). Following this is a particular case study, proffering an outline of the current participation of women in the Australian film industry. The chapter concludes with observations of what women filmmakers bring and offers strategies for improving the participation and status of women. Throughout there is reflection on the effects of the decline of women's representation in major creative areas of film, including what it means for Australian and global film industries, and the textures and sensibilities women bring to filmmaking.

WOMEN IN FILM AND TELEVISION INTERNATIONALLY

There are women in the Senate, women heading studios, and busloads of young women emerging from film school. So why are 96 percent of films directed by men (Goldberg, 2002, p. 1)? When the action director Kathryn Bigelow became the first and only woman to win an Academy Award for Best Achievement in Directing in 2010 (for *The Hurt Locker*, 2008/9), the international status of women in film fell into sharp relief. While Bigelow has made films that have virtually excluded women (*Point Break*, 1991, for example), she also made *Blue Steel* (1990) critiqued by Yvonne Tasker as "an attempt to put a woman at the centre of a movie predominantly occupied by men" (Tasker, 2002, p. 63). From a feminist perspective, Tasker also argues the interest of Bigelow's work "has as much to do with its capacity to underline the limitations of thinking about certain kinds of genres and styles as 'masculine'" (Tasker, 2002, pp. 60–61).

While Bigelow's success placed a spotlight on the issue of gender, researchers in recent times also have increasingly turned their attention to gender in relation to filmmaking (and other media industries). In what follows, I examine international research, finding across a number of Western industrialized countries that women have not achieved equity (through equal opportunities, or proportional opportunities for participation), and the status, or representation, of women in these film industries has generally remained static or has declined.

An American survey (Lauzen, 2008) found that women represent between 4 and 23 percent in any of the following roles: director, executive producer, producer, writer, cinematographer and editor (thus remaining significantly under-represented). Very few substantial gains have been made in achieving employment in top grossing American films, and in several areas women have been losing ground (writer, executive producer/producer, editor). In all categories, women's participation declined in the period between 1998 and 2007. While this appears to be improving again in the current period, this dip in participation in the early 2000s has also occurred in other countries, such as the United States and Australia.

Lauzen's 2008 survey of the employment of 2706 individuals working on the top 250 domestic grossing films in America (excluding foreign films) noted a decline in women's participation from 2001, which began to recover (increase again) from 2007. Lauzen's 2008 American survey further found that 22 percent of films released in 2008 did not employ any women in the key creative roles of director, executive producer, producer, writer, cinematographer, or editor. A comparison over ten years (1998–2008) showed that women's employment as directors and cinematographers remained stable while percentages of female writers, executive producers, producers, and editors slightly declined.

A study conducted in the United Kingdom in 2007 (Bhavnani) indicated that women were underrepresented in the film industry in relation to the general UK workforce. It found gender inequity in screenwriting, camera, and technical areas. The researchers concluded that

> under-represented groups in the film industry are not always equitably represented or treated, whether in the workforce, among audiences, or in portrayal. The sector is dominated in leadership positions by white, male middle-aged, able-bodied men. However there is a business case for greater diversity in the industry, as well as a legal and ethical case. (Bhavnani, 2007, p. 9)

An example of this lack of equality can be seen in a 2008 study (Skillset) of the film and television workforce in the United Kingdom. It revealed a pay equity gap, finding that the earnings of men and women in the industry were different, with women earning "on average substantially less than men— £29,016 per year compared with £34,669."

Sinclair et al.'s 2006 study of women screenwriters (1999–2003) in the United Kingdom found that although films written by women were as likely to gain release as those written by men, and the box office return on a British film with a female writer was slightly higher than films with a male writer (Sinclair et al., p. ix), women screenwriters were still only credited on less than 15 percent of UK films. The study found that women wrote in all genres, were overly represented (compared to their industry participation) in industry-accredited screenwriting courses, and cinema audiences were ap- proximately evenly balanced between men and women—so none of these factors (experience in genre, training, or audience demographic) could ex- plain the finding that women writers made up only 26 percent of the total writing for film, and 38 percent of the total in audiovisual media other than film. It also noted that only 8.6 percent (47 of 549 films) had a female director, and 70 percent of those had a female writer as well, but that the majority (24 out of 33) were writer directors (only 9 out of 33 were directors working with women writers) (p. 10). This would suggest that a significant pathway to directing for women is also to be the writer on the project.

A Danish study of gender and work in relation to Danish feature films (Knudsen & Rowley, 2005) revealed a marked imbalance. In film, women made up 0 percent of cinematographers, 17 percent of screenwriters, 19 percent of producers, 20 percent of directors, and 38 percent of editors. Television had a similar picture. The Board of Directors (1991–2003) in Denmark's main public service TV station, DR, had only 17 percent women; and 4 percent on the Executive Board (1992–2002). The study also found female ghettos in children's documentaries (which appear to have discrimi- nated against men), with 83 percent of female employees. For children's features, however, no women were hired for fourteen out of twenty years. There was evidence of a decline in female participation: "[a]cross the board there were 78 percent men and 22 percent women in 1992, and 80 percent men and 20 percent women in 2002." The number of women in positions of influence in the world of Danish feature films decreased from 1992 to 2002 (Knudsen & Rowley, 2005). This indicates that the dip in participation found in the United States and Australia in the early 2000s is possibly a global phenomenon, although the Danish study (1992–2002) noted despite the de- cline in most areas, women improved their representation as directors (to 20 percent). While it is still a low figure, it varies from the decline shown in women directors' participation in Australia and New Zealand. A study of New Zealand films released into New Zealand cinemas (2003–2007) found that only 8 percent were written or directed by women (Evans, 2008), and figures from Screen Australia (2009) established that 18 percent of films were directed by women (1990/1991–2008/2009), a decline from the 1992 survey (Cox & Laura), which found women constituted 22 percent of directors.

Women in Western film industries experience numerous common barriers to progress and success in the film and related audiovisual industries. For example, Sinclair et al. (2006), who aimed to highlight priority areas for further research and action in relation to screen writing in UK television, found a number of barriers that are likely to be common to film given many women working across both film and television. These included a poor record on diversity in many areas of the workforce affecting women, as well as ethnic and disability groups, in content and portrayal. In hiring, there was found to be indirect discrimination. For example, men in positions of power were more likely to hire men, and those making decisions about hiring writers believed myths, "possibly unconsciously," that women "do not write the sorts of stories that sell" (Sinclair et al., p. xii). Women more often did not make the most of work cultures, failing to capitalize on networks, to feel comfortable to sell or promote their work, and often women were dissuaded more easily by early criticism, finding "this process more difficult than men as they tend to have less confidence in their work and are less tenacious" (Sinclair et al., p. xiii). In general, there was a lack of access, a paucity of support, and few efforts to improve gender imbalance.

Women's participation in the Australian film industry is still, according to a recent research project and survey of 135 industry members (French, 2012), declining; for example, women's numerical representation in key creative areas such as directing has slipped backwards over the last decade. Results of the study, which has a focus on the Australian state of Victoria, indicated that many of the gender issues visible in the last major survey of the industry (Cox & Laura, 1992) are still visible today. These include sexism in the form of stereotyped assumptions, expectations to be "one of the boys," exclusion from groups, and unequal division of tasks by sex; however, not just women but many of the men completing the survey also noticed these factors (although they were proportionately less visible). The industry still has gender segregation in some areas: technical fields are still more difficult for women to gain a foothold, and there was a clear bias toward males in the areas of production (43 percent), script (57 percent), and direction (57 percent). Women continue to achieve the highest numerical representation in areas such as producing and production management.

The survey (French 2012) revealed interesting results in relation to family. First, 76 percent of women reported family responsibilities were not a significant issue in relation to progress in the industry, which was a significant shift from the previous survey (Cox & Laura, 1992) where family responsibilities were rated as hindering ability to work in the industry (an issue for both women and men). However, 75 percent of women (compared to a little over half the men) are more able to maintain a career in the industry. Therefore, the female population in the industry has aged in Australia, given few women with dependent children are working in it (and arguably films telling stories of women with children would be less likely to be developed). Where they did have dependent children, women experienced a lack of career mobility. In addition, there were some indicators that there may be more single parents (both male and female) in audiovisual industries. Additional research might determine sole responsibility of children. There was some evidence of ageism for both younger women under twenty-five and those over forty-eight. Notably, women proportionately held more part-time work than men, and men had more job security as evidenced by more stable employment in that freelancers worked for fewer employers. Women reported (French, 2012) that while they may want to work in other industry jobs, they were prevented by lack of opportunities, experience, and contacts or mentoring, whereas the main reason preventing men shifting to other jobs was financial security.

Many of the issues and barriers found in the last major survey of the Australian industry (Cox & Laura, 1992) have not been addressed, and this may explain the Australian census figures indicating women are leaving the industry. While the majority of women agree that attitudes toward women have improved, only 4 percent agree the economic situation is better. Only 20 percent of women believe there have been improvements in the last five years, compared to 50 percent of men, indicating a gender inequity when it comes to views on improvements for women.

In summary, the international situation provides evidence that women are generally significantly under-represented in Western film industries. Not only have they stopped gaining ground, but in many instances their numbers have declined. There is some evidence of a dip in participation in the early 2000s but a slight recovery in the second part of the decade. In many key creative roles female participation is well below representation in the wider workforce, and gendered ghettos in some fields still exist (which are most often the technical or camera areas). Despite a trend for women to over-train, confirmed by their proportion in training, evidence suggests that they are often paid less. It appears that films with female directors are more likely to have female writers, often because women are able to direct a film when they are writer/directors. In summary, the declining status of women is a major concern for global film industries. As Tobias has observed:

As far as many of today's female screenwriters know, right now is the best it's ever been for women in Hollywood. It's a vast improvement over the situation even twenty years ago. What they don't know is that their ideal future, the one in which at least 50 percent of screenwriters are women, came and went nearly 70 years ago. (Tobias in Sinclair et al., p. 1)

Why is equality important? When the products turned out by our media are mainly created by men, it is not only a pity for the women in the business; it is a pity for all of us. Because the consequence is that all of us—both women and men—miss out on a lot more multi-faceted and much more interesting stories about our lives. (Knudsen, 2005, p. 7)

Business and cultural arguments demonstrate that equal representation in leadership positions in film and related industries such as television are essential. As outlined in a 2004 report on the Australian television industry, if "leaders are chosen from only half the population it will be harder to get the best person for the job every time," and "if the industry misses out on all these potential leaders, this certainly represents a real waste of talent, skills and experience" (AFC/Morgan, p. 8). There are implications for lack of diversity for content because when "decision makers come from only one part of society, they will only draw on a narrow range of experiences . . . [and it] will be harder for them to take into account the diverse television audience when they make decisions on programming and production" (AFC/Morgan, p. 8).

Where there are more women in leadership positions, more diverse leadership styles are possible. The 2004 AFC/Morgan Australian report on television (which is transferable to film because many Australian women work across both) found that men and women are freer to choose to use a communication style that suits them—often involving both masculine and feminine perspectives—and so inflexible styles that existed before are now not necessary to gain success (dominance, competitive behavior, and toughness). This points to a benefit for those who work in the industry, although it must be noted that men and women may not necessarily have different leadership approaches given that "women in senior leadership will have been selected and socialized to conform to the dominant organizational structure" (p. 10). On the other hand, some research has shown (Rhode) that women perform well in more interpersonally sensitive or collaborative approaches (as may some men). Rhode has noted that conventional gender roles have encouraged women "to develop interpersonal skills and sensitivities, which increase their comfort level with participatory styles" (Rhode, 2003, p. 20), and it follows that this would imbue changes in workplace cultures if such styles flourished.

There is arguably a link between the gender balance of a workplace and the retention of women. Bell has observed, "there is ample and consistent evidence that the organizational culture of the workplace plays an important role in retention and career advancement, especially for women" (Bell, p. 39). It could be observed from this that retaining women in audiovisual industries may be dependent, or directly related to, achieving a gender-balanced workforce.

It also appears that the number of women in the industry has a direct correlation with opportunities. An American study (2010) found that where women were equally represented as decision makers behind the scenes, "the number of female characters in a film increases," and "the number of female actors grows" (Smith, 2010). Other studies have supported this conclusion. One 2007 UK report observed, "when women are involved in writing, production, and directing, they create more female characters" (Bhavnani, p. 12). If one considers films that have women in these roles, one finds evidence that they not only create more female characters, but characters who make an outstanding contribution to the exploration and visibility of female experience; these films also tend to have more women than usual on the crew.

A 2006 UK study of screenwriters outlined a business argument for improving the representation of women in the screenwriting role. It observed that data showed "women write the sort of films that do well in the United Kingdom, that the films they make are as likely to gain a release, and their films are actually dollar for pound marginally more financially effective" (Sinclair et al., p. 15). The report also argued that the industry was potentially missing out on "new and interesting ideas, stories and storytelling innovation," and also causing social effects, for example, a lack of female perspectives resulting in the perpetuation of stereotypes (Sinclair et al., p. 15). It can be deduced from this that if film industries increase diversity (not just in terms of women's participation, but the participation of other minority groups), national cinemas will be less heterogeneous, and international cinema will be richer.

WOMEN IN THE AUSTRALIAN FILM INDUSTRY

> While women directors in film industries around the world are still seen as anomalous (if mainstream) or marginalised as avant-garde, the Antipodes have been home to an impressive cadre of female film-makers who negotiate and transcend such notions. Before the promising debuts of Ann Turner (*Celia*) and Jane Campion (*Sweetie*), Gillian Armstrong blazed a trail with *My Brilliant Career*. —Sarris in Barber, p. 6

Entering the first decade of the new millennium, Australian women filmmakers in the 2000s continued to achieve great success. In a variety of industry crafts Australian women made a substantial contribution on the international stage, many winning international accolades such as Academy Awards (for example, actors Cate Blanchett and Nicole Kidman, art/set/costume designer Catherine Martin, and producer Melanie Coombs). Australian women achieved international profiles in key creative roles; these include producers Jan Chapman (*The Piano*) and Jane Scott (*Shine*), editor Jill Bilcock (*Moulin Rouge!*), screenwriter Laura Jones (*Brick Lane*), cinematographer Mandy Walker (*Australia*), and production designer Janet Patterson (*Bright Star*). Although still a minority in all major creative positions, women shone at the Australian Film Institute Awards in the 2000s. In the feature categories over the last decade, Best Film was won 80 percent of the time by women producers (who are only 33 percent of the workforce); Best Direction awards went 40 percent of the time to women directors (who are only 18 percent of the workforce); and Best Original Screenplay awards went 50 percent of the time to women writers (who are only 20 percent of the workforce).

Despite these successes, Australian census figures indicate that women have been leaving the film, television, and audiovisual industries at a greater rate than men, and that the participation of women in the key creative areas of directing has slipped dramatically over the last decade. Data from the EOWA Census of Women in Leadership (AFC/Morgan, 2004) observed that only one director of television is a woman (although it should be noted that in Australia there are only a small number of such jobs); and that 8.3 percent of media sector board directors are women (lower than the Australian average of 8.6 percent). However, women in the media sector hold 15.4 percent of ASX2000 executive management positions, which is much higher than the Australian average of 10.2 percent (AFC/Morgan), and women hold a significant proportion of the head positions in state and federal government film funding agencies (in 2010 women were head of several government agencies: Screen Australia, Film Victoria, and Screen NSW).

Today, women in the Australian film industry are integrated at all levels; there are no longer affirmative action programs, such as women's film units (e.g., The Women's Film Fund run by the Australian Film Commission in 1976–1988), and there is no separate feminist filmmaking (as was visible in the 1970s with feminist filmmaking groups)—which is not to say that feminism is not alive and well, but rather that it is expressed in the textures, sensibilities, and viewpoints of more mainstream work. Many women felt that the female filmmaking collectives and organizations marginalized or ghettoized them, that women were talking to themselves, and that there was a need to enter the mainstream (although given the poor status of women in global industries, many of these affirmative action programs and support groups are arguably still required). Since the 1980s, women filmmakers in Australia have worked within the structures of mainstream film production. For instance, the work of Australian-based Jane Campion exemplifies filmmaking which is mainstream but which reflects concerns central to feminist theory: "the relationship of women to language, and to public and private histories; sexual difference . . . the limits and possibilities of desire; the relationship between women . . . " (Thornham quoted in Gamble, p. 82). As Michelle Citron has observed, such filmmaking in the mainstream creates "the opportunity to reach a larger audience [and] the potential of using mainstream culture to critique or subvert it" (Citron quoted in Gamble, p. 82).

Contemporary Australian women filmmakers have made a particular contribution as female authors interested in representing female experience, female subjectivity, and portraying relationships between women. Notably, these are also the most successful and internationally well-known Australian filmmakers, such as Gillian Armstrong, whose career has been dominated by her films about female experience, for example, the features *Little Women* (1994) and *Charlotte Gray* (2001), or the five 'seven-up' documentaries beginning with *Smokes and Lollies* (1975).

There are many other contemporary Australian women filmmakers who have made cinematic explorations from female perspectives, making "women's films" in the sense that they explore the cultural construct of the "feminine," and what it is to be a woman in the depicted society. Notable for their explorations of female experience are films examining the tensions and connections between sisters (*Little Women, The Last Days of Chez Nous, Radiance, Love Serenade, In the Cut*); the bonds between mothers and daughters and sometimes grandmothers (*Looking for Alibrandi, How to Make an American Quilt, High Tide, The Piano*); the strange nature of some female friendships (*The Well, The Portrait of a Lady*); the way men and women negotiate living together in the world (*Road to Nhill*); and the hold that romantic myths have over some women (*Love Serenade, Walk the Talk, An Angel at My Table, In the Cut*). The great talents that women bring on their merits as skilled filmmakers are significant and vital to the success of a global film industry. These stories, of sisters, mothers, daughters, and female friendships are those that male filmmakers would be less likely to make, and the kinds of stories that, despite their success, are those at risk if fewer and fewer women are able, or make the choice, to work in the film industry.

Moving forward, it is important that researchers collect qualitative and quantitative data that maps gender imbalance in order to provide overdue evidence bases for action. Further research is needed globally to gather and analyze key issues, examine industry practices, and look to support mechanisms. Support that might be significant in turning around the minority participation of women might be initiatives such as more flexible workplaces and support for career interruption due to child rearing. Programs to encourage women to plan careers and have the confidence to aim high and to understand their leadership potential are also important, along with mentoring. Recognition of what women contribute to the field, for example, via public awareness of contributions by women filmmakers (or further research on this), is also significant in fostering women's belief in themselves, as well as developing a larger picture of women's work.

ACKNOWLEDGMENT

I would like to thank the Academic Women's Writing Group for their helpful feedback on this paper (Mary Debrett, Hester Joyce, Brigid Magner, Gabrielle Murray, and Terrie Waddell).

REFERENCES

Andrews, N. (2003, October 18). FT Weekend Magazine—The Arts' *Financial Times*, p. 26.
Australian Film Commission/Morgan, L. (2004). Tuned into leadership: Women and television. Retrieved from afcarchive.screenaustralia.gov.au/downloads/pubs/tuned_into_leadership.pdf.
Barber, L. (2008, April 25–26). "Reel Women." *Australian (Review)*, p. 6.
Bell, S. (2009). Women in science in Australia: Maximising productivity, diversity and innovation. Retrieved from www.fasts.org/index.php?option=com_content&task=view&id=1.
Bhavnani, R. (2007). Barriers to diversity in film. Retrieved from www.ukfilmcouncil.org.uk/media/pdf/8/n/Barriers_to_Diversity_in_Film_DS_RB_20_Aug_07.pdf .
Cox, E., & Laura, S. (1992). *What do I wear for a hurricane: Women in Australian film, television, video & radio industries*. Sydney: Australian Film Commission & The National Working Party on the Portrayal of Women in the Media.
Cutler and Company. (2008). Venturous Australia: Building strength in innovation. Retrieved from www.innovation.gov.au/innovationreview/Documents/NIS_review_Web3.pdf.
Evans, M. (2008). *Background notes on women writers' and directors' participation in Australian feature film, from a New Zealand perspective*. Retrieved from www.wift.org/about/Marianper cent20Evanspercent20Notesper cent20Maypercent2008.pdf .
French, L. (Ed.). (2003). *Womenvision: Women and the moving image in Australia*. Melbourne: Damned Publishing.
French, L. (2012). Women in the Victorian film, television and related industries: Research Report, RMIT, Melbourne.
French, L., & Poole, M. (2009). Shining a light: 50 years of the Australian Film Institute. Melbourne: ATOM.
Gamble, S. (Ed.). (2006). *The Routledge companion to feminism and postfeminism*. London: Routledge.
Goldberg, M. (2002, August). Where are all the female directors? *Salon*, Retrieved from dir.salon.com/ent/movies/feature/2002/08/27/women_directors/index.html.
Knudsen, M. (2005). *Update on women in the industry*. WIFT Summit, Los Angeles. Unpublished paper supplied directly to the author of this chapter.
Knudsen, M. & Rowley, R. (2005). *Gender and work in Danish film & TV 1992–2002*. Retrieved from www.nywift.org/article.aspx?id=82 .
Lauzen, M. M. (2009). *The celluloid ceiling: Behind-the-scenes employment of women on the top 250 films of 2008*. Retrieved from www.wftv.org.uk/wftv/reports.asp?menu=reports&clean_search=yes.
Mayne, J. (1990). *The Woman at the keyhole: Feminism & women's cinema*. Bloomington: Indiana University Press.

Rhode, D. L. (Ed.). (2003). *The difference "difference" makes: Women and leadership.* London: Stanford University Press/Eurospan.

Screen Australia analysis of the credits of 395 Australian features, shot between July 1990 and June 2009. Supplied directly to the author of this chapter (unpublished data).

Sinclair, A., Pollard, E., & Rolfe, H. (2006). *Scoping study into the lack of women screenwriters in the UK.* London: UK Film Council & Institute for Employment Studies (IES).

Skillset. (2008). Why her? Factors that have influenced the careers of successful women in film & television. *AFTV & Alliance Sector Skills Councils,* UK. Retrieved from www.skillset. org/film/industry/article_7432_1.asp .

Smith, S.L. (2010). USC Annenberg study shows recent top films lack females on screen and behind the camera. Retrieved from annenberg.usc.edu/Newsper cent20andpercent20Events/ News/100223FilmGender.aspx.

Tasker, Y. (Ed.). (2002). *Fifty contemporary filmmakers.* London: Routledge.

II

Political Issues

Chapter Five

Mass Media Explain the Global Sex Trade

Anne Johnston, Barbara Friedman, and Autumn Shafer

The United States is a "source, transit, and destination" for human trafficking, which includes the sexual enslavement of women and children (U.S. Department of State, 2010). As part of a far-reaching global network, criminals trafficked more than twelve million adults and children for forced labor and prostitution in 2009, at a rate of 1.8 people per 1,000 worldwide. The sale of trafficked women and girls provides a significant source of revenue for criminal networks throughout the world, second only to narcotics and arms sales (U.S. Department of Health and Human Services, 2010).

The United Nations defines sex trafficking as:

> The recruitment, transportation, transfer, harbouring or receipt of persons, by means of the threat or use of force or other forms of coercion, of abduction, of fraud, of deception, of the abuse of power or of a position of vulnerability or of the giving or receiving of payments or benefits to achieve the consent of a person having control over another person, for the purpose of exploitation. Exploitation shall include . . . the exploitation of the prostitution of others or other forms of sexual exploitation. (United Nations, 2004, p. 42)

The definition provides that consent of the victim is irrelevant if any of the means described above are used. If none of the means described in the definition occur, but the victim is a minor, it is considered trafficking.

Trafficking "appears to be directly correlated with the increasing universal marginalization of women," Schauer and Wheaton have argued (2006, p. 146). Globalization, with its impact on vulnerable populations, also has been linked to an increase in the trafficking of women and girls for sex (Chuang,

2006; Risley, 2009; Stoecker, 2004). Undeniably, trafficking in the United States is a "domestic problem with transnational dimensions" (Hodge, 2008, p. 143).

As an upward trend with global implications, sex trafficking is worthy of news coverage for many reasons. (Itule & Anderson, 1994; The Missouri Group, 2007). The international aspect of the sex trade overlaps with a number of issues to which mass media have long been attentive: crime, abuses of power, immigration, violence, and war. Journalism's tradition of providing voice to the voiceless (Kovach & Rosenstiel, 2007) lends itself to coverage of the sex trade, whose victims are often among the world's most vulnerable individuals (Kelly, 2004). Further, journalists function as an independent monitor of power (Kovach & Rosenstiel, 2007), and thus, investigation and exposure of the corruption inherent in sex trafficking is an appropriate endeavor for news organizations that fulfill their watchdog role.

Although there has been little systematic research on mass media coverage of sex trafficking (Johnston & Friedman, 2008), some of the research from other fields acknowledges an important link between news coverage and anti-trafficking efforts. Scholars have noted that the mass media are influential contributors to a global discourse on sex trafficking that also includes policymakers (Berman, 2003; Wilson & Dalton, 2008). Yet, more often than not, news organizations are blamed for underreporting the problem, misrepresenting the problem, promoting ineffective solutions, and worse.

For example, when news organizations have turned a blind eye to trafficking, scholars have accused them of neglecting their important watchdog role, being complicit in allowing trafficking to flourish, and making women more vulnerable to the coercion of traffickers (Margolis, 2007). Hughes (2000) wrote that mass media should expose the tactics used by traffickers to lure women and children into the sex trade. In some countries, a "relative media blackout on the subject of trafficking" leaves "women without information about what is happening to women who have gone abroad" under false pretenses (p. 645). Indeed, with fewer official controls of its distribution of information, Western media may be best positioned to illuminate traffickers' international reach and thwart traffickers' practices.

On the other hand, "sensationalist media coverage of exceptional cases of murder and abuse, as well as the depiction of [women trafficked for sex work] as victims" has been blamed for misrepresenting the typical trafficked woman (Cwikel & Hoban, 2005, p. 309). In fact, critics argue that misrepresentation is common in news coverage of trafficking. For example, Hughes (2000) has noted the tendency to refer to women trafficked from the former Soviet Union as either "Russian" or "Eastern European," without further identification to indicate the specific country of origin. Thus, when executed poorly, news coverage of sex trafficking, as one indicator of women's status in the world, can "encourage racism" and promote stereotypes of women as victims (Kitzinger, 2004, p. 14).

Sensationalism or "incendiary language" (Berman, 2003, p. 38) in news coverage of trafficking may have additional consequences. It may alarm the public and promote rash or short-term solutions rather than policies or programs to address underlying causes, which research suggests are often transnational in nature. For example, Hughes (2000) has noted that globalization has been accompanied by technological advances that benefit criminal networks, by allowing them to more easily transfer and launder money gained from illegal activities such as sex trafficking. Another underlying cause with transnational dimensions is the desire to emigrate, an aspiration that traffickers exploit and mass media encourage. Throughout the world, a common thread in trafficking is the persistence of a "material culture that constantly provides the myth of glamour and allure that forces girls and women to seek what appears to be a path to fulfillment" (McCabe & Manian, 2010, p. 7). Hodge and Lietz (2007) have argued that the mass media's glamorized depictions of life in industrialized nations contribute to an environment that is conducive to trafficking.

Finally, scholars also have taken issue with the media's willingness to accept without verification the claims of special interest groups, which may exaggerate the rate of trafficking to attract media coverage and donor funding. While the existence of sex trafficking is not in question, the magnitude of the problem has been challenged (McDonald, 2004; Steinfatt, Baker & Beesey, 2002). For example, Weitzer (2007) has argued that an alliance between the religious right and abolitionist feminists has used "exaggerated, unverifiable, or demonstrably false" (p. 458) claims to win coverage and control the debate over trafficking. On the other hand, organizations that monitor trafficking are among those who have blamed careless and ahistorical reporting for perpetuating myths about trafficking (Feingold, 2005).

Mass media play a crucial role in explaining complex issues to the public (Carey, 1986). Sex trafficking is one such issue, with causes and consequences that radiate from and to the global community. As Hodge (2008) wrote, "It is difficult to understand sexual trafficking in the United States apart from the wider global context" (p. 144). This chapter analyzes the ways that U.S. newspapers have and have not covered the global facet of the sex trade.

METHOD

This chapter consists of a quantitative content analysis of the sex trafficking-related stories appearing in major U.S. print news sources in 2009. Although the focus is on U.S. news, the global facet of such coverage is implicit. Women and children in the American sex market are typically trafficked from other countries. Examining the ways that news media frame this important human rights issue can suggest how a society or culture views sex trafficking and may promote a particular interpretation among audiences. Because traffickers target women and girls disproportionately compared to other groups, news coverage also can illuminate the global status of women in the media.

The quantitative analysis is followed by an in-depth discussion of the qualitative elements in the articles. Texts such as news stories and the discourses contained in them are embedded with "ideas, ideology and referents that systematically construct both the subjects and objects of which they speak" (Hesse-Biber & Leavy, 2006, p. 293). When paired with quantitative analysis, a close examination of the news coverage provides a richer interpretation of the material related to sex trafficking. In studies that involve gender, as sex trafficking arguably does, textual examinations have been used to illuminate the systems of meaning that bolster representations of women in the mass media. For example, Walsh (2001) has shown how the masculinist discourse that pervades mass media coverage of politics reinforces the subordination and segregation of women, and Meyers (1997) found that myths and stereotypes suffused news coverage of violence against women and worked to blame women for their victimization and absolve men of responsibility for their violence.

SAMPLING

The news stories were gathered using LexisNexis Academic search for U.S. newspaper articles that included the word "sex" within one word of any variation of the words "traffic" (e.g., trafficking, trafficker, trafficked) or "slave" (e.g., slaves, slavery) or within one word of "trade." The search resulted in 1,069 articles published between January 1 and December 31, 2009, in 140 newspapers. Coders then reviewed each of the articles from the initial search and excluded eighty-one articles that contained a coincidental occurrence of the search terms that was inconsistent with the United Nations definition of sex trafficking or were duplicates. For example, there were several articles about a woman arrested for attempting to trade sex for World Series tickets (Caparella, 2009).

For the remaining 988 articles, coders determined if sex trafficking was a main focus of the story and then coded those articles for presence of transnational issues as well as sources quoted, dominant issues discussed, and whether the articles provided any discussion of what the causes, remedies, and consequences of sex trafficking were. These categories are informed by recent discussions of framing international issues by Entman (2004), who suggests that frames "perform at least two of the following basic functions in covering political events, issues, and actors: defining effects of conditions as problematic; identify[ing] causes; conveying a moral judgment; endorsing remedies or improvements" (p. 5.). Three coders developed and refined the coding protocol in three rounds of coding and then trained three additional coders. Each of the coders was then randomly assigned to code an average of 165 articles. Ten percent of the articles were double coded to check for inter-coder reliability. Strong inter-coder reliability was achieved (Cohen's kappa ranged from .22 to 1, with 60 percent of the units over .80).

RESULTS: QUANTITATIVE ANALYSIS OF ARTICLES

A total of 281 news articles in 2009 had sex trafficking as the main focus. Of those, slightly fewer than half (n=130) had references to international issues—the "transnational dimensions" of trafficking (Hodge, 2008, p. 148). There were a variety of ways that the articles addressed the transnational aspect of sex trafficking. In some instances, the articles focused on the trafficking of women from European, Asian, and Central American countries into the United States. Many of these articles included statistics about the numbers of women and girls trafficked into the United States, or included information about conditions that exist for women globally that might make them vulnerable to sex traffickers. In the following tables and charts, we compare how these articles with transnational references compared to those articles with no transnational references on several dimensions, including gender of writer, type of story, description of the ages of the trafficked persons, issues covered in the articles, sources quoted in the articles, as well as the causes, remedies, and consequences suggested by the articles.

As table 5.1 shows, we found that there were significant differences in those articles that featured transnational issues and those that did not reference transnational issues on several dimensions, including gender of reporter, type of story, and description of the trafficked females in terms of age.

Table 5.1.   Analysis   of   Domestic   versus   Transnational   Stories

		Domestic Stories[a]	Transnational Stories[b]
Gender of writer*	Female	29.5%	28.7%
	Male	38.9%	48.1%
	Can't tell	4.7%	10.1%
	No byline	26.8%	13.2%
Type of story*	News	48.3%	36.9%
	Commentary	7.9%	27.7%
	News brief	28.5%	8.5%
	Feature	11.9%	24.6%
	Other	3.3%	2.3%
Age of trafficked persons*	Minors	55.6%	28.5%
	Adults	9.3%	19.2%
	Both	30.5%	46.9%
	No age mentioned	3.3%	4.6%
	No trafficked persons mentioned	1.3%	.8%
Other information or detail included	Report on event, meeting, occurrence*	86.1%	67.7%
	Experiences of individual*	27.2%	40.0%
	Ties ST to larger health, societal, law enforcement issues*	15.2%	46.9%
	Reports on trends, background of issue, statistics, expert opinions*	18.5%	48.5%
	Counter viewpoints, multiple viewpoints	8.6%	8.5%
	Source quoted or cited		
	Law enforcement*	51.7%	34.6%

	Politicians / government workers	57.6%	53.8%
	Social worker	3.3%	6.2%
	Advocacy groups*	21.2%	40.8%
	Victim(s)*	11.9%	30.0%
	Traffickers / spokespersons	17.2%	15.4%
	Witness / non-expert	5.3%	8.5%
	Journalist / media	8.6%	8.5%
	Academic / expert	5.3%	6.2%

Note: * Chi-square is significant at p<0.05
[a] No references to international issues (n=151)
[b] References to international issues (n+130)

Men wrote almost double the number of transnational sex trafficking stories than did women. Most of the stories about sex trafficking were news stories focused on current or breaking events, although more commentaries and features were a part of the transnational coverage of sex trafficking. Much of the commentary about sex trafficking focused on the transportation of women and children from other countries into the United States. For example, the *New York Times'* Nicholas Kristof has devoted many of his columns to the personal experiences of women who have been sex trafficked and, in some cases, escaped to become advocates for other trafficked women (Kristof, January 1, 2009). Feature stories also tended to have transnational issues as these typically focused on the cases of women who had been trafficked and on the groups worldwide who were addressing sex trafficking issues globally. For example, a feature article in the *St. Petersburg Times* described how a trafficker lured a young woman from Guatemala into the United States as part of a transnational sex trafficking operation (Abel, March 15, 2009). Another feature article described a New Jersey church's international efforts to stop child sex trafficking with a series of concerts (Chadwick, Feb. 19, 2009).

As table 5.1 shows, over four-fifths of the domestic stories reported on some current event or meeting. Transnational stories also reported on sex trafficking by covering a specific event or meeting, but the transnational coverage also provided more attention to profiles and to the individual experiences of the persons involved in sex trafficking—primarily the trafficked and not the traffickers. The transnational stories also included more information on sex trafficking's connection to larger societal issues, and they provided more data on sex trafficking statistics and trends. In many ways, the transnational articles contained more contextual information than did the domestic articles.

Table 5.1 also provides information about the different types of sources quoted or referenced in the articles. Politicians and government workers were featured in over half of the sex trafficking articles, regardless of whether or not the articles referenced transnational issues. However, transnational sex trafficking articles quoted fewer law enforcement sources and more advocacy groups and victims of sex trafficking than did domestic stories.

In addition to these overall elements of how information about sex trafficking appeared in transnational versus domestic stories, we were also interested in the ways in which sex trafficking was positioned as an issue in news coverage. How was sex trafficking positioned in terms of the type of issue it was, as well as the causes, consequences, and remedies for sex trafficking?

Crime issues dominated both types of articles, but the transnational articles also covered human rights issues. Most of the sex trafficking articles did not identify a cause, and both types of articles addressed the deeper root causes (such as poverty, inequality of women, globalization) of sex trafficking in about one-third of the articles. In articles where transnational issues were discussed, the causes of sex trafficking were more likely to be identified as transnational reasons (immigration, conflict, and war) as well as demand and access reasons. In comparison to domestic articles, transnational articles also contained more discussion of bad laws or lack of concern by society as causes of sex trafficking.

The two types of articles were also different in their discussion of the consequences of sex trafficking, or the discussion of who or what suffered because of sex trafficking. Almost half of the domestic articles had no mention of the consequences of sex trafficking. This was true for only one-third of the transnational articles. Both types of articles were dominated by a focus on consequences such as violence, emotional trauma, and intimidation to the women and girls victimized by sex trafficking. Finally, both types of articles did not address consequences to public health, such as the spread of AIDS or other sexually transmitted diseases in their coverage of consequences. Transnational articles did contain more mention of public health consequences, but only in 10 percent of the articles.

Finally, the articles were different in terms of how often remedies were discussed in the stories. Overall, transnational articles had more discussion of different types of remedies to sex trafficking than did domestic articles. Sixty percent of the domestic articles had no mention of any remedy to the problem of sex trafficking; this was true for only 27 percent of the transnational articles. For domestic articles, the most frequently mentioned remedies were legislation and policy changes. The remedy mentioned most often in transnational articles was education and public awareness, followed closely by training and allocation of resources to those working with sex trafficking victims as well as to sex trafficking victims themselves. Increasing punishments for those who prey on the victims of sex trafficking was also featured as a remedy in about one-fourth of the transnational stories.

SUMMARY

Sex trafficking stories in which there were references to transnational issues were more likely to include a discussion of individuals and their experiences with sex trafficking, as well as a discussion of how sex trafficking might be tied to larger public health, societal, and legal issues. If sex trafficking appeared in transnational articles, then it was more likely to be contextualized beyond the event or meeting that was driving the story; it was more likely to be positioned in a story that included background information and reports on trends and statistics.

More types of voices were also heard in the articles that contained transnational references. Transnational articles quoted more sources and experts from a variety of backgrounds; they not only featured the opinions and voices of law enforcement officials and politicians but also included experts from advocacy groups and the voices of victims.

Transnational articles on sex trafficking also contained more discussion of the underlying causes of sex trafficking from issues such as immigration restrictions, problems of war and conflict, to issues such as demand and access and the lack of concern by society. In addition, transnational articles were more likely to present the consequences of sex trafficking, although both types of articles did address consequences to the victim such as violence and mental trauma.

Finally, transnational articles were probably most different from those articles with no transnational issues in the frequency with which remedies to the problem of sex trafficking were discussed. More transnational articles addressed a variety of solutions to sex trafficking, including educating the public to increase their awareness about sex trafficking; training and providing resources to victims of sex trafficking; and increasing the punishments for the people who prey on and profit from the women and girls being trafficked. If the story focused on sex trafficking as a domestic issue, then a reader would most likely not see a remedy to the problem or might understand the remedy as part of a narrow and localized range of options.

DISCUSSION OF QUALITATIVE ELEMENTS OF ARTICLES

Looking closer at the text of the transnational and domestic news coverage, several patterns emerged that help contextualize the quantitative findings. The primacy of victims' testimonials (particularly for transnational stories) became apparent, as did an overreliance of reporters on official sources, such as law enforcement figures and politicians. The proliferation and use of both of these kinds of sources—victims and officials—help to explain some of the criticisms of news coverage of sex trafficking.

Victims' testimonials were an important way to disprove the notion that trafficking was something that happened only in foreign countries or involved only foreign women smuggled into the United States (Johnson, Jan. 25, 2009). One reporter wrote, "It's not heard about often in West Michigan, but the occurrence of youth who are sexually exploited may be surprising" (Williams, Aug. 2, 2009, para. 18), and offered a victim's testimonial as evidence. A story about sex trafficking in Las Vegas led with a victim's testimonial. The reporter followed, "This happens every day. Here, in Vegas" (Lake & Curti, June 13, 2009). Thus, while news coverage might acknowledge trafficking as an issue with transnational dimensions, it could quickly shift the focus to a domestic issue.

While indeed the women's first-person accounts were sometimes graphic, they were not necessarily gratuitous. In fact, the testimonials of victims as eyewitnesses and human sources added the kind of emotional component that some practitioners and scholars have argued is necessary to make a story salient. Kovach and Rosenstiel (2007) have urged journalists to "get as close as you can to primary sources" (p. 106). Direct quotes from sources with firsthand experience with the issue being reported enliven and humanize stories, adding credibility and readability (The Missouri Group, 2008).

The testimonials in news coverage also could serve as a warning to others, as they sometimes related traffickers' strategies for enslaving the women or girls (DiMartino, Dec. 3, 2009; Kristof, May 7, 2009; O'Neill, November 19, 2009). This was particularly important for stories that addressed the trafficking of American girls in this country (Boudreau, June 4, 2009). In some instances, the victims' testimonials were juxtaposed with quotes from traffickers. For example, in a *New York Times* series about youth runaways, a trafficking victim described how she was lured into prostitution. In the same story, a convicted pimp tells the reporter how he identified his targets: young girls with low self-esteem, prior sexual experience, and few options. "With the young girls, you promise them heaven and they'll follow you to hell," he said (Urbina, Oct. 27, 2009, para. 36). Thus, the use of testimonials to warn readers of potential threats in their communities and to describe the forms those threats might take was a way for a news organization to fulfill a watch-dog role for a local audience.

The testimonials were also a way to cultivate reader sympathy for trafficked girls and women and frame them as victims, not prostitute-criminals, as they are often charged by police (Johnson & Wagner, June 28, 2009; Nealon, Feb. 15, 2009). In fact, the framing of trafficked women and girls as victims was robust. News stories laid blame primarily on traffickers but suggested also that negligent parents, corrupt police officers, and dysfunctional social services were at fault. Finally, victims' testimonials were often cited as a motivation by individuals who had become involved in the anti-trafficking efforts (Quinn, June 14, 2009).

With few exceptions, victims' testimonials in the studied news coverage originated with events that reporters covered, such as an anti-trafficking rally. There was nothing to suggest the women's stories had been verified; in many cases, the women's testimonials were given many years after the abuse had occurred. That is not to suggest their stories were suspect, but rather to point out there was little enterprise reporting among the news coverage studied; in most stories, victims were presented to reporters through intermediaries.

That fact helps explain some of the criticism leveled at the mass media for accepting without verification the evidence or claims of special interest groups (Weitzer, 2007). Kovach and Rosenstiel (2007) have noted that "the discipline of verification is what separates journalism from entertainment, propaganda, fiction, or art" (p. 79). Yet, the imperative of verification can present a dilemma for reporters who cover sex trafficking. Compelled to find sources to humanize and make more salient their stories, reporters may discover that victims are difficult to identify and interview for a variety of reasons: sex trafficking is an underreported crime; victims may be reluctant to tell their stories given the stigma associated with sex trafficking; and importantly, the groups that shelter victims may be disinclined to allow reporters access, believing they lack the special skills required to interview trauma victims. Perhaps as a result, trafficking victims' experiences were more likely to be related as part of a covered event.

Another way reporters related a victim's experience was to reconstruct it through the use of documents such as court records or police incident reports (Thalji, May 13, 2009). Yet, this method too, can be problematic and to blame for some of the criticism of coverage. Police reports, as journalism practitioners and scholars have noted, are one sided and frequently inaccurate

(The Missouri Group, 2008). Although those kinds of public records provide one form of verification, if they are not systematically corroborated with a range of other sources (Kovach & Rosenstiel, 2007), they may emphasize the primacy of institutions such as the courts and law enforcement and suggest to readers this is where remedies lie.

In addition to their reliance on public records, reporters relied over-whelmingly on official sources such as law enforcement figures and politicians in news stories that had a domestic focus. While local officials may be loath to admit trafficking is occurring in their communities, they appeared as sources in many stories reporting the successful efforts of anti-trafficking task forces and police raids (Daugherty, March 7, 2009; Rankin, April 18, 2009). An overreliance on official sources in crime stories has been cited as an obstacle to making the news relevant to audiences (Iyengar, 1994). In her study of Utah newspaper coverage of domestic violence, Bullock (2008) found that most stories relied on unattributed information and official sources, and neglected domestic violence, expert sources, and context. As a result, she argued, the authority of police and politicians was reinforced, and readers may have come to believe that domestic violence was an issue already being addressed; further thought about prevention and solutions was unnecessary.

Transnational stories about trafficking, then, had an advantage over domestic stories because they drew from a wider range of sources, arguably resulting in more in-depth news coverage exploring causes and remedies. Thus, where reporters acknowledged the global facet of the sex trade, stories did a better job of explaining this complex issue, as is the responsibility of journalists (Carey, 1986). As sources in an individual story, victims, traffickers, law enforcement, policy makers, advocacy groups, and academic experts could provide a spectrum of voices. Further, those sources could suggest a range of responses to trafficking.

CONCLUSION

The criticism of news coverage of sex trafficking—that it is sensational, that it misrepresents the problem, that it promotes ineffective solutions and worse—is deserved, at least in part. Based on the coverage studied here, coverage disproportionately focused on the domestic aspect of trafficking, to the neglect of the transnational facet. When reporters fail to acknowledge the transnational aspect of trafficking, they also may neglect potential remedies, or be unable to critically evaluate proposed remedies.

Further, reporters did tend to accept without verification the claims of certain groups regarding the rate of trafficking. To be fair, though, reporters always qualified those statements with the fact that no reliable statistics on the rate of trafficking exist.

Critics have argued that to frame women and girls as "victims" further stigmatizes the crime of trafficking and may promote stereotypes. However, that frame proved to be an important way to distinguish the women and girls as victims of traffickers in need of support and services, not prostitute-criminals to be jailed, prosecuted, and perhaps, deported. Their testimonials, whether as part of an organized event or reconstructed from official documents, did allow the women a platform with which to "tell" their own stories.

One obstacle to understanding and reporting the complex issue of sex trafficking has been the news routine—with its tendency toward episodic reporting (Iyengar, 1994) and crime coverage (Graber, 1980)—as an obstacle to understanding and reporting the complex issue of sex trafficking. A localized focus on raids, arrests, and court proceedings may obscure the root causes of trafficking, such as poverty and political instability, that originate in other countries (Johnston & Friedman, 2008). As another consequence of that focus, audiences may look for solutions to sex trafficking in more laws and tougher penalties for offenders. Law-and-order solutions to crime seem to be a particularly Western fixation that can misdirect funding and policy efforts where trafficking is concerned (Seidel & Vidal, 1997). Similarly, when news organizations focus on demand for, rather than the supply of, women and girls for sex, coverage tends to ignore or obscure the structural issues that may be keys to reducing or eradicating the sex trade (Hudgins, 2007).

In some ways, we could argue that the transnational articles did a better job of covering the range of problems, consequences, causes, and remedies to and of sex trafficking and that they provided more viewpoints in their use of sources. But another interpretation is that sex trafficking as a transnational story was positioned in the newspapers as an issue of greater concern and one that was more problematic. Sex trafficking covered as a transnational issue presented more dire consequences and was positioned as a problem urgently in need of more solutions or remedies. If this was a problem brought to the United States by outside forces, then we needed to be more aware of the problem. In stories that had no transnational references, the problem of sex trafficking was presented as one that could be understood by hearing from politicians and law enforcement experts and was an issue that did not have any particular solution or remedy. In these domestic-focused stories, sex trafficking was a criminal activity and best solved by stricter laws and best handled by experts in law enforcement.

REFERENCES

Abel, J. (2009, March 15). Downfall of a sex slave ring. *St. Petersburg* (Fla.) *Times*, pp. 1B.

Berman, J. (2003). (Un)popular strangers and crises (un)bounded: Discourses of sex trafficking, the European political community and the panicked state of the modern state. *European Journal of International Relations, 9*(1), 37–86.

Boudreau, J. (2009, June 4). In Vietnam, teenage daughters sold into sex slavery. *Contra Costa* (Calif.) *Times*.

Bullock, C. F. (2008). Official sources dominate domestic violence reporting. *Newspaper Research Journal, 29*(2), 6–22.

Caparella, K. (2009, Oct. 29). No sex needed to get her Series tickets. *The Philadelphia Daily News*, p. DN17.

Carey, J. W. (1986). The dark continent of American journalism. In R. K. Manoff & M. Schudson (Eds.). *Reading the news*. New York: Pantheon.

Chadwick, J. (2009, February 19). Local church takes on an international cause: Friday concert proceeds aimed at stopping child sex trafficking. *The* (Bergen County, NJ) *Record*, pp. L7.

Chuang, J. (2006). Beyond a snapshot: Preventing human trafficking in the global economy. *Indiana Journal of Global Legal Studies, 13*(1), 137–63.

Cwikel, J., & Hoban, E. (2005). Contentious issues in research on trafficked women working in the sex industry: Study design, ethics, and methodology. *The Journal of Sex Research, 42*(4), 306–16.

Daugherty, S. (2009, March 7). Police bust Mexican "brothel." *Maryland Gazette*, pp. A1.

DiMartino, M. F. (2009, December 3). Human trafficking a growing problem, especially exploiting the young. *Inland Valley Daily Bulletin* (Ontario, Canada).

Entman, R. (2004). *Projections of power: Framing news, public opinion, and U.S. foreign policy*. Chicago, IL: The University of Chicago Press.

Feingold, D. A. (2005). Think again: Human trafficking. *Foreign Policy* 150, 26–32.

Graber, D. (1980). *Crime news and the public*. New York: Praeger.

Hesse-Biber, S. N., & Leavy, P. (2006). *The practice of qualitative research*. Thousand Oaks: Sage Publications.

Hodge, D. R. (2008). Sexual trafficking in the United States: A domestic problem with transnational dimensions. *Social Work, 53*(2), 143–52.

Hodge, D. R., & Lietz, C. A. (2007). The international sexual trafficking of women and children: A review of the literature. *Affila: Journal of Women and Social Work, 22*(2), 163–74.

Hudgins, A. M. (2007). Problematizing the discourse: Sex trafficking policy and ethnography. In L. O'Toole, J. Schiffman, & M. Edwards (Eds.), *Gender violence: Interdisciplinary perspectives*, pp. 409–14. New York: New York University Press.

Hughes, D. M. (2000). Welcome to the rape camp: Sexual exploitation and the Internet in Cambodia. *Journal of Sexual Aggression, 6*(1–2), 1–23.

Itule, B. D., & Anderson, D. A. (1994). *News writing and reporting for today's media*. New York: McGraw-Hill.

Iyengar, S. (1994). *Is anyone responsible? How television frames political issues*. Chicago: University of Chicago Press.

Johnson, A. (2009, January 25). Horror of teen sex slavery not a foreign woe—it's here. *Columbus* (Ohio) *Dispatch*, pp. 1B.

Johnson, A., & Wagner, M. (2009, June 28). A new word for prostitute—victim. *Columbus* (Ohio) *Dispatch*, pp. 1A.

Johnston, A., & Friedman, B. (2008, April). Mass media's coverage of sex trafficking. Poster presentation at *Combating Sex Trafficking: Prevention and Intervention in North Carolina and Worldwide* (conference). Raleigh, NC.

Kelly, L. (2004). The perils of inclusion and exclusion: International debates on the status of trafficked women as victims. *International Review of Victimology, 11*(1), 33–47.

Kitzinger, J. (2004). Media coverage of sexual violence against women and children. In K. Ross & C. M. Byerly (Eds.), *Mass media and women*, pp. 13–38. Oxford: Blackwell.

Kovach, B., & Rosenstiel, T. (2007). *The elements of journalism: What newspeople should know and the public should expect.* New York: Three Rivers Press.

Kristof, N. (2009, January 1). The evil behind the smiles. *New York Times*, pp. A25.

Kristof, N. (2009, May 7). Girls on our streets. *New York Times*, pp. A33.

Lake, R., & Curti, L. (2009, June 13). Rally targets child prostitution. *Las Vegas Review-Journal*, pp. 1B.

Margolis, D. (2007, May 24). Media often abets sex trafficking. *People's Weekly World Newspaper*. Retrieved from www.pww.org.

McCabe, K. A., & Manian, S. (2010). Defining sex trafficking. In K. A. McCabe & S. Manian (Eds.), *Sex trafficking: A global perspective*, pp. 1–8. Lanham, MD: Lexington Books.

McDonald, W. F. (2004). Traffic counts, symbols, and agendas: A critique of the campaign against trafficking of human beings. *International Review of Victimology, 11*(2–3), 143–76.

Meyers, M. (1997). *News coverage of violence against women: Engendering blame.* Thousand Oaks: Sage Publications.

The Missouri Group (2007). *News reporting and writing* (9th ed.). Boston: Bedford/St. Martin's.

Nealon, S. (2009, February 15). Teen prostitution, the inland's dark underside. *The* (Riverside, Calif.) *Press-Enterprise*, pp. A1.

O'Neill, N. (2009, November 19). Miami pimp Hugo Gonzalez lavished gifts on his whores to keep them around. *Miami New Times*.

Quinn, C. (2009, June 14). Sex trafficking fight goes beyond streets. *Atlanta Journal-Constitution*, pp. 1B.

Rankin, B. (2009, April 18). Craigslist blamed in child pimping. *Atlanta Journal-Constitution,* pp. 3B.

Risley, A. (January 2009). *Perspectives on trafficking and the global sex trade.* Paper presented at the Southern Political Science Association annual meeting, New Orleans, LA.

Schauer, E. J., & Wheaton, E. M. (2006). Sex trafficking into the United States: A literature review. *Criminal Justice Review, 31*(2), 146–69.

Seidel, G. & Vidal, L. (1997). The implications of "medical," "gender in development" and "culturalist" discourses for HIV/AIDS policy in Africa. In C. Shore & S. Wright (Eds.), *Anthropology of policy: Critical perspectives on governance and power.* London: Routledge.

Steinfatt, T. M., Baker, S., & Beesey, A. (2002). *Measuring the number of trafficked women in Cambodia.* Paper presented to The human rights challenge of globalization in Asia-Pacific-U.S.: The trafficking in persons, especially women and children, Honolulu, HI.

Stoecker, S. (2004). Human trafficking: A new challenge for Russia and the United States. In S. Stoecker & L. Shelley (Eds.), *Human traffic and transnational crime: Eurasian and American perspectives.* Lanham, MD: Rowman & Littlefield.

Thalji, J. (2009, May 13). Sex slavery victims sought. *St. Petersburg Times*, pp. 1B.

United Nations. (2004). Protocol to prevent, suppress and punish trafficking in persons, especially women and children, supplementing the United Nations Convention against Transnational Organized Crime. Available at: www.unodc.org/documents/treaties/UNTOC/Publications/TOC percent 20Convention/TOCebok-e.pdf. Accessed on March 17, 2010.

Urbina, I. (2009, October 27). For runaways on the street, sex buys survival. *New York Times*, pp. 1A.

U.S. Department of Health and Human Services. (2010). Overview of human trafficking issue. Retrieved October 1, 2010, from www.acf.hhs.gov/trafficking/about/index.html#overview.

U.S. Department of State. (2010). *Trafficking in persons report.* Retrieved June 20, 2010, from www.state.gov/documents/organization/142979.pdf.

Walsh, C. (2001). *Gender and discourse: Language and power in politics, the church and organizations.* New York: Longman.

Weitzer, R. (2007). The social construction of sex trafficking: Ideology and institutionalization of a moral crusade. *Politics & Society, 35*(3), 447–75.

Williams, T. (2009, August 2). Hope Project to shelter the sexually exploited. *Muskegon* (Michigan) *Chronicle*, pp. A3.

Wilson, J., & Dalton, E. (2008). Human trafficking in the heartland: Variation in law enforcement awareness and response. *Journal of Contemporary Criminal Justice, 24*(3), 296–313.

Chapter Six

Gendered Construction of HPV

A Post-Structuralist Critique of Gardasil

Nicole Defenbaugh and Kimberly N. Kline

Approximately 20 million Americans are currently infected with HPV. Another 6 million people become newly infected each year. HPV is so common that at least 50 percent of sexually active men and women get it at some point in their lives. —www.cdc.gov/std/hpv/stdfact-hpv.htm#common.

In June 2006, the FDA approved a new vaccine that protects against four strains of Human Papilloma Virus (HPV), a virus that may cause many kinds of cancer. Despite the fact that HPV infects both women and men, even before the vaccine made the headlines, Merck's marketing campaign framed HPV as a women's issue. In 2005, Merck launched a series of campaigns to inform women about the connection between HPV and cervical cancer. The first wave of Merck's marketing activities, public education campaigns, asked women to "Make the Connection" and, later, to "Make the Commitment" to talking to their physicians about ways to reduce the threat of cervical cancer; the second wave asked women to "Tell Someone" about the connection between HPV and cervical cancer. Notably, though funded by Merck pharmaceutical company, none of these campaign efforts mentioned the HPV vaccine for which Merck was seeking U.S. Food and Drug Administration (FDA) approval. When the FDA finally approved Merck's HPV vaccine Gardasil, the media blitz began in earnest with a direct-to-consumer advertising campaign "One Less" (to be diagnosed with cervical cancer because "now there's Gardasil").

Cultural scholars have long recognized that advertisements "attempt to sell the product by associating it with certain socially desirable qualities" (Kellner, 1995, p. 127). This has been particularly troubling for women be-

65

cause such "socially desirable qualities" tend to mirror oppressive patriarchal expectations. As DeFrancisco and Palczewski (2007) explained, the "media interact with the institution of gender as they provide mechanisms through which representations of work, family, education, and religion are communicated" (p. 241). Our analysis of HPV vaccine marketing reveals a particularly gendered construction of the disease with problematic implications for women's health.

Here we examine four U.S. Gardasil advertisements that depict a diverse, seemingly empowered group of young women, the kind that feminist media critics might find progressive and appealing. However, we argue that these advertisements function as a form of commodity feminism. That is, advertisers have co-opted the "feminist ideas and icons . . . for commercial purposes, emptied of their political significance and offered back to the public in a commodified form" (Gill, 2008, p. 1). We argue that this form of feminism is utilized in multiple HPV vaccine commercials and that the particular aim of the advertisements is not awareness of HPV but the "selling" of fear-based rhetoric to persuade young women to get vaccinated (and mothers to take their daughters to get the vaccine).

LITERATURE REVIEW

In the past, feminist critiques of women in the mass media have been concerned with overtly anti-feminist representations and the "symbolic annihilation" of women by the mass media. Steiner (2000) explains that symbolic annihilation is "a two step finding: first, women and minorities are underrepresented in media content; second, when they are represented, women and minorities are trivialized, victimized, or ridiculed" (p. 1326).

One of the first anthologies of feminist media critiques related to women in the media focused primarily on the absence of women in the media. In the introduction to this anthology, Tuchman (1978) discussed how research from 1954 to 1975 consistently demonstrated that males dominated television depictions, including advertisements. As recently as 2003, Ganahl, Prinsen, and Netzley confirmed that women continue to be underrepresented in prime-time television commercials.

MEDIATED FEMALE STEREOTYPES

Beyond concern with mere presence or absence of women in the media, contemporary feminist media scholars have been troubled by sex role stereotypes (Steiner, 2000). Early on, Kilborne (1995) observed that in advertisements "Women are shown almost exclusively as housewives or sex objects" (p. 123; see also Jhally, 1989; Rakow, 2008). African American women, too, have been negatively stereotyped in the media. Boylorn (2008) details at length how these stereotypes, from the long-standing Mammy and Jezebel depictions to the "the recreations of the historical stereotypes, make room for new updated versions of Mammy [and Jezebel], with [fewer] restrictions" (p. 415).

Representations of women have long been held to be disempowering in the sense that women's work is trivialized and denigrated. With regard to representations of female health issues, victim-blaming is the more common form of disempowerment (Kline, 2003). The victim-blaming allegation presumes that a woman who suffers from a health threat does so because she has chosen not to engage in a recommended preventive behavior (i.e., she has breast cancer because she did not get a mammogram).

Contemporary feminist media research suggests that at least a few of these traditional stereotypes have been challenged. As demonstrated in their edited volume, Carter and Steiner (2003) assert that "an increasingly varied array of feminine messages and role models is now available, some of which offer progressive and sometimes challenging alternatives" (p. 13). Indeed, as we will demonstrate in our study, the stereotypical gender images censured by feminist scholars are not the predominant focus of Merck's HPV vaccine advertisements. Still, Steiner (2000) cautions that "what may first appear as exceptions to the finding of symbolic annihilation are in fact more complex processes of signification" (p. 1326). That is, she continues, "the manifestations of sexism are varied and demonstrate great ability to co-opt strategies and themes of the women's movement" (p. 1327). And yet, this gender inclusivity in the name of feminism comes at a price.

COMMODITY FEMINISM AS THEORETICAL FRAME

Goldman, Heath, & Smith (1991) in their well-known article, "Commodity Feminism," explore the use of feminist ideologies as a marketing strategy in selling advertisements. As a ploy to sell products to women, advertisers purport to give women confidence and power—feminist components—if they buy their product. Gill (2008) explains, "Goldman argued that advertisers' response was . . . an attempt to incorporate the cultural power and energy of feminism while simultaneously domesticating its critique of advertising and the media . . . It turns social goals into individual lifestyles, and has fetishized feminism into an iconography of things: a product, a lot, a style" (p. 2). Goldman (1995) uses an example from *Ms.* magazine to explain how "the *Ms.* Pitch to advertisers . . . makes 'buying power' the motive for postfeminism" (p. 89). In this sense, the female body functions as a site of power. The message? If you want to have power—over yourself or others—then you buy the product. This message would not work without the cultural stereotype of feminism as a means of possessing power and a patriarchal system that supports this perceived empowerment as long as it is purchasable and does not defy normative standards of femininity. The authors (Goldman et al., 1991) go on to state, "the formula, though self-contradictory, can be expressed quite simply: Self-fetishization supposedly offers women an avenue to empowerment" (p. 335). By spending more time and money focusing on the self—often in the form of beautiful enhancement—women will not only look more confident, but they will feel confident as well.

In this commodified form, "feminism is reduced to the status of a mere signifier or signified, so it may be re-encoded by an advertiser . . . [and] worn as a stylish sign" (Goldman et al., 1991, p. 336). This feminist "sign" is also applied once the product is purchased. Rapp (1998) explains how advertisements transform "feminism *social* goals [in]to individual *life-style*[s]" so that feminism is "depoliticized" (p. 32). Feminism, once viewed as a means for social change and equality, is now purchasable in a bottle to be applied to one's face, clothes, house, and possessions. As Goldman et al. (1991) note, "when framed by ideologies of possessive individualism and free choice, feminism in its 'new' commodity form forgets its origins in a critique of unequal social, economic, and political relations" (p. 336). Simply put, advertisers use feminist ideologies as a marketing tool to persuade their audience that these principles can be consumed. As long as female consumers desire empowerment through self-fetishization (p.335), advertisers will continue to present feminism as a purchasable good.

Feminism as a marketing strategy transforms into an ironic reification of stereotypical feminine gender norms and hegemony disguised in a pink bottle of empowerment. Feminism is defined through its commodities (Goldman et al., 1991), the signifier for perceived individuality and empowerment that must be bought in order to be possessed.

METHOD

We use qualitative textual analysis following guidelines set forth by Sonja K. Foss (2004) in her discussion of generative rhetorical criticism to identify and assess the latent content of Merck's HPV awareness and Gardasil advertisements (see appendix at the end of this chapter). The intent of generative rhetorical criticism is to consider which of many meanings the media source means to privilege. This qualitative textual method of analysis assumes that unique interpretations provide insight into the ways rhetoric invites audience members to make meanings from a text. We used an inductive approach; through an intensive, in-depth, and comprehensive reading of the texts, we identified relevant themes reflected and constituted by representations of women in these Gardasil advertisements and assessed the linguistic strategies employed to construct HPV as a gendered disease.

FINDINGS

(Sexual) Health as Women's Work

According to du Pré (2010), women are the primary audience for advertisements because of their role in health care and family. In her article *Health as Women's Work*, Barnett (2006) explains the social history behind women's health in magazines as second wave feminism and health as a consumerist product.

> Both are concerned with locus of responsibility for health. The health consumer movement positions good health as an undertaking—a task a person must accomplish—while the women's movement has encouraged women to learn more about health as a means of taking control of their bodies and their lives. (p. 1)

Despite the fact that HPV affects men as well as women and men spread the disease to women through sexual contact, Merck's message is that it is a woman's responsibility to take charge of her health and care for the health of others (in this case, other women). Except for a few brief appearances by men in the "One Less" commercial, women are the only characters shown in all Merck ads. In the "Get Connected" commercial, for example, professional women in business suits, the jogger, mothers and daughters, the main narrator, Elisabeth Rohm (famous actor), and even the police officer are all women.

To some extent, Gardasil ads seem to correct past stereotyped images of women in the media by blurring gender boundaries. For example, a young girl plays the drums and speaks to the camera while flipping her drumsticks, an untraditional portrayal in advertising. Gardasil further challenges the feminine role with a girl shooting hoops on an outdoor basketball court in her "One Less" shoes, another skateboarding on her "One Less" inscribed skateboard, and a female soccer player hitting the soccer ball—all depictions of athleticism less common in commercials targeting female audiences.

Moreover, unlike the ads of the past, women in Gardasil ads represent an array of ethnic and racial backgrounds. In the "Get Connected" commercial, an Asian woman in a business suit talks about the number of diagnoses of cervical cancer in the United States. The next scene shows an African American woman jogging followed by a female police officer of unknown ethnic background. Although the narrator of the commercial is a well-known Caucasian actor (Elisabeth Rohm), the other actors represent a plethora of racial, ethnic, and even occupational diversity. In both "I Chose" commercials and "One Less," the advertisers portray women of color (mostly African American). Although the women in the first "I Chose" commercial appear to be middle-to-upper class, their racial backgrounds seem somewhat diverse, with Caucasian, African American, and Latina actors. Notwithstanding the seemingly progressive representations of women, the Gardasil ads revert to traditional feminine roles to sell their product.

PRIVILEGING THE MOTHER/DAUGHTER RELATIONSHIP

The mother-daughter relationship, commonplace in most female-targeted ads, takes center stage for Gardasil. In the "Get Connected" commercial, a woman in her forties is shown walking and talking with a young woman in her mid-to-late teens, presumably her daughter. The actor directs the following statement not to the camera but the teenager next to her: "Help others make the connection between cervical cancer and human papillomavirus." As she begins the statement we see her hand briefly touch the young woman's back as they walk, side by side, past the camera. In the last shot of the encounter we see the young woman smile, not having uttered a single word. Similarly, the "Una Menos" commercial focuses primarily on the mother-daughter relationship. A woman is talking about the vaccine when a young girl (early middle school age) comes out of school and walks over to the woman. We see the woman embrace and kiss the young girl, presumably her daughter, before taking her hand and walking away. In the same commercial, a mother is shown adjusting her daughter's wrap in a clothing store, and the next "mother" depicted is reading about Gardasil in a magazine to her daughter while sitting on a bench. In the second "I Chose" commercial, the mother-daughter role is the primary marketing device, whereby a "mother" interacts with her "daughter" in virtually every frame. In these commercials, the makers highlight gender normative behavior between mothers and daughters as sensitive and caring (Wood, 2009, p. 179). Mothers kiss their daughters, brush and braid their hair, look at magazines, and cook together, or simply sit in the kitchen, do their daughter's nails, and play chess—though games of strategy are typically portrayed by boys (Wood, 2009, p. 126). The reoccurring theme is one of touching and communication. We see the mothers and daughters sitting in close proximity to each other, touching each other's hands, hair, or face, and discussing the vaccine while laughing or smiling.

GETTING CONNECTED BY COMMUNICATING

These feminine behaviors aim to "create and maintain relationships . . . establish egalitarian relations with others . . . use communication to include others . . . and use communication to show sensitivity to others" (Wood, 2009, p .127). The emphasis is clearly on creating relationships and communicating when having fun and engaging in girls' games. The playful, feminine, and relationship-focused commercial functions as a powerful marketing tool, encouraging the audience to see themselves as one of the girls listening to their mother's advice: get the vaccine, protect yourself against HPV and cervical cancer, and be "One Less" statistic.

The commercial's primary message? "Get Connected." At the bottom of the screen "maketheconnection.org" scrolls by, reinforcing the gender stereotype that women desire connecting with other women and are the primary source of that connection. As Wood (2009) states, "feminine people use language to foster *connections*, support, closeness, and understanding" (italics added) (p. 128). One of the primary goals of feminine speech, as depicted in the commercial, is to create connections with others. The author also states that friendships among women are defined through communication. "Many women share their personal feelings, experiences, fears, and problems in order to know and be known by each other. By sharing details of [their] lives, women feel intimately *connected* to one another" (italics added) (Wood, 2009, p. 214). As both quotations from Wood demonstrate, feminine communication styles reinforce the creation and maintenance of connections or relationships with other women. The Gardasil ad reinforces these ideologies with the "Get Connected" theme and website shown during the advertisement.

AGENCY AND EMPOWERMENT AS A MEANS TO SELL GARDASIL

Functioning within a framework of commodity feminism, the marketers of Gardasil use "I Chose" and "One Less" as the primary message for their ads. One commercial in particular has almost every actor repeat "I Chose" throughout the commercial and "You have the power to choose," reinforcing the message of empowerment and self-identity. The ad purports that by *choosing* to get the vaccine, women are *choosing* the option of protection against four types of HPV and, more importantly, cervical cancer (although the vaccine doesn't protect against all forms of HPV and only protects against cervical cancer under specific, limited conditions). By espousing a feminist ideology of self-empowerment, the makers of Gardasil are selling the vaccine as a feminist tool, a product based on cultural "attitudes which they can then 'wear'" (Goldman et al., 1991, p. 336). As the signifier for female empowerment, the vaccine sells choice and the need for self-identity (Goldman et al., 1991) among young women of a perceived sexually active age group.

In the "I Chose" advertisement, for example, we clearly see commodity capitalism in conjunction with commodity feminism. In the first frame we hear the sound of a camera, similar to the camera sounds associated with modeling shoots. The women, all in their late teens and early twenties, are shown in apartment complexes or similar dwellings with stylish furniture and artwork, wearing up-to-date, stylish clothing. In accordance with commodity feminism is the understanding that "commodity logic consists of a series of interpretive maneuvers where we abstract a desired relationship out of a lived context" (Goldman et al., 1991, p. 334). The relationship between young viewer and young model is one of envy and desire for a healthy body free of HPV or cancer and a lifestyle filled with material goods. In these images we see how "self-fetishization supposedly offers women an avenue to empowerment" (Goldman et al., 1991, p. 335) through the assembly of "signs which connote independence, participation in the work force, individual freedom, and self-control" (p. 337). The women are shown alone in their houses or apartments, surrounded by their material goods and the occasional dog. One cannot help but notice how *all* the women in the "I Chose" commercial are sitting on new-looking couches, surrounded by matching wooden coffee tables and chairs, bicycles, and computers.

Interestingly, the womens' employment centers around the arts and humanities, which are often associated with women and feminine identity. The commercials also suggest employment or hobbies as painters, sculptors, clothing designers, writers, photographers, and actors, with paintings, an easel, a mannequin, a "Broadway" sign, and framed photos strewn around their rooms. In the "Una Menos" commercial a young woman is shown playing the bongos in a very large studio. Donned in stylish clothing and jewelry, the woman sits alone practicing her instrument. In the same commercial, another woman is sculpting a large clay figure. The final two clips are of women dancing or preparing to dance: a group of girls in colorful costumes and jewelry preparing for a party or festival, and a female flamenco dancer practicing in a large studio. In the "One Less" commercial, four girls rehearse what appears to be stepping (a form of African American dance of rhythmic footsteps and handclapping), and three girls participate in jump rope or Double Dutch.

CONCLUSION

Merck advertisements for Gardasil sell the vaccine by suggesting that young women counseled by their mothers are empowered by "choosing" to get this vaccine. This may be viewed as a "progressive" move from a feminist stand-point. However, we argue that Merck has appropriated the feminist ideal of empowerment in what amounts to commodity feminism. Thus, the presumed privileging of women deflects attention from important absences in the ad-vertisements.

Given the feminist critique that women largely have been ignored in advertising, representing women exclusively in Gardasil ads might be viewed as an avant-garde move. However, this focus on women is a rhetori-cal strategy that deflects attention from the absence of men in this discussion of HPV. Likewise, a feminist perspective might find it progressive that wom-en's sexuality is *not* the focus of Gardasil ads. Ironically, the inattention to women's sexuality is also a rhetorical strategy that deflects attention from the fact that HPV is a sexually transmitted illness (STI). Thus, it is the *absence* of men and the absence of discussion about women's sexuality that is proble-matic because this avoidance does not allow for talk about sex. If women truly wish to reduce their odds of contracting HPV, it is imperative that they understand safer sex practices.

Gardasil ads appear to avoid the victim-blaming so common in health-related rhetoric. Instead of calling women out for not choosing safer sex or not getting the vaccine, the ads frame "choosing" to get the vaccine as a means of empowerment—a way to take charge of reducing one's risk of cervical cancer. The notion of empowerment for women "has been central to the evolution of women's movements since the late 1960s" and defined, among other things, as "access to information" (Bunch & Frost, 2000, p. 554). In the case of Gardasil ads, however, the focus on presumed empower-ment deflects attention from the *lack* of information in the ads about HPV and cervical cancer.

We do not think it productive to recount ongoing debates about the over-all threat of cervical cancer to U.S. women. Regardless, if actual risk was the rationale, it would necessitate a discussion of sexual activity, which would invite rejection of getting young children (girls and boys) vaccinated against an STI. The bottom line is that Merck's ads appropriate empowerment to sell the product; agency becomes *the* rationale for getting the vaccine. We cer-tainly do not advocate victim-blaming (i.e., that women may not "choose" to get the vaccine is not in any way indicative that they should then be blamed for contracting HPV), but this does not alter the fact that contracting HPV is related to sexual activity. Indeed, framing the Gardasil vaccine as a "choice" is not only an appropriation of feminist ideals to sell the product; it may set the stage for later victim-blaming rhetoric.

The bottom line is that talk about an HPV vaccine is the one time where we need to represent men as much as women, and we must talk about sex even if it means attending to women's sexuality. Ultimately, we should include men in the discussion about HPV (not just because it affects women, but because it affects men, as well). We should talk about women and sex, and we should acknowledge the consequences of not choosing safer sex practices. And we should challenge advertisers who would use feminist ideals to sell their product. Advertisers recognize that in the new millennium it is not only traditional feminine ideals that sell products, but a new feminism that privileges empowerment. Commodity feminism is the latest marketing tool, and women deserve to know that it is merely that, a marketing tool.

REFERENCES

Barnett, B. (2006). Health as women's work: A pilot study on how women's magazines frame medical news and femininity. *Women and Language, 29*(2): 1–12.

Berger, J. (1972). *Ways of seeing.* London: Penguin.

Boylorn, R. M. (2008). As seen on TV: An autoethnographic reflection on race and reality television. *Critical Studies in Media Communication, 25*, 413–33.

Bunch, C., & Frost, S. (2000). Empowerment. In C. Kramarae & D. Spender (Eds.), *Routledge international encyclopedia of women: Education: Health to hypertension* (vol. 2, pp. 554–55). New York: Routledge.

Carter, C., & Steiner, L. (2003). Mapping the contested terrain of media and gender research. In C. Carter & L. Steiner (Eds.), *Critical readings: Media and gender* (pp. 11–35). Maidenhead, England: Open University.

DeFrancisco, V. P., & Palczewski, C. H. (2007). *Communicating gender diversity: A critical approach.* Thousand Oaks: Sage.

du Pré, A. (2010). *Communicating about health: Current issues and perspectives* (3rd ed.) New York: Oxford University Press.

Foss, S. K. (2004). *Rhetorical criticism: Exploration and practice* (3rd ed.). Prospect Heights: Waveland.

Ganahl, D. J., Prinsen, T. J., & Netzley, S. B. (2003). A content analysis of prime time commercials: A contextual framework of gender representation. *Sex Roles, 49* (9/10): 545–51.

Gill, R. (2008). Commodity feminism. *Blackwell reference online.* Retrieved June 16, 2010, from www.blackwellreference.com/public/book?id=g97814051/31995/yr2010/97814/0513/ 1995.

Goldman, R. (1995). Constructing and addressing the audience as commodity. In G. Dines & J. M. Humez (Eds.), *Gender, race and class in media: A text-reader* (pp. 88–92). Thousand Oaks: Sage.

Goldman, R., Heath, D., and Smith, S. L. (1991). Commodity feminism. *Critical Studies in Mass Communication, 8*: 333–51.

Jhally, S. (Ed.). (1989). *Advertising, gender and sex: What's wrong with a little objectification?* Retrieved from www.sutjhally.com/articles/whatswrongwithalit.

Kellner, D. (1995). Reading images critically: Toward a postmodern pedagogy. In G. Dines & J. M. Humez (Eds.), *Gender, race and class in media: A text-reader* (pp. 126–32). Thousand Oaks: Sage.

Kilborne, J. (1995). Beauty and the beast of advertising. In G. Dines & J. M. Humez (Eds.), *Gender, race and class in media: A text-reader* (pp. 121–25). Thousand Oaks: Sage.

Kline, K. N. (2003). Popular media and health: Images, effects, and institutions. In T. L. Thompson, A. M. Dorsey, K. I. Miller & R. Parrott (Eds.), *Handbook of health communication* (pp. 557–81). Mahwah, NJ: Erlbaum.

Rakow, L. F. (2008). Women in the media, images of. In W. Donsbach (Ed.), *The international encyclopedia of communication*. Indianapolis, IN: Wiley-Blackwell.

Rapp, R. (1988). Is the legacy of second wave feminism post-feminism? *Socialist Review, 98*, 31–37.

Steiner, L. (2000). Media: Overview. In C. Kramarae & D. Spender (Eds.), *Routledge international encyclopedia of women: Global women's issues and knowledge* (Vol. 3, Identity politics publishing, pp. 1324–31). New York: Routledge.

Tuchman, G. (1978). The symbolic annihilation of women by the mass media. In G. Tuchman, A. K. Daniels & J. Benet (Eds.), *Hearth and home: Images of women in the mass media* (pp. 150–74). New York: Oxford University.

Wood, J. T. (2009). *Gendered lives: Communication, gender, and culture* (8th ed.). Belmont, CA: Wadsworth.

APPENDIX

Merck Advertisements for HPV Awareness and Gardasil HPV Vaccine.

Merck & Co., Inc. (2006, November 13). *One Less* (Gardasil commercial). Retrieved October 11, 2009, from www.youtube.com/watch?v=hJ8x3KR75fA.

Merck & Co., Inc. (2007, October 16). *Una menos* (Gardasil commercial). Retrieved October 11, 2009, from www.youtube.com/watch?v=f66nM-UbQQc.

Merck & Co., Inc. (2008, June 6). *I Chose #2* (Gardasil commercial). Retrieved October 11, 2009, from www.youtube.com/watch?v=ZHUamYNSH9c.

Merck & Co., Inc. (2008, June 11). *I Chose #1* (Gardasil commercial). Retrieved October 11, 2009, from hwww.youtube.com/watch?v=ehvxbEOgNEM.

Merck & Co., Inc. (2008, August 15). *Get Connected* (HPV commercial). Retrieved October 11, 2009, from www.youtube.com/watch?v=OMbvhug7CGU.

Chapter Seven

Who's Afraid of the Pink *Chaddi*?

New Media, Hindutva, and Feminist Agency in India

Saayan Chattopadhyay

THE PINK *CHADDI* CAMPAIGN

On a sleepy Saturday afternoon of January 24, 2009, a mob of some twenty men attacked a group of young women partying inside Amnesia Pub at the Hotel Woodside in the busy Balmatta area of Mangalore. According to newspaper reports, the men kicked and slapped the young women and shoved them to the ground in full view of a camera crew from a local television network invited to capture the event (Gopal, 2009). Following the attack at the Amnesia Pub, Sri Ram Sene, a right-wing Hindu group, as well as the Bajrang Dal, a radical Hindu organization, and the youth wing of the Vishwa Hindu Parishad (VHP) [World Hindu Council] claimed responsibility. Bajrang Dal activist Prasad Attavar claimed the attack was a "spontaneous reaction against women who flouted traditional Indian norms of decency."

The Sri Ram Sene [The Army of Lord Rama] has been the principal "moral policing" group in Mangalore led by Pramod Muthalik. In recent years, they have targeted inter-religious relationships and issues such as cow slaughter. The pub attack was the first moral and cultural policing attack to be carried out (Johnson, 2009). Undaunted by the outrage over the attack on a Mangalore pub, Muthalik, who was released on bail, threatened to forcibly "marry off" couples dating in public on Valentine's Day. However, ahead of Valentine's Day, the Karnataka police arrested key leaders of the Sri Ram Sene in Mangalore as a preventive measure (ENS, 2009).

In reaction to these events, a few days later, a young female journalist from Delhi, Nisha Susan, who was working as a special correspondent for *Tahelka.com*, started a Facebook group titled the "Consortium of Pub-going, Loose and Forward Women," "as a faintly bitter joke." However, to her surprise, within five minutes "two women had signed up laughing. Twenty-four hours later the campaign sent pink *chaddis* [panties] to Pramod Mutha-lik. The joke was now richly sweet" (Susan, 2009c). Susan also points out that it was actually the Sri Ram Sene's threat of violence on Valentine's Day following the Mangalore pub attack that motivated her. "All spectators understood that the Sene, a new and unwelcome franchise of India's favorite corporation, the moral police, was announcing a play for greater power" Susan explains, continuing, "While Karnataka's BJP [Bhāratiya Janatā Party] Government watched to see whether Muthalik could pull off his boast, we decided to give the Sene some attention."

Five hundred visitors joined the online campaign on the first day. Within a week, forty thousand had joined. Susan remarked, "From Puerto Rico to Singapore, from Chennai to Ahmedabad, from Guwahati to Amritsar, people wrote to us, 'how do I send my chaddis?'" Meanwhile, "the campaign had gone offline" with collection centers for pink undergarments. Many people, including men, supported the cause. In the words of one visitor who posted his comment in the official blog: "Deep down, this gesture doesn't just stand for a right to raise a mug in toast, but for an ideology, for freedom and for justice, for liberation from oppression and the right to dignity" (Supertrampo, 2009).

The Pink Chaddi Facebook Group and Susan's account, after being re-peatedly hacked, was suspended and transformed into blogs. The mainstream print and electronic media covered the campaign with a reasonably affirma-tive stance, and in the process bolstered its popularity and reach. The beliefs behind this movement initiated by "pub-going, loose and forward women" is to some extent explained by Susan (2009b):

> How wonderful it is to accept that you are an urban woman. The privileges you
> have will shame you everyday, but there are few you will give up. Most
> importantly, you are that loose and forward woman, the slur you have tried to
> avoid your entire life. And now you are sending your underwear to an avowed
> fundamentalist. "Be grateful you are not walking 15 kilometres for water,"
> used to come as the response from friends anywhere on the political spectrum,
> each time you complained about something. This week, many of us found
> ourselves done with gratitude. Our fundamental rights are not to be taken
> away, like gifts with strings.

WOMEN AND THE NEOLIBERAL PUBLIC SPHERE IN INDIA

How do we understand this "successful" feminist campaign, given India's emerging new media? What are the implications for the mobilization of urban women's agency in the online public sphere of India? If the recent report by the Internet and Mobile Association of India (2007) is any indication, then the number of women online in the country has crossed the twelve million mark. The year 2007 was declared the "Year of the Broadband," a positive trend "heralding women's participation in the Internet revolution." However, only 23 percent of Internet users in India are women. Men and children continue to use the personal computer in the house more than women, even in households of diverse socioeconomic levels. Many studies show that women use the Internet to keep in touch with family members through emails or to help their children with their homework. "The incentive to use the Internet grows out of their family roles" writes Vinitha Johnson (2010, p. 162), noting in her recent study, "role definition underlies the reasons why women do not make ample use of technology and restricts their interests in such a way that they do not seek to fulfill their individual needs and their own growth." The media and society continuously define the role of women in the family. Subordination is often self-imposed. And as Johnson argues, a woman outside her home may use the computer and the Internet at the workplace as part of her job, "motivated by the need to perform better, but will rarely use them for herself or in her own interest." In the case of working class women, the additional disadvantage continues to be not only attitudinal but also economic.

Nisha Susan and others like her are not constricted by such limitations. The young, urban, educated (often well-employed) women living in a cosmopolitan city like Mumbai, Delhi, or Mangalore negotiate agency and activism differently from the ordinary housewife living in a suburban household with access to the Internet. The category of urban working women sidesteps the pressing notion of a digital divide in a developing country like India.

POLITICAL ACTIVISM ON NEW MEDIA: AGENCY, CULTURAL HEGEMONY, AND THE POLITICS OF BELONGING

Susan's agency as an urban, independent working woman, active in both online and offline socializing, may point to four significant aspects in the interplay of media, hegemony, and urban women's activism. Firstly, the online media and the web services provide the space and tool respectively for advocacy, where the personal can truly be political. Wendy Harcourt (2002, p. 154), citing incidents from India, Mexico, Thailand, Armenia, and East

Timor, argues that women are increasingly developing an influential layer of support through the Internet from moments of need and social crisis, "to safe spaces where personal struggles can be discussed and solutions shared." The new media has been utilized as a ready lobbying tool to prevent violations against women. Harcourt claims, "Local women's groups gain strength from support solicited at the global level." Along these lines the pink *chaddi* campaign (PCC), emerging out of a local incident, received substantial national and global support.

In spite of the indubitable limitations and apprehension around access and control, women, especially in the urban regions, are increasingly adapting the new media and using it as a potent tool for women's place-based politics in developing countries. Movements like these disseminate women's collective experiences and invest in the realignment of the political domain for gendered social change.

Moreover, symbolic solidarity legitimizes the movement. For instance, a number of posts in the PCC blog have received more than a thousand comments (Susan, 2009b). One visitor from Singapore posted, "What an idea! I am joining in. I live in Singapore but will be proud to be a part of this!!!!" Another from Orange County wrote, "Brilliant idea! I am sending pink chaddis." Still another commentator states, " . . . I want to send my friends's chaddi from Miami to Mumbai. . . ." In a symbolic sense, this global textual participation builds solidarity through technology.

In addition, the politics of belonging becomes crucial for the understanding of the interplay of media, hegemony, and urban women's activism. To differentiate between "belonging" and the "politics of belonging," Nira Yuval-Davis (2009, p. 8) points out that "belonging" is about emotional attachment, about feeling "at home" and about feeling "safe." The politics of belonging includes engaging in particular political projects to create a collective consciousness. The difference between belonging and the politics of belonging is especially crucial for the study of gender relations and the construction of the feminine and the masculine. Jay (2009), one of the commentators in the blog, writes,

> I am not a woman. I do not drink and so do not go to pubs either. But I support this campaign because this is a campaign for freedom. It is not necessarily a campaign for the freedom of women or their right to go to a pub, but it is a campaign to stop a bunch of hooligans from appropriating the soul of this country. . . . I have two daughters, and I do not intend to allow them to go to a pub until they are adults and old enough to make decisions on their own and understand what going to a pub entails.

The feminist political struggles aimed at women's emancipation, Yuval-Davis (2009) explains, depend on the denaturalization and debiologization of women's roles. One visitor to the blog remarked (Susan, 2009a), "Most middle class women scoff at your idea of adopting underwear as a symbol of protest. Do you really think it's a nice idea?" Often political projects of belonging attempt to constitute differences between "us" and "them." Civilized or moral "us" versus barbarian or immoral "them" is at the heart of different constructions of gender relations (Yuval-Davis, 2009, p. 9). For instance, Sudeshna Niyogi (2009) candidly remarks in her comment in the PCC blog:

> These people are "terrorists" in the real sense of the word. Why point at other nations or other religions, when such shameless acts of terror are being allowed within our country and by the very people who are claiming to defend the Hindu culture and religion. . . . I feel sorry for them . . . because these men are not capable of understanding the purity and sanctity of love . . . and the spirit of a nation.

PCC constructs the rhetoric of us and them, and paradoxically, the overtly conscious inclination toward transcending the us-them binary reinforces such distinctions. In response to a post that alleges the people behind PCC are not serious, one individual (Susan, 2009a) writes, "Don't you get it? *These* people are actually you and us! How about not trying to segregate people into groups for once and learning from history! Act together. Put that lovely mob mentality to use, man!" Another individual echoes his concern by stating, "You are absolutely right. These people are us. I should not have fallen into the us/them rhetoric. Apologies!"

Clictivism is a form of activism that uses social media to build political support. These movements such as the PCC serve as surrogate activism and not merely as clicktivism. The "successful" transition from an entirely online communication to offline communication and the corresponding transition from token protest, resistance, and support to tangible, material confrontations are necessary to tread outside the elusive sphere of clicktivism. New media serve as a surrogate social-political space needed for gradual legitimization and for solidifying the politics of belonging prior to the deployment of the movement. A number of supporters voiced their concerns in reply to the lack of usefulness of such a campaign: "Those of you who are criticizing the initiative for lack of seriousness—please think about any action that you have taken to try and counter the right wing forces since the Mangalore pub attack on women took place. . . . Please respect the efforts of those who have organized the initiative" (Susan, 2009a). These movements may not only be defined in terms of gender but can be applied to any online community or collectivity to understand the reconfigurations of agency.

HINDUTVA AND FEMINISM FOR A HETEROGENEOUS TIME

The PCC needs to be understood in the context of a rising Hindutva move-ment in India. Although not a powerful force in the immediate post-indepen-dence years, Hindu nationalism has reemerged as a popular and influential movement in the last three decades. Hindu images have started to appear in popular media. Hindu "values" have become a key ingredient in the rhetoric of many political parties, including the supposedly secular Congress Party. The question of women remains central in the discourse of Hindutva, espe-cially amidst its patriarchal structure. Radical Hindu nationalist groups do not omit women from their organizations. The construction of womanhood, however, draws on images of ideal mother, chaste wife, and compliant and dutiful daughter as part of Hindutva rhetoric.

As educated women enter the labor force, gender norms are disrupted. Nevertheless, women like Nisha Susan can express themselves, albeit in a limited manner since the government, whatever its ideological positions may be, has not put an injunction on women's legal rights in India. Banerjee (2005) notes, "the presence of a lively watchdog press seems to check, bar-ring the explosion of some political catastrophe, any tendency of these par-ties to roll back existing laws (however inadequate) protecting women's rights."

Nevertheless, Hindutva ideologues through meetings, press, and electron-ic media continue to disseminate their ideology and extend their political movement. The media plays a significant role for the supporters of Hindutva as well. Scholars like Corbridge and Harriss (2000) agree that the fundamen-tal patronage for the Hindu nationalist movement comes from India's middle classes or Indian elites. A U.S.-based Hindu population provides significant support for Hindu nationalism. The Internet, in particular, seems to be the preferred medium for the Hindu nationalists working in technology to pro-mote Hindutva. They assist in maintaining over five hundred websites with their messages of Hindutva, Hindu history, and Muslim-bashing (Chopra, 2006, p. 194).

Thus, it is essential to take account of this rereading of Hindu values within the framework of neoliberalism by the transnational elite, endorsing an essentialized ethno-religious identity. Serious allegations have been ex-pressed in the PCC blog against Susan's religious association and even her political motives. According to one such allegation, "Her campaign was funded by churches, bishops . . . And her employer is getting funds from churches." One allegation asserts that Susan and the media house where she works have links with SIMI (Students Islamic Movement of India), a former-ly banned Islamic student organization believed by many, including the government of India, to be involved in terrorism. A similar blatant allegation comes from an anonymous individual who claims, "This blog is surely created by Pakistani terrorists. . . . After the Mumbai attack they are scared to attack directly so they use blogs to spoil our country . . . Jai Hind" (Susan, 2009b). Some of the comments posted on the official blogs and other websites note that Susan's identity as an upper-class, English speaking, working woman is crisscrossed with her Christian surname, her alleged indulgence toward drinking, implicit disregard of religion, supposed "lack of seriousness," and of course, her "loose" sexuality.

Shalilendra (Susan, 2009a), a participant in an open-to-all chat with Susan, arranged by a popular Indian news portal, asks:

> Hello Mam, Don't you think you are just over doing things here . . . First thing is that the logo used is generally used by Hindus at holy place and instead of Om sign you have kept a "Pink chaddi" Its not justified . . . Don't you think that we are losing our rich culture in an attempt to grab modernization.

Her socioeconomic identity becomes the target for another comment that says, "Girls who won't dirty their hands in helping a woman fallen on the street are out here now, shouting to save pub-going girls and their alcoholism. What an irony." Hinting at the "sexually liberated" nature that the urban feminist women are believed to embody, Sadashivn (Susan, 2009a) rather mockingly wrote, "I am for the following: wife swapping, prostitution, drugs, and gambling. Can you please start a similar campaign for rights of people like me? I appreciate your leadership skills." A cursory look at the official PCC blog might indicate that those in favor of this urban radical feminist movement outnumber the staunch radical Hindu nationalists, though Hundutva-related sites give a completely opposite picture.

CONCLUSION

In this chapter I have explored the notion of new media in India as it provides a surrogate space for urban women's activism. Focusing on the PCC, I have examined the mobilization of urban women's agency in India through social media amidst the prevalent Hindutva movement and pointed out the challenges of such movement in a densely heterogeneous time. Debates about the public visibility of women, their participation in employment, and their subsequent emancipation have occupied center stage in post-liberalized narratives of nation building. The constitution of Indian new media must be positioned within the context of wider social processes such as globalization, changes in the sphere of cultural politics, and the emergence of the transnational elites as agents of new forms of the politics of identity in a networked society. Media may appear to be the least reliable when it comes to momentous long-term women's movement, but it would be gravely erroneous to consider it as an entirely futile space for effective politics. On the contrary, it opens up new modes of belonging and perhaps equally atypical ways of approaching politics, sexuality, and cultural difference.

REFERENCES

Anderson, B. R. O'G. (1998). *The spectre of comparisons: Nationalism, Southeast Asia, and the world.* New York: Verso.

Babajaba. (2009, February 9). Chaddi campaign: What next? Message posted to thepinkchaddicampaign.blogspot.com/2009/02/chaddi-campaign-what-next.html.

Banerjee, S. (2005). *Make me a man! Masculinity, Hinduism, and nationalism in India.* New York: State University of New York Press.

Butalia, U. (1993). Women and alternative media (India). *Reports and Papers on Mass Communication* (UNESCO), *107*: 51–60.

Chatterjee, P. (2004). *The politics of the governed.* New York: Columbia University Press.

Chaudhuri, M. (2000). "Feminism" in Print Media. *Indian Journal of Gender Studies*, 7(2), 263–88.

Chopra, R. (2006). Global primordialities: virtual identity politics in online Hindutva and online Dalit discourse. *New Media Society*, 8(2): 187–206.

Corbridge, S., & Harriss, J. (2000). *Reinventing India: Liberalization, Hindu nationalism and popular democracy.* Malden, MA: Blackwell.

Express News Service. (2009, February 13). Muthalik arrested to save V-day in Karnataka. *Express India.* Retrieved from www.expressindia.com/latest-news/Muthalik-arrested-to-save-VDay-in-Karnataka/423184/.

Garfinkel, H. (1967). *Studies in ethnomethodology.* Englewood Cliffs, NJ: Prentice Hall.

Gopal, N. (2009, February 1). Mangalore mayhem was violent politics. *Deccan Chronicle.* Retrieved from www.deccanchronicle.com/big-story/mangalore-mayhem-was-violent-politics-920.

Greenspan, A. (2004). *India and the IT revolution: Networks of global culture.* New York: Palgrave Macmillan.

Harcourt, W. (2002). Women and the politics of place. *Development*, 45(1): 7–14.

Internet and Mobile Association of India Statistics. (2007). Women Internet users cross the 12 million mark in India. *IAMAI.* Retrieved from www.iamai.in/section.php3?secid=16& press=id=817&mon=2.

Jay. (2009, February 9). Welcome! Message posted to thepinkchaddicampaign.blogspot.com/2009/02/welcome.html.

Johnson, N. T. (2009, January 27). Rama Sene, Bajrang Dal vie for "credit," extortion under scan. *Indian Express.* Retrieved from www.indianexpress.com/news/rama-sene-bajrang-dal-vie-for-credit-extortion-under-scan/415576/0.

Johnson, V. (2010). Women and the Internet: A micro study in Chennai, India Indian. *Journal of Gender Studies*, *17*: 151–63.

Mitra, A. (2002). Virtual commonality: Looking for India on the Internet. In S. Jones (Ed.), *Virtual culture: Identity and communication in cyberspace*, pp. 55–79. Thousand Oaks, CA: Sage.

Niyogi, S. (2009, February 9). Welcome! Message posted to thepinkchaddicampaign.blogspot.com/2009/02/welcome.html.

Ong, A. (2006). Mutations in Citizenship. *Theory Culture Society*, *23*(2): 499–505. Retrieved from www.guardian.co.uk/commentisfree/2010/aug/12/clicktivism-ruining-leftist-activism.

Sarkar, T, Roy, K., & Chakrabarty, K. (2005). *The Vedas, Hinduism, Hindutva.* Kolkata: Ebong Alap.

Sundaram, R. (2000). Beyond the nationalist panopticon: The experience of cyberpublics in India. In J. T. Caldwell (Ed.), *Electronic media and technoculture*. New Brunswick, NJ: Rutgers University Press.

Supertrampo. (2009, February 9). Welcome! Message posted to thepinkchaddicampaign. blogspot.com/2009/02/welcome.html.

Susan, N. (2009a). IBN Live Chat transcript. *IBNlive.in*. Retrieved from features.ibnlive.in. com/chat/view/243.html.

Susan, N. (2009b). The pink chaddi campaign. Retrieved from thepinkchaddicampaign. blogspot.com/.

Susan, N. (2009c, February 28). Valentine's warriors: The pink chaddi campaign: Why it began and how. *Tehelka Magazine* 6(8). Retrieved from www.tehelka.com/story_main41.asp? filename=Op280209valentine_warrior.asp.

White, M. (2010, August 12). Clicktivism is ruining leftist activism. *The Guardian*.

Yuval-Davis, Nira. (2009). Women, globalization and contemporary politics of belonging. *Gender Technology and Development*, *13*(1):1–19.

III

Westernizing Women

Chapter Eight

Women of China Magazine

The "Modern" Woman in a Discourse of Consumerism

Wei Luo

Scholars who engage in Chinese cultural studies have been fascinated by changing images of Chinese women in media representations over several historical eras. They have noted that looks and body images of Chinese women are deeply implicated in cultural and gender politics and stand out as a dynamic site on which tradition, politics, and consumer ideology are played out (Andrews & Shen, 2002; Croll, 1995; Evans, 2000; Hall, 1997; Johansson, 2001; Ko, 2000; Li, 1998; Roberts, 1997). For instance, images of women's bound feet are perceived by Western thinking as an atrocious means of enforcing a separate sphere for men and women and a manifestation of women's oppression in feudal hierarchy (Ko, 2000; Roberts, 1997). By contrast, images of the "iron woman," who wore androgynous outfits and seemingly embraced Mao's policy of austerity, raised doubts about the Chinese Communist Party's imposition of gender egalitarianism.

The most debated images remain those of the "modern" Chinese woman who, with a fashionably dressed body (Li, 1998) and a "sweet and gentle femininity" (Evans, 2008, p. 369), found herself immersed in consumer culture and market narratives of post-Mao economic reform. The "modern" woman's beauty in post-Mao media texts reflects a "re-feminization" (Johansson, 2001, p. 99), dramatically altering gender politics. The Chinese woman herself, as Johansson (2001) points out, carries the feminine signifier with dual meanings—simultaneously "representing a global 'modernity'" and safeguarding "the Chinese way of life" (pp. 97–98). Evans (2000) and Li (1998) share similar concerns about the interplay of global and local forces producing new sets of bodily prescriptions while reshaping the modern outlook of Chinese womanhood. These theorists are reluctant to interpret media images of women in the 1990s as a sign of enlightenment or empowerment. The "modern" Chinese woman thus stands as a perplexing icon, especially among other "modern" women in Asia (Munshi, 2001). Munshi's (2001) germinal anthology entitled *Images of the "Modern Woman" in Asia* addresses a complex discourse about "modern" womanhood in Asia's postcolonial contexts. Modernity, although commonly believed to originate from "European and American enlightenment, enabled and universalized by imperialism" (p. 7) is "produced and engaged with . . . a great variety of historical trajectories in the world" (p. 7). I concur with Munshi (2001) and other contributors (such as Chaplin, 2001; Donald & Lee, 2001; Johansson, 2001; Leichty, 2001) that the "modern" woman in Asia is entangled in tension-ridden representations of new social gender identity formation in her country. I particularly agree with Munshi's perspective that the "modern" woman is "always in progress" because she stands for "a potential subjective position" rather than "a 'real' one" (p. 6). This perspective extends the scholarly conversation about media representations of "modern" Chinese womanhood. I argue that post-millennium images of women are no longer the same as those analyzed (e.g., Evans' and Johansson's research mentioned above) within the 1990s sociocultural milieu when China first ushered in global commodities and media artifacts (and when mass consumer culture first emerged) especially from the West.

The millennium has witnessed China's accelerating economic growth; its successful entry into WTO, in particular, signifies a new historical and cultural era in which the political goal of "Xiao Kang" ("moderately prosperous society") has been established and pursued (Ministry of Foreign Affairs Official Report, 2008). Global commodities and media artifacts have become part of consumers' lives, and an affluent upper-middle class is gaining more and more cultural capital and economic power. Contextualizing my study of representations of the "modern" Chinese woman in the zeitgeist of post-millennium consumerism, I ask the following questions: In what ways do the images of the "modern" Chinese woman circulated in the local consumer culture of the post-millennium converge and diverge from those propagated in the 1990s? To what extent have gender politics been redefined? How do women's images speak to the tensions women face against the backdrop of China's intensifying interactions with the outside world?

By analyzing the images of Chinese womanhood depicted in *Zhongguo Funü* (*Women of China*), a leading official women's magazine published by All China Women's Federation, I will attempt to answer these issues. My textual analysis focuses on the publications in the 2000s—almost a decade after Johansson's (1998, 1999, 2001) thorough studies of the same magazine. I examine two types of theme-based texts for my investigation: the woman on the magazine cover (both her image and life story), and a series of essays depicting the local woman. Following Roy (2005), I employ selected texts to serve as "representative anecdotes" in Burke's term (1969, cited in Roy, 2005, p. 4). I will use the selected texts to shed light on the magazine's portrayals and the broader discourse of consumerism in post-millennium China.

Based upon my reading of these specific texts, I contend that the magazine, which used to distribute feminist texts to engage women of previous generations in social productions, now adopts a new formula of representations, following what Western scholars theorize as "post-feminist" media representations (Goldman et al., 1991; Vavrus, 2000; Arthurs, 2003; Stillion Southard, 2008) to privilege "meritocracy and elitism" (Vavrus, 2000). Post-feminist representations in Chinese contexts point to a growing pattern of illuminating the rising upper-middle-class Han majority. The "modern" woman is represented in the *nouveau riche* role model for her female readers. I further argue that despite the empowerment enabled by the confluence of local marketplace and global modernity, this role model creates a divisive, and even marginalizing, social force, especially in light of the official magazine's alleged long-term mission to propagate gender equality. I posit that such representation of "modern" womanhood is not an anecdote but a strategic alignment with the market logic of redefining women's gender and social identities in a discourse of profit-driven consumerism, as well as showcasing China's ever-increasing economic power to the outside world.

My argument begins by prefacing Western feminist scholars' theorizing of post-feminism in media texts. Then, I introduce *Women of China* as a microcosm of media representations, describe women's changing images portrayed in different decades, and explain my understanding of post-feminist representations in Chinese contexts. Next, I analyze the portrayals of the woman on the cover, and the local woman, highlighting the new characteristics of "modern" Chinese womanhood. I conclude this chapter through discussing the ideological implications underlying the representations of the "modern" Chinese woman, especially her complex, paradoxical effects in a discourse of consumerism.

POST-FEMINISM IN MEDIA REPRESENTATIONS

Post-feminism is a loaded notion in Western feminist scholarship, as the parameters of its definition are still under debate (Ouellette, 2002; Stillion Southard, 2008). In the political terrain, the label suggests an intentional detachment from the second-wave feminist movement and identity "based upon an assumption that women's material needs have, for the most part, been met and that a politics of feminism is no longer necessary for women's advancement" (Vavrus, cited in Stillion Southard, 2008, p. 152). In media representations of women, post-feminist sentiments more saliently manifest in such woman-centered dramas as the controversial *Ally McBeal,* and *Sex and the City* (Arthurs, 2003; Dubrofsky, 2002; Ouellette, 2002; Stillion Southard, 2008). These dramas presented the "liberal, heterosexual, white, metropolitan career woman" (Arthurs, 2003, p. 83), who is seemingly empowered by her financial security and individual choices over name brand commodities, fashion, lifestyle, and even men. Such a woman is dramatically exemplified by Carrie, Charlotte, Miranda, and Samantha in *Sex and the City*, women who can afford to indulge themselves in a romantic lifestyle. Besides popular dramas, advertising also abounds in similar portrayals. As Goldman, Heath, and Smith (1991) observe, the Esprit jeans commercial showcases a modern woman having a choice to (re)define her "elegance and style" via "fashion and luxury," thus creating a façade of transcending the "constraints of patriarchy" (p. 347). Vavrus (2000) identifies Western mainstream media's deployment of a set of "ideals and tactics" that privilege "a mostly white, middle-class to elite, straight perspective on women's lives" (p. 425). Such skewed representations of women, as Vavrus (2000) further contends, constitutes the concept of "post-feminist solipsism," which refers to "generalizing about women using particular women's voices and concerns to the exclusion of others" (p. 413).

While post-feminism and its politics have received notable criticism from Western media and feminist scholars, such a conception has not been examined in a non-Western discourse. My examination of the Chinese women's magazine reveals what I call a "post-feminist representational formula" that implicitly and quietly constructs the "modern" Chinese woman's images and identities. Post-feminism in Chinese media contexts lacks scholarly visibility mainly because the culture partook in a different historical trajectory in women's movements than those in the West. The first, second, and third wave feminist movements and discussions about their successes and flaws remain contained within Western circuits. Although Chinese women (if viewed as a collective group) experienced a fundamental liberation from feudalism (e.g., liberation from foot-binding practice and the polygamy system), ordinary women themselves have hardly been labeled as "feminists." Current official historical textbooks circulated in mainland China, for example, signify Chinese women's emancipation as one of the indelible achievements of the Communist Party's leadership instead of a result of feminist victory. I contend that this previous lack of visibility of feminist discourse in Chinese contexts makes post-feminist representations more intriguing.

WOMEN OF CHINA MAGAZINE AND THE CHANGING DEPICTIONS OF WOMEN

Women of China provides a rich reservoir of Chinese women's portrayals. In circulation for more than seventy years, the magazine has gained historical prestige by witnessing every social change and depicting the growth of several generations of Chinese women. Since its inception in 1939, *Women of China* has remained the most influential official women's magazine published by the All China Women's Federation. In the past decades, the magazine carried the political responsibility of publicizing the central government's policies on issues of women and gender (Johansson, 2001). Reading the magazine as a microcosm in a larger system of cultural representations (Barthes, 1968; Emmison & Smith, 2000), I highlight the changing portrayals of Chinese women along with the editorial and stylistic transformation of the magazine. I intend to show the transformation of the magazine from a political mouthpiece with significant feminist messages to an arguably depoliticized artifact of consumerism.

A general contrast of the magazine's 1970s, 1980s, 1990s, and 2000s publications points to two salient patterns of transformation. First, themes, subject matter, and stylistic features have gradually changed over time, as the magazine simultaneously mirrors and constructs China's social realities. Specifically, since its renewed publication in 1978, three historical/social eras have signified paradigm shifts in Chinese women's social lives (Luo & Hao, 2005). The political messages for women readers of the 1970s, for example, were explicitly conveyed in the magazine's editorial reports. In the Communist Party briefing of the Fourth National Women's Congress, the reports focused on the development of the service industry, the importance of revolutionary and traditional education for women and children, and the rationale for one-child birth control. By contrast, the economic reform era ushered in commercialization, manifested by dramatic increases of commercials and captions. The mid-1990s marked the beginning of advertisements by Kan Yue-sai's international cosmetics company. The editorial reports became less didactic and focused more on personal storytelling about women's lives and careers, including women's challenges as mothers, and women's development of new hobbies (such as cooking, writing, and making household decorations). The globalizing era's subject matter ranged from discussions of specific social issues such as global warming, interpersonal relationships in the workplace, and engineered/generic food to narratives on media celebrities' lives, beauty editorials, and individualized stories about women's emotions, loves, and marriages. Advertisements of all sorts, selling women's fashion, cosmetics, lingerie, furniture, and medicine now appear regularly. The magazine has strategically positioned itself as part of the discourse of a newly developing consumerism, ostensibly introducing new themes, yet subtly depoliticizing the messages for women about women's media images.

The second noticeable transformation lies in the visual representations of women in tandem with the three eras' social and cultural changes. In the post-revolutionary era, women's images were somewhat sparse. In photos, women were mostly depicted as "being together," usually wearing clothing that obviously displayed their social identities: workers' outfits, farmers' outfits, police uniforms, army uniforms, or ethnic costumes. Women also were seen working side by side with their male colleagues in farms and factories. These images reinforced Mao's slogan that women finally "held up half of the sky" (Barret, 1973, p. 193; Li, 1998, p. 81). The cover images of the July 1978 issue, for example, fell into the category of "theme covers," which portrayed group activities instead of highlighting each individual on the cover (Lehnus, 1977; Luo & Hao, 2005). This cover specifically depicted President Hua Guofeng (Mao's immediate successor after his death) and a group of six women, including Han. The other five women were minorities, wearing colorful ethnic costumes. Hua and the women were smiling despite their ethnic differences, thus conveying a sense of group cohesion. However, the physical appearance of each individual was not depicted in detail. Such theme covers were characteristics of the late 1970s and early 1980s issues. In the reform era, "theme covers" were replaced by what Lehnus (1977) categorized as "character covers," which magnified the individual's features (Luo & Hao, 2005). On the cover of the April 1990 issue, for example, the woman was young and beautiful and her enlarged photo was a facial close-up, which, according to Johansson (1998), was a novelty in Chinese magazines of the 1990s. Noticeably, she had well-trimmed, painted eyebrows, shining eyes highlighted by mascara and eye shadow, and rosy lips colored by lipstick. Also, she wore a pair of earrings of the same color as her glossed lips. She smiled brightly and her head tilted to one side of her shoulders, a pose that appears to enhance her feminine look. A white dove was sitting right on the other side of her shoulders, and the bird's snow-white features very well matched her light-colored skin. Her curly hair was tied up in a fashionable knot. Typical in the 1990s issues, such images were aligned with those in commercials launched during Kan Yue-sai's massive marketing campaign. These commercials showcased Chinese/Oriental models, selling a range of cosmetics products: sunblock, moisturizing lotion, whitening cream, and lipstick, all of which were not available in the previous decades. In the global era, women's images were even more glamorous. Movie stars and television celebrities replaced the anonymous cover girls who modeled in the 1990s. Whereas women of the previous decade started to experiment with self-beautification, the affluent women in the post-millennium are portrayed as consumers of both local and global name brands, as well as experts in cosmetics who know how to choose, purchase, and apply makeup to beautify their facial features and protect their skin.

From theme covers to character covers, from defeminization to refeminization of women's body images, and from portrayals of women workers/ farmers to women celebrities/consumers, the textual and visual changes in *Women of China* magazine reflect the process media representations negotiated during the country's social transition from Maoist ideology to market-driven consumerism. By modifying their looks, women have redefined their gender and social identity. The magazine has shifted from a political artifact which upholds feminist ideals of gender equality to a popular cultural artifact that strategically promotes personalized consumption (as displayed in the outlook of the glamorous, affluent cover women). In the next sections of this chapter, I look at the ways the magazine constructs the "modern" Chinese woman via the formula of post-feminist representations. As I show through my analysis, this "modern" woman of the post-millennium stands out differently from her 1990s counterpart. Portrayed as a role model, she now embodies the rising, dominant upper-middle Hang class, seemingly empowered by the confluence of local consumerism and global modernity. Ironically, she has become a symbol of oppression herself. Specifically, I examine the portrayals of women on the magazine's covers, their personal stories, and the series of essays entitled "Local Woman."

COVER WOMEN

A magazine's cover conveys the most significant messages of and about the magazine because it serves as a "genre identifier, semiotic system, and frame" (McCracken, 1993, p. 37). As the "face" of a magazine (Moeran, 1995, p. 114), the cover, through the photographic and linguistic text, creates a genre identity for the whole magazine. The cover is also a semiotic system in the sense that its texts interact to construct new systems of meanings (McCracken, 1993). Even more importantly, the cover provides readers an interpretive frame for reading the materials inside. In Hall's terms, it presents "pre-embedded definitions" and connects various events and themes that follow (Hall, 1973, p. 13). My analyses of the cover pages of *Women of China* show that the magazine skillfully utilizes the functions of its covers to construct a "modern" Chinese woman who is capable of integrating her external and internal beauty. This Chinese woman, expected to be a role model for other Chinese women (especially as suggested in the magazine's mission statement), has it all: beauty, career, love, and/or children. I argue that this perfect woman is a post-feminist icon, representing China's economic prosperity. My argument is based upon my deciphering of the montage created by a combination of the woman's images and her personal stories.

The deliberation to represent the modern Chinese woman is noticeably reflected in the standardized layout of the covers. The covers in the postmillennium issues consistently follow the same patterns of layout. On the cover of every issue, the title "Zhongguo Funü" is written in traditional Chinese characters in calligraphy and placed at the upper left corner of the magazine. The title is then translated into English as "Women of China" and positioned at the very top of the magazine, and the English words are bigger and more striking than the Chinese characters. The image of the Chinese woman occupies about two-thirds of the cover's space. On her left side some of the eye-catching headlines of the issue's major articles are listed. While the title in Chinese characters is juxtaposed horizontally with the woman's face, the title in English is either right behind her head, partially covered by her hair, or right in front of her head, covering part of her hair. The positioning of the title in both Chinese and English and its connection with the woman's image creates a strong perception that the title "Zhongguo Funü" ("Women of China") labels both the magazine and the model. The model represents Chinese women.

Unlike those beautiful yet anonymous cover girls of the 1990s, the individual models are now public figures well known to Chinese audiences. Their professions fall into two major categories: award-winning actresses/singers (Gong Li, Zhang Jingchu, Zhouxun, Xu Jinglei, Song Zuying, and Cheng Chong,); and television show hostesses (such as Yang Lan, Jing Yidan, Zhou Yingqi, and Wang Xiaoya). These individuals embody China's *nouveau riche*, as they have become famous and wealthy. These glamorous women conjure up the image of a modern woman's physique. She wears traditional Chinese Qipao, or high-fashion name brand Western-style clothing. She confidently displays the upper part of her face and body. Her "refined," porcelain skin, painted eyebrows, shining eyes, rosy lips, and white sparkling teeth, along with her hair, demonstrate the height of fashion. Most striking is her steady, calm, and self-contained gaze. Rather than being gazed upon, she gazes back, looking into the beholder's eyes, often with disconcerting straightforwardness. A sense of empowerment is especially conveyed through her body posture. In his study of gender and advertisements, Goffman (1979) views women's body positions in advertising as suggesting a "ritual of subordination." Goffman (1979) argues that the subordination ritual is embodied in such postures by females as "body cant," "passive withdrawal," "knee bend," and "head cant" (pp. 45–46). Other poses such as lying down, lowering the head or body, and having a childish look and manner can also reflect the women's sexual appeal and subordinated status.

In contrast to Goffman's characterizations, this cover woman stands straight, holds her body erect, her head high, and gazes directly into the camera. Yet, her overall image represents hyperfemininity.

Seemingly, the Chinese woman represented on the cover is empowered by her own beautiful physique and upscale socioeconomic status. Such representations, when magnified under the critical lens of a feminist perspective, however, are quite problematic. I first questioned the representational strategy of an "empowered 'female gaze'" (Ouellette, 2002, p. 326). Drawing from Bordo (1997), Ouellette (2002) says in her analysis of Ally McBeal that "reserving the gender of the objectifying gaze at the level of representation does not necessarily reverse power hierarchies or hegemonic understandings of femininity and masculinity" (p. 326). In the case of the cover woman, her gaze, powerful as it appears, establishes an even more subtle level of hierarchy between her and other Chinese women. Long gone are the minority women who used to stand in their ethnic costumes, proudly being part of the portraits on the covers. Now this celebrity woman, whoever she actually is, comes to represent the Hang majority and especially its meritocracy. In this regard, her gaze negates those who do not belong to her privileged group. The representation of the elite woman with an empowered gaze is one of the ostensible manifestations of post-feminist solipsism that Mary D. Vavrus (2000) critiques. Expressing concerns for the absence of the less privileged and disadvantaged women in media, Vavrus (2000) notes that the "normative messages" post-feminism conveys to women "have a strong, but unspoken, class component: middle-class to elite women are those who fit the dominant definition of womanhood constructed in mainstream media accounts" (p. 425). Vavrus's (2000) criticism helps to shed light on the empowerment of the modern Chinese woman on the magazine's covers but the simultaneous disempowerment of many others.

In her study of Chinese commercialism and femininity of the 1990s, Evans (2000) observes "a frequent disjuncture in women's magazines between visual and written versions of femininity" (p. 232). As Evans (2000) further explains, the visual depicted a "romantic beauty (the agent of desire)" whereas the written depiction pointed to the "normative standards of feminine conduct" such as a woman being expected to be an "ideal wife" who should put her own interests after her husband's (p. 232). In media representations of the previous decade, the "external beauty" of a woman was not aligned with the same woman's "internal beauty" (Evans, 2000, p. 218). The representations of the modern Chinese woman have undergone a significant shift. The modern Chinese woman integrates both internal and external beauty. The magazine's visuals showcase her beautiful, feminine facial and bodily features while the text details her "internal beauty." The Chinese notion of "internal beauty" ("Lei zaimei") refers to normalized feminine conduct (or virtue), which is being ascribed to the woman through storytelling. Thus, the integration of the woman's internal and external beauty creates a role model who reinforces her role as a post-feminist icon, further demonstrated through my reading of the cover woman's personal stories.

As a regular reader of Chinese magazines, I notice that most women's lifestyle magazines use linguistic texts to serve the function of what McCraken terms as "anchorage and relay" (1993, p. 27), that is, using a story or a scenario to at least briefly gloss cover images. Adopting this common strategy of glossing the cover, *Women of China*, however, elaborates upon the cover woman's success stories, thus upholding her as a role model for contemporary Chinese women, and especially highlighting and normalizing her feminine conduct—her internal beauty.

My reading of the women's stories (as representative anecdotes) shows more commonalities about these women than differences. Told in a third-person perspective by an essayist and/or journalist, apparently based upon each woman's interview accounts, all the narratives attempt to trace the cover woman's growth as a successful public figure. Here is a glimpse of a revealing list:

1. She has an unforgettable childhood, privileged upbringing, and elite education. (For example, Yang Lan, Xu Jinglei, Tao Hong, Ju Xue, and Yu Feihong are among many others who have intellectual parents to nurture their interests in music, art, and/or literature and to encourage them to pursue their higher education and later their career.)
2. Under the influences of her family (especially her parents), she has developed strong family values. (Even when Gong Li, Cheng Chong, Yang Lan, and Zhang Zhiyi live abroad for the sake of their studies or careers, their hearts are tied to their families in the home country.)
3. She has both the look and the luck to facilitate her career pursuits. (While Zhao Ling is quoted as "accidentally becoming a TV hostess and later on unexpectedly turning into a promising actress," Song Zhuying has the fortune of joining the army's performance crew, which has enabled her to develop into a professional classical singer. Even Xue Jinglei, well known for her multiple talents in acting, film directing, and writing, says she has not endeavored to gain fame in the entertainment industry.)
4. She is intelligent, independent, hard working, and perseverate, all qualities valued in Chinese culture.
5. Despite her independence, she is attached to her husband or boyfriend, without whom she would not view herself as being successful.

This long list of commonalities are interwoven to add the final touch to the glamorous picture of the woman on the cover; she is close to perfection, beautiful, well rounded, in control of her own life, and capable of balancing her career with love and family. In these women's stories, men are temporarily removed to underscore the women's success. While Song Zuying boasts of her husband as being a loving partner and friend, Zhou Yingqi proudly announces that her husband is the one who most touches her heart. While Cheng Chong has a comfortably well-off Chinese American doctor- husband who emotionally and financially supports her acting career, Ju Xue has a famous film director-husband who takes pride in his wife's acting and her love and passion for life. As for Yu Feihong, Zhao Ling, and Xu Jinglei, their emotional lives provide them with the strength and inspiration to achieve their grand career goals. Although these women appear as if empowered in their career and personal relationships, they are quite constrained within their gender roles. These women are much like the women on *Sex and the City*, who cannot feel fulfilled without a man.

Yang Lan's success story establishes the prototype of what this cover woman can do and should be like. Because of her beautiful look, graceful demeanor, and eloquence in both Mandarin and English, she was selected among more than two thousand candidates to become the hostess of the popular TV show *China Arts and Entertainment* in 1990. When she became a household name in her twenties, she quit her thriving position to pursue her master's degree in International Affairs at Columbia University. Upon returning to China in 1997, Yang joined Hong Kong Phoenix Satellite TV and established the TV talk show *Yang Lan Workshop*, through which she interviewed world leaders and celebrities from various cultures and backgrounds. At the peak of her career, she made the significant decision of starting Sun Media, her own media company, and becoming one of the major entrepreneurs of China's media industry. As her biography shows, Yang has navigated through every phase of her life with grace and ease. What makes Yang most successful, as Su (writer of Yang's story) (2004) suggests, is not only her skillful management of her business but her ability to maintain a balance between her hectic career and her serene family life. Besides the cover, more pictures of Yang are placed intertextually in Su's essay. One shows her sitting comfortably on an antique chair. The caption states in English: "New Year's plan for thirty-five-year-old Yang Lan means the plan for her parents, husband, kids, and career. None will be left out in her plan." The other picture shows her holding her husband Wu Zheng's arm and smiling contentedly. The caption on this picture reads, "Career and family life is equally important; to begin with, Yang Lan has never pursued merely one or the other." To emphasize her attention to her family life, Su continues to talk about Yang's plan to take her daughter horseback riding, seek a drawing tutor for her son, and accompany her husband on a vacation by the ocean. In Su's narration, Yang's career has never conflicted with her role as a wife or mother.

From this snapshot, Yang's silhouette resembles what Western scholars identify as the "hallmarks" of a "post-feminist vision" (Dow, 2002, p. 260). On the one hand, like Ally McBeal in Dow's (2002) and Dubrofsky's (2002) analyses, this post-feminist woman has (or wants to have) it all: "career, femininity, love, husband, babies—not just a career" (Dubrofsky, 2002, p. 271); in the Chinese version, she has external and internal beauty, as well. Even more problematic, her success stories are deliberately personalized, as if telling her women readers that social achievements can be made by simply relying on personal decisions and endeavors (or sometimes fortuitous forces such as accidental opportunities), yet disregarding any societal and institutional constraints on women. I concur with Dubrofsky (2002) that in post-feminist representations, "when the personal is looked at without any kind of political inflection, and when the political is personalized—all we are left with is something superficial, melodramatic, and empty" (p. 279). The image and life story of the woman on the cover is depoliticized, thus sidestepping any gender inequality and social challenges that less privileged women have to face in consumer culture. The cover woman reflects and deflects a beautiful yet oppressive construction of the modern Chinese woman. She represents China's elite socioeconomic class. She internalizes normative conducts of femininity and negates those less privileged.

THE LOCAL WOMAN AND HER REGIONAL TRAITS

Whereas the woman on the cover is strategically represented as the ideal, elite role model, the "local woman" depicted in a series of essays embodies a more individualistic nouveau riche lifestyle, enjoying local and global fashion and luxury. In this section, I look into another post-feminist icon that manifests itself in these essays.

The 2004 issues of *Women of China* added a series of third-person narratives, which attempt to capture the so-called "regional characters" and "special traits" of women from such cosmopolitan cities as Changchun, Beijing, Shanghai, Guangzhou, Changsha, and Kunming, to name a few. These essays consistently focus on three aspects. First, the essays describe the appearance of the local women, who are said to have special physical features and beauty which distinguish them from women of other cities. Second, the essays depict the way that local women's lifestyles are influenced by both local cultural norms and global consumption. Finally, stories of one or two individuals (with pseudonyms) are told to exemplify their local traits. The following descriptions give a glimpse of some of the riveting yet problematically framed scenarios that attempt to reflect the local woman's beauty and self-beautification.

The Changchun Woman

The Changchun woman is described as a blooming red flower among a stretch of greenness, very eye-catching. She has delicate and distinct facial features. She is tall and winsome. Her beauty is like the scenery of Changchun's Clear Moon Lake and can touch the hearts of those who gaze at her. She applies bright color makeup like the Japanese woman does and appears graceful and elegant. With her makeup perfectly matching various occasions, she appears clean, sharp and modern. Beauty is said to have become the tradition and norm of Changchun. (Liu, 2004, pp. 16–18)

The Beijing Woman

The Beijing woman is confident, independent, and self-centered, all of which are also part of the tradition of Beijing as a cosmopolitan capital city. She is compared to Beijing's climate, having distinctive seasonal changes with short transitions in between. She transforms herself in one way or another the year round and will not stick to the same fashion. (Cheng, 2004, pp. 18–19)

The Shanghai Woman

The Shanghai woman has absorbed the essence of both Chinese and Western cultures and integrates the two in her makeup and her lifestyle. She is compared to Shanghai, which is cosmopolitan, materialistic, and romantic, and embraces both the old and the new in terms of architecture, cultures, and lifestyles. The Shanghai woman fits nicely into the old costume of Qipao due to her light-colored and tender skin tone, and her small, slim, curvy body shape. (Li, 2004, pp. 26–27)

The Changsha Woman

The Changsha woman's beauty includes her physique, her skin tone, and her ways of dressing up and applying her make up. Her skin, in particular, is pale in color, smooth, moist and refined, making her even more feminine. Among other things, she is very trendy and loves to follow fashion. Her favorite clothing and makeup is from Guangzhou, the biggest city in South China. (Xiao, 2004, pp. 24–25)

While focusing on the local woman's physical beauty and lifestyle, these essays show that *becoming* (instead of *being*) a beautiful local woman involves a keen sense of fashion, a persistent process of beautification, and constant investment in that beautification. Although they live in different Chinese cities, these women are all avid consumers of foreign beauty and fashion products, as they also endeavor to beautify themselves and keep abreast of international fashion trends. The Changchun woman emphasizes that a woman turns into a beauty through her own efforts. She experiments with L'Oreal, Shiseido, and Lancôme cosmetics, believing that her expensive investment is worthwhile. The Beijing woman's charm is closely linked to her keen sense of fashion and her modern lifestyle. She uses a high-class Louis Vuitton suitcase and trendy cell phone to match her white-collar status and display her successful career. Like the Changchun woman, the Beijing woman relies on her makeup to refine her skin and beautify her face. Her beauty is a result of what she consumes. The Changsha woman's obsession with beauty makes her sensitive to the fashion trends in the cosmopolitan cities of South China. Like women from other regions, she cannot miss the latest fashion and popular cosmetics.

As reflected in these accounts, the magazine constructs a notion of beauty that goes hand in hand with women's consumption of beautification. To some extent, these portrayals create an artistic picture of the local woman, who is said to have feminine beauty and can uphold the alleged regional characteristics and traditions. Through the theme of the local woman, the magazine showcases the diverse local traditions in different locales. The woman's regional differences, however, become negligible in the consumer market. She resembles her beauty-cautious counterparts elsewhere, all of whom seem to have sufficient purchase power to enjoy upscale commodities and fashion from home and abroad. Indeed, the woman has become an emblem of the rising middle-upper class who skillfully navigate between the local traditions and global modernity, managing any possible tensions in the discourse of consumerism. This emblem constitutes another aspect of post-feminist representations. In Chinese contexts, the construction of the modern Chinese woman is aligned with the market logic of profit-driven consumption. The magazine and the consumer market benefit by redefining the modern woman as an upscale cosmopolitan who can modify her look and lifestyle. Such a woman is capable of promoting consumerism and presenting a model of economic prosperity and progress to the outside world.

Ironically, however, the woman as a post-feminist icon serves as a problematic synecdoche, masking the social realities of ordinary local women's everyday lives. As a native Chinese who grew up in mainland China, I have witnessed and experienced what Ouellette (2002) states as "structural power dynamics that shape and constrain diverse women's experiences and choices" (p. 320). Paraphrasing Tan, Evans (2000) explains, "economic reform has diversified employment opportunities and choices for women; it has simultaneously exacerbated gender differences in power, income, and status" (p. 224). Like Evans, I question the absence of the actual women underlying the magazine's representations of the "modern" Chinese woman. Missing from this equation include women of ethnic minorities, rural farm women, women who have been laid off and cannot fit into the market economy, and women who work long hours in sweatshops. Whereas Evans (2000) speaks of a hierarchical divide "between the rural (backward/victim/suffering) and the urban (modernized/fulfilled/successful) apparent in many discussions about gender and social transformation" (p. 228), I note that such a divide is quietly missing in the construction of the feminine, equal, and empowered "modern" Chinese woman. Like the cover woman, the local woman, positioned in the confluence of local and global encounters, creates illusory expectations for those who do not have a similar share of the consumer culture, pointing to the hegemonic process of gender and social identity construction in China's consumerist discourse.

CONCLUSION

My reading of the covers and series of essays on the local woman reveals that *Women of China* magazine strategically constructs a "modern" Chinese woman. Whereas the older images of the "modern" woman in Johansson's (2001) research depict "an obedient traditionally minded housewife but also a consumer who cares about her looks" (p. 120), the post-millennium "modern" woman has taken on some new traits that diverge from those of the past. First, she is no longer portrayed as a shy, obedient, or traditional housewife. Instead, she is a bold and independent woman who enjoys her career, love, and family. Second, she no longer shies away from displaying her femininity in the public domain. Third, she is affluent. Finally, she is capable of integrating her beautiful looks with her "internal beauty." Arising from these depictions is a new notion of femininity that has been redefined by the confluence of local tradition and global modernity. This seemingly empowered "modern" woman constructed in the mediated texts, as I have argued, epitomizes a post-feminist icon with significant political and ideological implications. This icon contributes to a discourse of globalization and consumerism, in which femininity promotes gendered consumption. This female icon, situated in the tensions between local tradition and global consumption, contributes to China's grand project of achieving modernity. Although her outlook has been modified, the "modern" Chinese woman, like her other Asian counterparts (explained in Munshi's 2001 collection), still shoulders the responsibility of showcasing the country's newly gained prosperity in a postcolonial era. Indeed, this woman needs an "empowered" gaze and enhanced economic status.

Paradoxically, implicated in the redefined gender politics and consumerist ideology, the woman and her life stories are depoliticized. As reflected in the narratives about the cover woman, her success appears without struggle against oppressive gender rules or institutional power. Representing the privileged, educated, Han, middle-to-upper-class woman, the "modern" Chinese woman (with her modified outlook and new traits) has unfortunately become a symbol of oppression in this microcosm of media representations. My analysis points to the importance of examining post-feminist media texts in non-Western contexts, which have not yet drawn much scholarly attention. A feminist critique, as this chapter demonstrates, can shed light on the hegemonic process of globalizing consumerism that constrains and disempowers non-Western women situated within a sophisticated web of local and global relationships.

REFERENCES

Andrews, J. F., & Shen, K. (2002). The new Chinese woman and lifestyle magazines in the late 1990s. In P. Link, R. P. Madsen, & P. G. Pickowicz (Eds.), *Popular China unofficial culture in a globalizing society* (pp. 137–62). Lanham, MD: Rowman & Littlefield Publishers, Inc.

Anonymous (2008). *China's progress towards the millennium development goal 2008 report.* Ministry of Foreign Affairs of the People's Republic of China & United Nations System in China. Retrieved July 1, 2010 from www.un.org.cn/cms/p/resources/30/809/content.html.

Arthurs, J. (2003). *Sex and the City* and consumer culture: Remediating postfeminist drama. *Feminist Media Studies, 3,* 83–98.

Barrett, J. (1973). Women hold up half of the sky. In M.B. Young (Ed.), *Women in China: Studies in social change and feminism* (pp. 193–200). Ann Arbor: Center for Chinese Studies, the University of Michigan.

Barthes, R. (1968). *Elements of semiology.* London: Cape.

Bordo, S. (1997). *Twilight zones: The hidden life of cultural images from Plato to OJ.* Berkeley: University of California Press.

Burke, K. (1969). *A grammar of motives.* Berkeley, CA: University of California Press.

Chaplin, S. (2001). Interiority and the "modern woman" in Japan. In S. Munshi (Ed.), *Images of the "modern woman" in Asia: Global media, local meanings* (pp. 55–77). Surrey: Curzon Press.

Cheng, T. (2004). Shui ye hua bu chu de Beijing nüren [The Beijing woman: Nobody could portray] *Zhongguo Funü [Women of China],* 638 (December), 18–19.

Croll, E. (1995). *Changing identities of Chinese women.* Hong Kong University Press.

Donald S. H. & Lee, C. (2001). Mulan illustration? Ambiguous women in contemporary Chinese cinema. In S. Munshi (Ed.), *Images of the "modern woman" in Asia: Global media, local meanings* (pp. 123–37). Surrey: Curzon Press.

Dow, B. (2002). *Ally McBeal,* lifestyle feminism, and the politics of personal happiness. *Communication Review, 5,* 259–64.

Dubrofsky, R. (2002). *Ally McBeal* as postfeminist icon: The aestheticizing and fetishizing of the independent working woman. *Communication Review, 5,* 265–84.

Emmison, M. & Smith, P. (2000). *Researching the visual: Introducing qualitative methods.* London: Sage Publications.

Evans, H. (2000). Marketing femininity: Images of modern Chinese women. In T. B.Weston & L. M. Jensen (Eds.), *China beyond the headlines* (pp. 217–44). Lanham, MD: Rowman & Littlefield Publishers, Inc.

Evans, H. (2008). Sexed bodies, sexualized identities and the limits of gender. *China Information, 22*(2), 361–86.

Goffman, E. (1979). *Gender advertisements.* Cambridge: Harvard University Press.

Goldman, R., Heath, D., & Smith, S. (1991). Commodity feminism. *Critical Studies in Mass Communication, 8,* 333–51.

Hall, S. (1973). The structured communication of events. *Media Series, 5,* 13–24.

Hall, S. (Ed). (1997). *Representation: Cultural representations and signifying practices, culture, media and identities.* London: Sage Publications.

Johansson, P. (1998). White skin, large breasts: Chinese beauty product advertising as cultural discourse. *China Information*, XIII (2/3), 59–84.

Johansson, P. (1999). Consuming the other: The fetish of the western woman in Chinese advertising and popular culture. *Postcolonial Studies*, 2(3), 377–88.

Johansson, P. (2001). Selling the "modern woman": Consumer culture and Chinese gender politics. In S. Munshi (Ed.), *Images of the "modern woman" in Asia: Global media, local meanings* (pp. 94–122). Surrey: Curzon Press.

Ko, D. (2000). Bondage in time: Footbinding and fashion theory. In R. Chow (Ed.), *Modern Chinese literary and cultural studies in the age of theory: Reimagining a Field* (pp. 199–226). Durham, NC: Duke University Press.

Lehnus, D. J. (1977). *Who's on Time? A study of Time's cover from March 3, 1923 to January 3, 1977*. New York: Oceana.

Liechty, M. (2001). Women and pornography in Kathmandu: Negotiating the "modern woman" in a new consumer society. In S. Munshi (Ed.), *Images of the "modern woman" in Asia: Global media, local meanings* (pp. 34–54). Surrey: Curzon Press.

Li, S. (2004). Shanghai pai nüren [The Shanghai woman: The Shanghai brand.] *Zhongguo Funü [Women of China]*, 616 (January), 26–27.

Li, X. P. (1998). Fashioning the body in post-Mao China. In A. Brydon & S. Niessen (Eds.), *Consuming fashion: Adorning the transnational body* (pp. 71–89). Oxford: Berg.

Liu, L. (2004). Changchuan nüren: Aimei dao xin hua lu fang [The Changchun woman: To love beauty to her heart's content]. *Zhongguo Funü [Women of China]*, 618 (February), 16–18.

Louie, K. (2008). Defining modern Chinese culture. In K. Louie (Ed.), *The Cambridge companion to modern Chinese culture* (pp. 1–19). New York: Cambridge University Press.

Luo, Y. J., & Hao, X.M. (2005). Mei ti nüxing xingxiang yu shehui biange—Zhongguo Funü zazhi fengmian renwu xingxiang de shizheng yanjiu [Construction of female images in the media and social changes: A case study of the cover images in the magazine "Women of China."] *Zhongguo Chuanmei Baogao [China Media Report]*, 87–99.

McCracken, E. (1993). *Decoding women's magazines: From* Mademoiselle *to* Ms. New York: St. Martin's Press.

Moeran, B. (1995). Reading Japanese in *Katei Gaho*: The art of being an upperclass woman. In L. Skov & B. Moeran (Eds.), *Women, media and consumption in Japan* (pp. 111–42). Surrey: Curzon Press.

Munshi, S. (2001). Marvelous me: The beauty industry and the construction of the "modern" Indian woman. In S. Munshi (Ed.), *Images of the "modern woman" in Asia: Global media, local meanings* (pp .78–93). Surrey: Curzon Press.

Ouellette, L. (2002). Victims no more: Postfeminism, television, and Ally McBeal. *Communication Review*, 5, 315–35.

Roberts, C. (Ed.). (1997). *Evolution & revolution: Chinese dress 1700s–1990s*. Sydney: Powerhouse Publishing.

Roy, A. (2005). The "male gaze" in Indian television commercials: A rhetorical analysis. In T. Carilli & J. Campbell (Eds.), *Women and the media: Diverse perspectives*. Lanham, MD: University Press of America, Inc.

Stillion Southard, B.A. (2008). Beyond the backlash: *Sex and the City* and three feminist struggles. *Communication Quarterly*, 56, 149–67.

Su, Y. (2004). Fengmian renwu: Yang Lan xinnian meiyou jiu dashuan [Person on the cover: Yang Lan, new years without old plans]. *Zhongguo Funü [Women of China]*, 616 (January), 12–14.

Traube, E. (1992). *Dreaming identities: Class, gender and generation in 1980s Hollywood movies*. Boulder, CO: Westview.

Vavrus, M. D. (2000). Putting Ally on trial: Contesting postfeminism in popular culture. *Women's Studies in Communication*, 23, 413–28.

Walters, S. D. (1995). *Material girls: Making sense of feminist cultural theory*. Berkeley: University of California Press.

Xiao, D. D. D. (2004). Changsa nüren: ban shi huoyan ban shi shui [The Changsha woman: Half fire half water]. *Zhongguo Funü [Women of China]*, 630 (August), 24–25.

Chapter Nine

From *"Babushki"* to *"Sexy Babes"*

The Sexing-Up of Bulgarian Women in Advertising

Elza Ibroscheva

In a popular 1980s Wendy's TV commercial, an imaginary Soviet catwalk is enacted. In the tradition of commercial parody, we hear the boorish voice of the female announcer, who is dressed in a military uniform. In a heavy Russian accent, she shouts out the dress line to be featured on the runway— "Pay attention, thank you, day vear, evening vear, swim vear . . . " Following the announcement, a large, unattractive "babushka" appears, dressed in a grey coverall, strolling the runway in a casual manner. As the announcer shouts out the different outfits to be modeled, all we see is a new accessory added for each occasion, without a single change in the look of the commu- nist dress—a flashlight for evening wear, a beach ball for swim wear. "Very nice," the female announcer says in a heavily accented inflection. The tagline is spoken by the voice-over: "Having no choice is no fun." And while the humorous spin on the communist concept of advertising and fashion is not lost on the audience, the fascinating aspect of this popular and much loved commercial is its portrayal of the Soviet woman—matronly, shapeless, asex- ual, unattractive, and, overall, unfeminine. In short, the featured fashion model is anything but fashionable. The depiction of her in this ad is a glaring example of the visual stereotypes which occupied the collective imagination of communist femininity in the West—the mother/worker, political function- ary, and strong woman, who is full of patriotic pathos and revolutionary spirit. These deliberate images, propagated by the Communist Party, have become a ready-made, cookie-cutter visual symbol of Soviet womanhood over the years of the Cold War.

And if this advertisement is indeed a comical pronouncement on the exploitive power of Soviet gender ideology, it also reflects the widely popular Western misconceptions about the socialist woman and her social positioning. During the years of ideological division between East and West, one thing that the East was often seen excelling at and, quite frequently, was envied for, was the status of women in the Soviet world. Women from the former Soviet bloc enjoyed rights and privileges which Western women could only dare to imagine. Laws that provided three years of maternity leave, widely available state-sponsored childcare, abortion rights—these were just few of the "protectionist" laws established by the socialist states of the Soviet Union and Eastern Europe in their attempt to resolve what they termed the "women's question" in a truly Marxist fashion (LaFont, 1998). Naturally, to support these ideas the powerful propaganda machine of the communist state disclosed pictures of women in hard hats, women technicians, and women doctors, widely supporting the illusion that women in the Communist countries had indeed been liberated and had found the perfect balance between handling a professional career and raising a family, becoming an object of envy of all Western feminists.

Today, while the particulars of women's status differ from country to country in Eastern Europe, patterns of marginalization are obvious all across the region: diminished labor market access, increasing vulnerability to crime, loss of family-oriented social benefits, exceedingly low parliamentary presentation, irresolvable social pressures (Hunt, 1997). What is more, during this period of transition, ever more blatant and disturbing gender-biased social practices have become deeply entrenched, and these practices have had a dramatic impact on the identity of women in Eastern Europe.

Given the unique set of social, economic, and cultural factors which define the reality of Eastern Europe, women in these transitional societies are faced with significant challenges in defining their role and their social identity. In her analysis, Rotkirch (1997) argued that after the end of communism, in Russia and other communist states, there has been a strong movement toward what she called the "aggressive masculinization" of society. Two manifestations of this phenomenon—the prevalence of images of domesticated women in the media, and I would argue, more importantly, the commercial eroticization of the female body in advertising—are particularly relevant to this chapter.

This has been a particularly fascinating trend, considering the fact that nowhere else is the cultural identity of gender more contested than in the visuals of advertising. As Sender (1999) pointed out, advertising serves a twofold function—"to provide role models with whom we can identify and through whom we can aspire to appropriate constructions of ourselves as social beings, and to guide us towards what the marketplace considers to be desirable kinds and quantities of purchasing in an increasingly commodified social environment" (p. 172). Therefore, because advertising is one of the major "factories" of visual images and has been seen as reflecting the social and cultural norms of a given society, studying the evolution of portrayals of women in advertising will present a revealing look at how post-communist female identities are being engendered and constructed. In addition, advertising becomes an extremely interesting media arena to study because it only made its first major appearance as a powerful cultural force in Bulgaria after the sweeping economic and social changes following the collapse of communism in Eastern Europe. Prior to that, advertising was seen as unnecessary and unhealthy promotion of commercialism and decadent social values. As a commercially motivated enterprise, advertising was thought to be "a particularly capitalist phenomenon incompatible with socialism" (Markham, 1964, p. 31), and therefore, was used scarcely, only in its propaganda function, promoting a very deliberate and engineered view of the Soviet society, which had no bearing on the reality of daily life.

Today, the Eastern European woman is anything but the imagined "babushka" of communist propaganda. Eastern European women have adopted a new, highly sexual identity—one that allows them to occupy both the position of the consumer, and more importantly, the position of the "consumed," widely and readily offering their sexualized bodies for consumption. This explores the current trends of "sexing-up" the look of women in Bulgarian advertising in an attempt to analyze the gender identity transformation that has taken place during the post-communist transition in Eastern Europe and has fundamentally affected the social, economic, and political positions of women in the former Soviet bloc. This chapter is important because it addresses an area of international media and cultural studies which largely has been overlooked in academic research and which offers a vitally important critical dissection of the process of establishing and constructing gender identities in a unique set of social, economic and cultural conditions as witnessed in Eastern European countries. While there have been studies discussing the economic conditions and the burden of the social roles and stereotypes of Eastern European women (Einhorn, 1993; Roman 2001, 2003; Funk & Mueller, 1993; Corrin, 1992), very few studies (Azhgikhina, 1995; Ibroscheva, 2006, 2007; Skoric & Furnham, 2003) have looked at the specific gender sexual stereotypes and sexualized portrayals in advertising.

Communism and the Images of Women in Eastern Europe

For a long time, the status of women in the Soviet bloc presented a unique mix of cultural, political, and social conditions that fascinated Western scholars and provided fruitful grounds for feminist studies. Among those scholars, Einhorn (1993), in perhaps the most widely read and cited book on the issue of Eastern European women, writing about the expectations of Western feminist scholars for the future development of the women in Eastern Europe, put it succinctly: ". . . [I]n the short run, at least, women in East Central Europe stand to lose economic, social welfare, and reproductive rights. The image of the female tractor driver is out, as is Superwoman wearing [a] hard-hat on a building site," Einhorn wrote (p. 1).

Kotzeva (1999) explored the images of women in Bulgaria to conclude that while Bulgarian society was under communist rule, two conflicting images of women were constructed—the socialist Amazon—a female-android, a mechanical woman, a heroine of a socialist modernization project—and the woman as mother and caregiver for children. Kotzeva's investigation reveals a higher degree of convergence in the self-identification strategies pursued by Bulgarian women. Her study demonstrated that despite theoretical approval of gender equality and emancipation, women predominantly identify themselves with motherhood and family, and women's self-esteem, dignity, emancipation, or unfair treatment get passed over in silence by an overwhelming number of Bulgarian women.

Mamonova (1994) offers yet another interesting look at the sexual identity and objectification of the Soviet and Eastern European woman. The eroticization of the female body by men has become the patriarchy's international norm, the author argues, and the opening of the former communist society for this kind of expression of male dominance has allowed sexism to move on to a more blatant, visual form. Beauty contests, Mamonova asserted, are the ultimate testimony to this change. She provides an excellent example to support her argument—the budget for the final contest at Miss Russia was around 1.5 million rubles. The organizers, naturally, were counting on a substantial return. "They planned to use the winners of the show for commercial purposes, which means good money, including hard currency" (Mamanova, 1994, p. 161). Thus, men have transformed the female body into immovable—or movable—property and have objectified it in the most obtrusive and materialistic manner.

Roman (2001) also offers a compelling look at post-communist developments in theories of gender representation in Eastern Europe. Roman describes the complex and often contradictory myriad of influences which women in Eastern Europe become exposed to: rise in traditional Orthodoxy, pre-communist village values, and more importantly, "a provocative *feminine mystique* of Western origins stressing beauty as a paramount goal" (Roman, 2001, p. 56) (emphasis by the author). These conflicting influences, Roman argues, have led Eastern European women to a rather unexpected turn—the women of post-communism have adopted a new understanding of being feminine that includes rejection of modernization and all the turmoil that it brings, and with it, rejection of Western feminist ideas. "If, for feminists following the Western model, emancipation means autonomy and taking a public job, for the average woman emancipation means dependency and the right to be a housewife, thus returning to the private sphere" (Roman, 2001, p. 56).

The main argument so far appears to be that the historical circumstances which determine the image and the identity of the Eastern European woman are dramatically different from those determining the lives and sense of self-worth of women in the West. In this vein, a number of Eastern European gender scholars have argued that the social and cultural identity of Eastern European women is drastically different from that of Western women since feminism is the product of a particular culture, of a particular country, and of a particular social system. Thus, for example, women's return to domesticity observed during the transition should not be interpreted as a backlash against feminism and emancipation but as a response to a regained sense of liberation and personal choice. As Siklova (1993), a well-known Czech dissident and a women's rights advocate, said: "As the enforced false ideology breaks down, many people welcome the freedom to return to traditions once forbidden. Young girls and boys are becoming nuns and monks; women are opting to stay at home. Freedom takes on different forms. This may give the impression that we are returning to patriarchy, but it is more a reaction to our recent past" (p. 76).

Parallel to their tendency to return to the home, women in Eastern Europe have also found a new sense of empowerment through embracing sexuality as an expression of femininity, which departs from the traditions of patriarchy and Soviet ideology. This has been further demonstrated in the predominance of sexualized images of women in visual media, and specifically, in advertising. In fact, as another well-known Czech social scientist, Jirina Smejkalova, noted, the asexual nature of the Soviet woman was seen by women in Eastern Europe as just another oppressive social restriction of the communist ideology. To explain the trend of hypersexualization of women in the Eastern European media, Smejkalova (1996) contended:

> Shall we call for censorship of pornography in a country whose entire modern history is built on an excessive fight for freedom of expression? Could anyone that at least once opened a fashion journal issue in Prague in the 1970s filled with sexless figures wrapped in colorless fabric seriously mobilize against abuse of women's bodies in the fashion industry and advertising? (p. 98)

While the literature suggests a variety of important factors influencing the image and character of the Eastern European woman, it seems apparent that her sense of self-identity was suppressed and constrained by the limits of quasi-Marxist feminism and solid Orthodox and Oriental patriarchy. As Petrova (1993) argued, "the everyday life of women was furrowed with ripples of formal equality and emancipation in a seemingly endless patriarchal ocean" (p. 22). What is even more, the revolution of 1989 left the patriarchal system of power intact, transforming its more superficial manifestations—from bad to worse.

ADVERTISING AND THE SEXING-UP OF BULGARIAN WOMEN

Commercial advertising is a fairly new phenomenon in Bulgaria and in most Eastern European countries. During the decades of central planning prior to the collapse of communism, the role of advertising in Bulgaria, as in most Eastern European countries, was very limited because for the most part, demand significantly exceeded supply (Millan & Elliot, 2004). In fact, the Soviet approach to advertising was clearly a result of the ideological incongruity of a planned socialist economy and a consumption-based, capitalist free market. In the large *Soviet Encyclopedia*, for instance, it was stated that advertising in capitalist countries was caused by unrestrained competition; "and the conclusion is that the huge sums spent on advertising in these countries become a burden on the consumer" (Markham, 1964, p. 31). In fact, following communist directives, until World War II, advertising was rejected as "bourgeois capitalist excrescence which artificially stimulates the economy by forcing people to buy what they don't need and what they can't afford" (Markham, 1964, p. 31).

Western-style advertising was understood only as reflected through the lenses of the class struggle and was considered to be one of the major tools enabling the unbridled growth of conspicuous consumption and the very foundation of capitalism. However, non-commercial forms of advertising were widely employed in the Soviet world. Some of these advertisements were concerned with publicizing important cultural events, such as theater performance, radio shows, and so forth, while others were used to encourage savings in the state banks, the production of more crops, and generally, all economic activities that would benefit the society at large. More importantly, most advertising which was non-political in nature was predominantly oriented toward the woman. In fact, as Reid (2002) contended, because women were seen both as the main decision makers in the household and the most active users of goods and consumer products, "construed as both housewives and consumers, women were ascribed the leading role in the production of aesthetic value and social meaning" (p. 245).

With the transition to democracy and a free market economy, advertising debuted in its purely commercial, revenue-driven form on the Bulgarian market, introduced mainly by international companies looking for profit in newly emerging markets. This, in turn, led to fundamental changes in the advertising landscape. As Millan and Elliot (2004) point out, during the formative years of the commercialization of the economy, immediately following the opening of the post-Soviet markets, advertising in Bulgaria developed under conditions of general institutional instability and lack of regulations.

Today in Bulgaria advertising expenditures have risen from $4.3 million in 1996 to $322 million in 2006, with this trend of phenomenal growth expected to continue (*Trends in Advertising*, 2006). More importantly, the fundamental shift in the consumer mentality of the socialist citizen, which was intrinsically tied to the penetration of capitalism on the local scene, brought along with advertising very deliberate images of gender, class, and social status, which were seen by the majority of men and women both as a sign of Westernization and breaking away from the past. In this sense, advertising became not only a vehicle of commercial success, but also a forum for cultural pedagogy, where new ideas of what it means to be a "modern" woman, what it means to be a successful businessman, and many other new cultural symbols could be learned. This pedagogical aspect of advertising has become particularly gendered and alluring with images of beauty, luxury, and socials norms often in direct clash with established cultural traditions of the past. It is this cultural shift in identity formation, triggered by advertising images and messages and combined with the economic hardships and social pressures of the transition, that has resulted in what Hughes (2005) argues are profound psychological changes in the self-esteem and self-worth of women across the former Soviet Union and the countries of the Eastern bloc. Combined with an increasingly sexualized appearance, seen by many as an empowering rejection of the "frumpy babushka" image of the communist past, Eastern European women are caught in an identity crisis—between the communist ideals and the capitalist realities, between the exploitive sexuality of today and the asexual aesthetic of the communist past, with no clear end in sight.

The visual space of Bulgarian media, and specifically Bulgarian advertising, is crowded with sexualized depictions of womanhood. Women's bodies have in fact become commodified and transformed into valuable currency that can be used to sell virtually any product. The majority of billboards feature an endless array of women's sexualized bodies, selling anything from latex paint to hunting accessories and weaponry to alcohol. Confident, young Bulgarian women stare from the billboards, daringly displaying their well-cultivated bodies. Interestingly, the paradox of this heightened sexuality on display stems not only from the collapse of the cultural and moral norms that characterized the post-communist transition, but also from the fact that Bulgarian women, and perhaps, most women in Eastern Europe, found a new form of rebellion against the established, artificial aesthetic norms and stagnant gender roles prescribed by the communist ideology. And while this rebellious spirit of what some called "the new sexual revolution" might have been a refreshing way to face the challenges of the disintegration of communist ideology, the new sexual mores of the post-communist transition were quickly politicized, and the sexual liberation of women was "highjacked" and used as a visual token of the new anti-authoritarian spirit ready for social change. Thus, beauty contests and wet T-shirt contests accompanied political protests while the opening of the first striptease bar in town was celebrated as important cultural news.

The sexing-up of women could indeed be seen as a reaction, albeit a fairly drastic one, to the stifling sexual politics of the communist ideology. However, it is also important to note that the market economy emerged at the time when female images turned out to provide a most profitable commodity in the conditions of unbridled capitalism. One obvious example, which well demonstrates the profitability of the sexing-up of Bulgarian media, is the fact that newspapers covering the first-ever beauty contest in the country sold better than the others. After 1991, the image of the fashion model and the beauty queen came to reign supreme in the mass media, successfully replacing the politicized woman functionary. Interestingly, this change, as Azhgikhina (1995) points out, occurred very smoothly, "since the consciousness fostered in the totalitarian system, as well as the surreal view of the world previously offered, had prepared the audience to accept yet another stereotype, instead of any real heroine of the time" (para. 10). Beauties in bikinis, fashion models' interviews, and press coverage of beauty contests started to appear not only in "lightweight" publications, but also in "respectable" ones and soon enough became the standard for any publication with business savvy.

The advertising industry was quick to take notice of this opportunity, which was further aided by the sudden interest in investing in Eastern Europe expressed by Western companies who saw immense profit potential in the new emerging markets of the former Soviet bloc. Naturally, media conglomerates and advertising giants were among the first to test the ground. And while the production value of print and outdoor advertisements at the onset of the transition was questionable, ads did not shy away from featuring sexualized females aimed to grab the attention of the eager consumers, selling anything and everything—from air conditioners to vitamins—with a sexy twist. The very idea of promoting goods for the sake of consuming out of pleasure and choice, rather than out of necessity and force, posed a novel challenge to Bulgarian advertising companies, which had a lot to learn from their Western counterparts. In this vein, it is important to note that at the initial stages of introducing commercial advertising to the Bulgarian market, there was a general void of creative approaches to promoting consumer goods. Because many eager young women wanted to see their faces on public display, the sexy model was the simplest, cheapest, and most immediate solution.

With the passage of time, however, the production quality in the advertising industry markedly improved; and with it, so grew the level of sexing-up the woman's body. Today the hypersexualization of Bulgarian women is common in all forms of advertising and for all consumer needs. For example, some of the most popular ads featuring female models are for alcoholic beverages. Billboard ads frequently feature attractive young girls posing topless, whose essential body parts are covered by succulent pieces of exotic fruit, seductively offering the consumer a shot of vodka or gin. Other advertising campaigns took an even more daring spin on the theme of sexual adventure and women's bodies. An advertising campaign for Vodka Xtaz (in Bulgarian, short for Ecstasy) featured both a controversial TV spot and multiple print ads resembling scenes from Stanley Kubrick's sexually charged drama *Eyes Wide Shut*. Absent the context of the dramatic dialogue and character development of the original movie, the thirty-second TV commercial was nothing more than a highly stylized "sexploitation" of the female body, which promised wild adventures and bloodthirsty temptresses if the viewer chose this vodka brand over others. The ad was indeed so controversial that it triggered one of the first complaints to the Council of Electronic Media from the Trade and Consumer Protection Commission and the Bulgarian Parents' Association. According to the Trade Commission, the commercial contained pornographic elements and incited people to violence—a claim which was dismissed by the director of the video Georgi Markov, who argued that the real problem is the timing of the broadcasts. "If the advertisement is aired during a night show, no one will be shocked," he said. Taking the focus away from the sexual violence and exploitation of women featured in the video, Grisha Ganchev, the owner of the company which produced the vodka, also stated in the same report that the main purpose of any ad is to produce publicity, and whether it is good or bad, it does not matter when everyone is talking about the brand.

The sexing-up of the Bulgarian woman takes an even higher degree of commodification when a printing company which offers design and publicity services advertises its own business by sending its customers Christmas cards featuring a young woman posing seductively in black lace lingerie and wishing everyone "Happy Holidays!" Here, advertising creativity takes on a whole different level—to beat the competition, and perhaps, to create a new sense of fascination with the concept of sexual tantalization. Christmas wishes take on a whole new, and very sexy, meaning. Perhaps the ultimate manifestation of the degree to which this sexualization has taken on the public imagination of the Bulgarians is the fact that a recent campaign initiated by the online publication *Vagabond* to elect the cultural symbols that truly represent contemporary Bulgaria included the following category: "Thousands of stunning babes dressed in clothing that leaves nothing to the imagination—all whilst working as lawyers, doctors, and managers. You wouldn't find that even in Venezuela!"

CONCLUSION

Gender identities in the countries under post-communist transition are in a state of flux. In the atmosphere of confusion and political disarray which characterized the collapse of the communist system, gender identities were caught in a crisis. This identity crisis, while clearly serving as a new source of empowered sexuality, is also an indication of the consequences of the penetration of global capitalism in the region. With the growing influx of capital in the media and with multinational corporate investments in advertising, women become the prime target as both models and consumers of goods advertised in a hypersexual fashion. In fact, scholars argue that along the sweeping media reform which opened Eastern Europe to the West, providing millions in market shares and advertising revenues, prostitution, and the sex trade can perhaps be defined as the other economic "boom" that has brought Eastern Europe into the global economy (Kligman & Limoncelli, 2005). "The body is a profitable commodity which satisfies all manner of fantasies in all manner of ways" (Kligman, 1996, p. 77). The marketing of the body, prior to democracy, a hidden and often condemned currency characteristic of the decadent commercial West, now easily translates into a legitimate "labor value," reinvigorating a new sexual revolution, now categorized as "sexploitation" (Shreeves, 1992).

This is a particularly dangerous trend in post-communist Bulgaria, and perhaps in the rest of the post-communist societies of the Eastern bloc, because Eastern European women are now exposed to a steady diet of exploitative, sexually provocative depictions of women, which in turn feed a poisonous trend in women's and girl's perceptions of their bodies and their sense of self-worth in the absence of alternative role models. This transformation into an oversexed, hyperfeminine body produces a feeling of empowerment, a feeling of having set out on the road of a different kind of life, one that will be less strenuous and more modern. Some scholars have linked these trends of "modernizing" gender with the massive transformation of the post-Soviet economy and the aggressive marketing of "beauty" as the utmost desired commodity, noting that pursuing beauty is seen in the East as both empowering and Westernizing (Rathner, 2001). However, this sense of empowerment, at minimum, rests on shaky grounds—among other things, it is based on some rather stereotypical and patriarchal definitions of femininity, which often reinforce rather than transform the relations of inequality and repressive gender identity in Eastern Europe. The danger here also lies in the political economy underlying the import of Western images of the perfect, sexed-up body, which creates in turn a new type of stereotype of the Eastern

European women—sexy, hungry for attention, frail, waiting to be rescued (or discovered) by a rich, powerful man, producing new masked politics of domination and subordination.

REFERENCES

Azhgikhina, N. (1995). Women as presented by the Russian media. A report for the *United Nations Department of Economic and Social Affairs (DESA).* Retrieved January 13, 2008, from un.org/documents/ecosoc/cn6/1996/media/rmediaen.htm .

Corrin, C. (Ed.). (1992). *Superwomen and the double burden: Women's experience of change in Central and Eastern Europe and the former Soviet Union.* London: Scarlet Press.

Einhorn, B. (1993). Imagining women: Literature and the media. In B. Einhorn (Ed.), *Cinderella goes to market: Citizenship, gender and women's movements in East Central Europe* (pp. 216–56). London: Verso Publishers.

Funk, N., & Muller, M. (Eds.). (1993). *Gender, politics and post-communism: Reflection from post-communism and the former Soviet Union.* New York: Routledge.

Hughes, D. M. (2005). Supplying women for the sex industry: Trafficking from the Russian Federation. In A. Stulhofer & T. Sanfort (Eds.), *Sexuality and gender in post-communist Eastern Europe and Russia* (pp. 209–26). New York: The Haworth Press.

Hunt, S. (1997). Women's vital voices: The costs of exclusion in Eastern Europe. *Foreign Affairs 76*(4), 1–7.

Ibroscheva, E. (2006). The new Eastern European woman: A gold-digger or an independent spirit? *Global Media Journal* 5 (9). Retrieved from lass.calumet.purdue.edu/cca/gmj/fa06/gmj_fa06_ibroscheva.htm.

Ibroscheva, E. (2007). Caught between East and West? Portrayals of gender in Bulgarian television advertisements. *Sex Roles, 57*(5/6), 409–18.

Kligman, G. (1996). Women and the negotiation of identity in post-communist Eastern Europe. In *Identities in transition: Eastern Europe and Russia after the collapse of Communism,* edited by University of California Press/University of California International and Area Studies Digital Collection, 93, 68–91.

Kligman, G., & Limoncelli, S. (2005). Trafficking women after socialism: From, to, and through Eastern Europe. *Social Politics: International Studies in Gender, State and Society, 12,* (1), 118–40.

Kotzeva, M. (1999). Reimagining Bulgarian women: The Marxist legacy and women's self-identity. In C. Corrin (Ed.), *Gender and identity in Central and Eastern Europe* (pp. 83–99). London: Frank Cass Publishers.

LaFont, S. (1998). *Women in transition: Voices from Lithuania.* New York: State University of New York Press.

Mamonova, T. (1994). *Russian women's studies: Essays on sexism in Soviet culture.* Oxford: Pergamon Press.

Markham, J. W. (1964). Is advertising important in the Soviet economy? *Journal of Marketing 28,* 31–37.

Millan, E., & Elliot, R. (2004). Offensive advertising, public policy and the law: The rulings on the *Zagorka* case. *Journal of Consumer Policy, 27,* 475–93.

Petrova, D. (1993). The winding road to emancipation in Bulgaria. In N. Funk & M. Mueller (Eds.), *Gender, politics, and post-communism: Reflections from Eastern Europe and the former Soviet Union* (pp. 15–22). London: Routledge.

Rathner, G. (2001). Post-communism and the marketing of the thin ideal. In M. Nasser, M. A. Katzman, & R. A. Gordon (Eds.), *Eating disorders and cultures in transition* (pp. 93–111). New York: Taylor & Francis.

Reid, S. (2002). Cold War in the kitchen: Gender and the de-Stalinization of consumer taste in the Soviet Union under Khrushchev. *Slavic Review, 61*(2), 211–52.

Roman, D. (2001). Gendering Eastern Europe: Pre-feminism, prejudice, and East-West dialogues in post-communist Romania. *Women's Studies International Forum, 24*(1), 53–65.

Roman, D. (2003). *Fragmented identities: Popular culture, sex, and everyday life in Post-communist Romania.* Lanham, MD: Lexington Books.

Rotkirch, A. (1997). Women's agency and the sexual revolution in Russia. Paper presented at the research seminar on Women's Active Citizenship University of Joensuu, Dept of Social Policy and Philosophy, September 11, in Helsinki, Finland.

Sender, K. (1999). Selling sexual subjectivities: Audiences respond to gay window advertising. *Critical Studies in Mass Communication, 16*, 172–96.

Shreeves, R. (1992). Sexual revolution or sexploitation: The pornography and erotica debate in the Soviet Union. In S. Rai, H. Pilkington, & A. Phizacklea (Eds.), *Women in the face of change: The Soviet Union, Eastern Europe and China* (pp. 130–46). New York: Routledge.

Siklova, J. (1993). Are women in Central and Eastern Europe conservative? In N. Funk & M. Mueller (Eds.), *Gender, politics, and post-communism: Reflections from Eastern Europe and the former Soviet Union* (pp. 74–83). London: Routledge.

Skoric, M., & Furnham, A, F. (2003). Gender role stereotyping in television advertisements: A comparative study of British and Serbian television. In J. Z. Arsdale (Ed.), *Trends in social psychology* (pp. 73–89). Hauppauge, NY: Nova Science Publishers.

Smejkalova, J. (1996). On the road: Smuggling feminism across the post-iron curtain. *Replika*, special issue, 97–102.

World Trends in Advertising. 2006. Published by the World Advertising Research Center (WARC).

IV

Political Individuals

Chapter Ten

For and About Women

Dorothy Jurney and "The Woman's Network"

Steven Carl Smith

In an address to the Michigan Woman of Achievement Awards banquet in 1984, Dorothy Jurney, reflecting on her career in a male-dominated profession, noted the early development of her identity while working at the *Washington D.C., News* from 1944 to 1946.[1] "It was at the *News* that I had my consciousness raised," she said, recalling how it bothered her that she was not promoted to the position of city editor. "Dorothy, I would like to make you the city editor," John O'Rouke apparently said, "but I don't think it would work. You know what I mean? Yes, because you're a woman."[2] This experience in 1946 had a lasting effect on Jurney, and she carried this rejection through her tenure at the *Miami Herald,* where she directed the women's page, aptly titled "For and About Women," and later at the *Detroit Free Press*, where she reported "on the cutting edge of what was happening, of what people were thinking about, and what people wanted to happen." At the *Detroit Free Press*, Jurney identified "women in the labor movement, women in politics, women in business, women in the arts, and women in Detroit's great universities and colleges," who were "black, Jewish, WASP, and from the many ethnic groups that comprise Detroit."[3]

As a result of the barriers she faced, Jurney developed a heightened awareness to the need for female journalists to develop a professional counterpublic.[4] "Professional organizations," she reminded the audience at the Michigan Woman of Achievement Awards banquet, "are important in expanding your vision."[5] In response to the predominantly male professional organizations, Jurney envisioned a network for and about women that would counter what she considered to be an "informal 'old boys' network' that created yet another hurdle for women's advancement in journalism."[6]

121

While acknowledging that women during this period began questioning gender roles in a patriarchal society through studies of the transformation of women's pages in the context of the second wave, scholars, however, have neglected the efforts by women to create professional counterpublics that challenged male control of journalism.[7] Citing the lack of centralized, informed "communities" of women journalists with common identities and shared concerns, pioneers such Jurney—working within a larger trend that witnessed women confronting sexual inequality in the workplace—created "The Woman's Network" that served not only young women seeking that elusive first job but the experienced journalist hoping to advance up the pay-scale.[8] Utilizing the National Women and Media Collection at the Western Historical Manuscripts Collection, this chapter examines the struggle over inclusion and exclusion in journalism by discussing Jurney's effort to create a professional counterpublic that would enable greater individual and collective advancement, placing women on par with men in journalism.

"THE WOMAN'S NETWORK"

Dorothy Jurney, described by Jean Gaddy Wilson as the "godmother of the transformation of the women's pages" from society club information and conveyer of new-and-improved diets to actual "substantive news," was also, for a time in the late 1970s, a guide for women entering into and trying to advance in the profession.[9] A firm believer in the centrality of newspapers to American social and political life and the unique perspective that women offer public discourse, Jurney maintained that "newspapers and the readers need to have the benefit of the creativity of women," even though for much of her professional life she and her colleagues encountered gender discrimination "because we have lived for a long time in a male dominated world."[10] Professional objectivity in both hiring and promotional practices, in her mind, was essential for the advancement of women in the field. "There's got to be more professional objectivity," she asserted, because, she thought, women could "contribute so much to the kinds of stories that get into newspapers."[11]

The problem, according to Jurney, was that women did not have the same opportunities for gaining employment with newspapers or advancing within the professional ranks that men did. As a result, after being prodded by Catherine East, who told her, "you know, you ought to do something about getting women into better jobs on newspapers," Jurney formed what she called "The Woman's Network," a national talent search firm based in Pennsylvania in which she operated "as a headhunter in finding women who were trained and would be suitable" for newspapering jobs.[12] Given her long career working on newspapers such as the *Gary Post-Tribune*, the *Miami News*, the *Washington, D.C., News*, the *Miami Herald*, the *Detroit Free Press*, and the *Philadelphia Inquirer*, in positions ranging from women's page editor to assistant managing editor from 1939 until her retirement in 1975, Jurney was in a unique position to help women find jobs and then advance in their careers. She was on good terms with numerous newspaper editors and was adept at approaching editors and managers in a direct, if not forceful, manner on behalf of women. For example, in a tense letter to Derick Daniels, the assistant managing editor of the *Miami Herald*, Jurney chastised Daniels and his male colleagues, "[The managing editor] is patronizing towards women employees, and he doesn't have the intellectual capacity I want in a superior," she wrote. "[Marie Anderson] tells me that when she tries to discuss anything of moment with [the managing editor] he doesn't hear her," merely patting "her on the shoulder" saying "there, there, little girl." [13]

In addition to her relationships with editors, Jurney had an interest in helping women advance in journalism based on her firsthand knowledge of the lack of women in newspaper management. Prompted by her belief that the American Society of Newspaper Editors should recognize the need to redirect their efforts to hire qualified women, Jurney began a yearly statistical analysis of "the number of women who had any kind of an executive or administrative post on all of the newspapers in the country, regardless of size." [14] The studies, which were published in the ASNE *Bulletin* from 1977 until 1986, were compiled from listings of men and women directing editors in the ASNE *Editor and Publisher* yearbook. Each entry in the *Bulletin* consisted of three to four pages of explanatory text followed by Jurney's data, broken into two tables: the gendered percentage of directing editorships on all U.S. daily and Sunday newspapers, categorized by circulation, as well as a table devoted to breaking down the various occupations and the percentage of women currently employed in those positions. [15] After relinquishing the reins of the yearly study to the National Federation of Press Women in 1987, Jurney recognized the significance of what she was doing in advocating professional advancement for women journalists:

> I continued this for ten years . . . it aroused considerable interest through the ASNE. I always tried to write the introduction to the tabulation to bring out the facts, but in a way that would not turn off the male editors, because if women were going to get ahead in newspapering, we needed their goodwill. We needed only to convince men that there were women of expertise out there that they, for one reason or another, had not recognized. So that I think that our approach was not one of alarm, but one of steady pressure. [16]

Her first study of the number of women in managerial positions with U.S. newspapers corresponded with the founding of the Woman's Network, and an analysis of the data she compiled in 1977 indicates her concern with projecting an image of gendered professionalism for women seeking either to gain employment in various newsrooms or advance in the profession. Men controlled 94.8 percent of directing editorships on all daily and Sunday newspapers in 1977, regardless of circulation. That percentage varied depending on the size of the paper, with women having significantly less influence at larger newspapers.

The gender imbalance in newspaper managerial positions was staggering. Although women seemed to be able to gain some headway at smaller newspapers with circulations ranging from 25,000 to 100,000, men dominated the profession in 1977. Jurney, therefore, resolved to counter this imbalance with the formation of the Woman's Network. The Network was conceived on the belief that "women in the field of journalism and publications have no good mechanism for reaching each other when job opportunities occur . . . men have long had an unofficial 'old boy's network' because they have predominated in managerial jobs," and when job opportunities become available "the men turn to each other to learn who is in the market and to get an evaluation of the potential candidate."[17] This is an example of what Barbara B. Reagan and Martha Blaxall define as "occupational segregation," in which a distinct gender imbalance in the workplace "results from the interaction of a well-entrenched and complex set of institutions that perpetuates the inferior position of women in the labor market."[18] In light of these larger societal concerns, Jurney indicated that she hoped to "recommend women with proven ability and those who show real potential" while evaluating the hiring practices of various newspapers regarding the hiring of women.[19] Jurney professed her unique qualifications for such a massive undertaking in the memo she circulated to hundreds of newspaper offices throughout the United States:

> The Woman's Network is conceived as a mechanism to make the talent of top professional women known to editors seeking to fill such jobs. Through 40 years of experience in newspapers in Indiana, Florida, Washington, D.C., North Carolina, Michigan, and Pennsylvania, I have come to recognize the qualities that mark the unusual, talented, creative editor or writer. And I am fortunate to be well known professionally. I am known to management through my participation in the ASNE and the APMEA. Over a period of 20 years I was a frequent lecturer at the American Press Institute. . . . Newspaper women know me from those organizations and from seminar appearances at the University of Missouri, the University of Michigan, and at various press associations. I was made especially aware of this in my present contact with the National Commission for International Women's Year. As I talked with women's news editors around the country, I was astonished at how many recognized my name. The Woman's Network should fulfill a need in bringing

supply and demand together with careful evaluation of both the women who are available for top positions and of the organizations which are seeking top professionals. [20]

Even more perplexing, perhaps providing an even greater impetus for establishing the Woman's Network was the lack of progress in decreasing the gender gap in managerial positions. Regarding the hiring of women for leadership jobs, journalism was woefully behind industries such as durable and non-durable manufacturing, retail trade—which included department stores, hardware stores, food stores, motor vehicle establishments, and liquor stores—financial institutions such as insurance and real estate, the service industry, transportation and public utilities, and public administration. For example, the percentage of female leadership in all U.S. industries increased from 17.6 percent in 1972 to 24.6 percent in 1979, with similar increase in the service industry, which saw a rise from 27 percent women in 1972 to 34 percent in 1979, as well as transportation and public utilities, which doubled the percentage of women managers from only 10 percent in 1972 to 20 percent in 1979. [21] The only industry with a larger gender gap in managerial positions was the construction industry, in which women held only 4 percent of leadership roles, compared to 6.5 percent in journalism. [22]

In addition to her knowledge of the profession and what to look for to place women in appropriate situations, Jurney required newspapers subscribing to her service to pay a nominal fee. The Network was set up as a "one-woman operation" to help "newspapers find women for news management positions." Jurney worked for, and was paid by, newspaper clients—not the women she was placing in jobs, an important distinction. [23] Jurney conceptualized the Woman's Network as a counterpublic in which newspapers negotiated with Jurney for finding women to fill positions. "Our fees are exceedingly modest," she wrote in one of several memos to newspaper offices, asserting that "since I am motivated to help newspapers find able women, I have kept the fees low." [24] Jurney requested that newspapers pay her a small percentage based on the first-year earnings of women she placed in newspapering jobs. She had no intentions, however, of making money through the Woman's Network. "I have undertaken this project not to make money," she wrote. "It is rather an attempt to be of service and to keep my mind alert." [25]

Reaction to Jurney's undertaking was initially positive, as demonstrated by the myriad of correspondence she received in 1977 and 1978. Jurney's colleagues wrote to offer encouragement as she embarked on this new, monumental endeavor. For example, Mary Ann Grossman asserted in a February 1977 letter that the Woman's Network seemed like "a fine idea, especially for younger women," while Reg Murphy noted "the Woman's Network is a good idea . . . because newspapers . . . need it." He added that those in the profession "need to encourage more women to seek careers in journalism." [26]

Moreover, Virgil Fassio, the vice president and general manager of the *Seattle Post-Intelligencer*, after learning of Jurney's retirement from the journalism profession, realized that she would not remain inactive for long.

> I had read earlier that you had retired and knew that you would be doing something very active. I think the business that you've started sounds like a great opportunity to continue your activity in the newspaper business, while at the same time helping outstanding experienced newswomen advance in their profession.[27]

Lastly, in a letter intended to justify Jurney's fee structure for the Woman's Network, JoAnne Roslansky not only reaffirmed Jurney's intention of charging newspapers a nominal fee for her services, she asserted that Jurney was "providing a service that answers a *real* need that exists now," maintaining that Jurney was conducting the service "in a most professional way."[28]

The Jurney manuscript collection points to the process by which she helped women gain employment with newspapers and help other women advance in their careers. When resumes arrived at her Philadelphia office, Jurney added them to her file of women seeking employment in journalism.[29] By June 1977 Jurney indicated in a letter to Gordon Hanna that she had "built up a file of about 300 names," and that "many of the women are of exceptional ability with experience as writers and editors in hard news and feature sections," as well as experienced administrators.[30] If candidates seemed to be fit for particular positions, she would then write to newspapers to see if they were interested in discussing the possibility of an interview. For example, Jurney wrote to Reg Murphy, the editor and publisher of the *San Francisco Examiner*, about an opening for the food editor position, paying particular interest to the requirements of the position. "Are you ready to move yet on the Food Editor's job?" she asked. "I have uncovered a couple of persons who might interest you in that both of these women have cooked for their families, an important qualification you specified."[31] Jurney eventually recommended Alice Powell for the position.

> As you can see by the enclosed material, Mrs. Powell is 48 years old and has been at the *Toledo Blade* for 24 years. During most of this time she was married and bringing up three stepchildren. She was cooking for them and for her husband, and thus her home became a test kitchen for the recipes and food stories she was producing in the *Blade*. Now she wants to leave Toledo in order to move ahead in her career. Having been divorced four years ago, and the children grown, she is at least free to do this.[32]

In addition to actively seeking out job opportunities for women, Jurney also turned to various editors for recommendations of women either seeking employment or advancement. In a letter to John McMullen, the executive editor of the *Miami Herald,* Jurney wondered if McMullen could "build up a stable" of "competent" women who left the *Herald.* "I am interested in names even though the women don't seem to be immediate prospects," she wrote. "They might be in time and I would like them listed in my files."[33]

Jurney and the Woman's Network helped raise awareness for the availability of talented women journalists. She was often able to find employment for women at newspapers while at the same time receiving rejection letters for women who did not impress managing editors. For example, she was able to secure jobs for Leslie Davis and Theasa Tuchy at *Newsday* on Long Island. In response to this good news, she wrote to Anthony Insolia, the managing editor of *Newsday.* "I am delighted to know that you were pleased with both Leslie Davis and Theasa Tuchy," Jurney wrote. "We strive very hard to screen our candidates before recommending them to a newspaper."[34] She was not always successful at landing women at newspapers, however, as evidenced by a letter from Kurt Luedtke, executive editor of the *Detroit Free Press.* "For individual reasons, neither Autret nor Christenson nor Heffley wind up being what we think we're looking for," he wrote, asserting that Christenson was a bad writer, Autret was void of objective thinking, only producing "opinion and description," and Heffley had "no critical intelligence evidenced in the reporting."[35]

CONCLUSION

Although Dorothy Jurney maintained that she discontinued the Woman's Network in 1980 after experiencing "moderate success," evidence indicates, however, that she did at least create awareness among newspapers about the availability of talented women which, as a result, enabled women to secure jobs at an increasing rate.[36] For example, the number of women occupying various directing editorships at U.S. newspapers increased from 165 in 1977 to 212 in 1979, rising to 232 in 1980, and although the percentage of these positions held by women remained dreadfully low—and would for the entirety of Jurney's study of occupational segregation in American journalism, capping at 12.4 percent in 1986—there was nevertheless a noticeable increase.

It is reasonable to assert in this instance, given the data compiled by Jurney, that the Woman's Network fostered a more refined image of gendered professionalism by creating communities of female journalists that transcended race, class, geographical, and economic barriers, occupying a space typically dominated by men, thus allowing women to gain a stronghold in professional communications. As this chapter has demonstrated, women journalists during the second wave of the women's movement struggled with notions of inclusion and exclusion in journalism, thus necessitating the creation of a professional counterpublic in order to bring female journalists from the periphery to the center. Although a 1975 study of 264 newswomen demonstrated that various jobs and assignments in newsrooms were still inherently linked to traditional gender roles and opportunities for advancing in the profession was limited to male notions about woman's abilities, Jurney's Woman's Network made strides in shifting stereotypes in order to decrease the gender gap in journalism. [37]

NOTES

1. For a recent biographical piece on Jurney, see Kimberly Wilmot Voss, "Dorothy Jurney," *Journalism History* 36, no. 1 (2010).
2. Dorothy Misener Jurney, "Keynote Address Delivered at the Michigan Woman of Achievement Awards Banquet," 1984. The Marie Anderson Papers, WUNP5551, Box One, National Women and Media Collection, Western Historical Manuscripts Collection, Columbia, MO. Hereafter cited as Anderson Papers.
3. Interview with Dorothy Misener Jurney by Anne S. Kasper, Women in Journalism Oral History Project of the Washington Press Club Foundation, 16–19 January and 7 September 1990, 73, in the National Women and Media Collection of the Western Historical Manuscripts Collection, Columbia, MO. Hereafter cited as Jurney Oral History; Jurney, "Keynote Address," Anderson Papers.
4. For a discussion of the concept of "counterpublics," see Nancy Fraser, "Rethinking the Public Sphere: A Contribution to the Critique of Actually Existing Democracy," in *Habermas and the Public Sphere*, edited by Craig J. Calhoun (Cambridge: The MIT Press, 1989). For the public sphere, see Jürgen Habermas, *The Structural Transformation of the Public Sphere: An Inquiry into a Category of Bourgeois Society*, translated by Thomas Burger and Frederick Lawrence (Cambridge, MA: The MIT Press, 1989).
5. Jurney, "Keynote Address," Anderson Papers.
6. Dorothy Misner Journey, "The Woman's Network," n.d., The Dorothy Misener Jurney Papers, C3904, Box One, folder 22, National Women and Media Collection of the Western Historical Manuscripts Collection, Columbia, MO. Hereafter cited as Jurney Papers.
7. Maurine Beasley, "The Women's National Press Club: Case Study in Professional Aspirations," *Journalism History* 15, no. 4 (1988), Rodger Streitmatter, "Transforming the Women's Pages: Strategies That Worked," *Journalism History* 24, no. 2 (1998), Kimberly Wilmot Voss, "Revising Newspaper History: A Reframing of the Women's Movement," *The Web Journal of Mass Communication Research* 7, no. 3 (2004), Kimberly Wilmot Voss, "Making the Personal Political: Florida Women's Page Journalists Spread News of a Movement," *South Florida History* 34, no. 3 (2006), Kimberly Wilmot Voss, "The Penney-Missouri Awards: Honoring the Best in Women's News," *Journalism History* 32, no. 1 (2006), Kimberly Wilmot Voss, "Vivian Castleberry: An Editor Ahead of Her Time," *Southwestern Historical Quarterly* 110, no. 4 (2007), Kimberly Wilmot Voss and Lance Speere, "A Women's Page Pioneer: Marie Anderson and Her Influence at the Miami Herald and Beyond," *Florida Historical Quarterly* 85, no. 4 (2007), Norman P. Lewis, "From Cheesecake to Chief: Newspaper Editors' Slow Acceptance of Women," *American Journalism* 25, no. 2 (2008).
8. See especially a special edition of *Signs: A Journal of Women in Culture and Society* titled "Women and the Workplace: The Implications of Occupational Segregation," 1, no. 3 (1976): 1–317. For the notion of "communities" with shared identities, see Benedict R. O'G Anderson, *Imagined Communities: Reflections on the Origin and Spread of Nationalism* (London: Verso Editions/NLB, 1983).
9. Kasper, "Jurney Oral History," p. 120.

10. Kasper, "Jurney Oral History," p. 116.
11. Kasper, "Jurney Oral History," p. 116.
12. Kasper, "Jurney Oral History," p. 96.
13. Dorothy Jurney to Derick Daniels, 12 April 1971, Anderson Papers, WUNP5551, Box One, Anderson-Jurney Correspondence folder.
14. Kasper, "Jurney Oral History," p. 93.
15. The first table, titled "Directing Editorships on All Daily U.S. and Sunday Newspapers by Gender," was broken into columns of under 25,000, 25,000–50,000, 50,000–100,000, 100,000–250,000, and over 250,000, with percentages for both men and women. The second table, "Numerical Listing by Job Titles," used the same circulation columns and percentages for men and women, adding to the equation the various newsroom jobs: Editor in Chief, Senior Editor, Editor, Associate Editor, Assistant Editor, Executive Editor, Asst. Exec. Editor, Managing Editor, Associate M.E., Assistant M.E., Deputy M.E., and Editorial Chiefs.
16. Kasper, "Jurney Oral History," p. 94.
17. Jurney, "The Woman's Network Circulated Memo," n.d., Jurney Papers, C3904, Box 1, folder 22, and Jurney to Marie Anderson, 7 February 1977, Anderson Papers, WUNP5551, Box One, Jurney-Anderson correspondence folder.
18. Barbara B. Reagan and Martha Blaxall, "Occupational Segregation in International Women's Year," *Signs* 1, no. 3, *Women and the Workplace: The Implications of Occupational Segregation* (Spring 1976), 2.
19. Jurney to Anderson, 7 February 1977, Anderson Papers, WUNP5551, Box One, Jurney-Anderson correspondence folder.
20. Jurney, "The Woman's Network Circulated Memo," Jurney Papers, C3904, Box 1, folder 22.
21. See "From Elizabeth Waldman, Senior Economist, Bureau of Labor Statistics," Jurney Papers, C3904, Box 2, folder 87.
22. Ibid. See also "Numerical Totals and Percentages of Women and Men Directing Editors in the Decade, 1977–1986," Jurney Papers, C3904, Box 2, folder 91.
23. Jurney, "The Woman's Network Circulated Memo," Jurney Papers, C3904, Box 1, folder 22. Jurney sent out at least four standard memos with no dates, and this one is separate from the one cited above.
24. Jurney, "The Woman's Network Circulated Memo," Jurney Papers, C3904, Box 1, folder 22. This memo, the third I've discussed so far, outlines the fee structure.
25. Jurney to Byron B. Harless, 14 March 1977, Jurney Papers, C3904, Box 1, folder 23.
26. Mary Ann Grossman to Dorothy Jurney, 9 February 1977, Jurney Papers, C3904, Box 1, folder 23; Reg Murphy to Dorothy Jurney, 18 July 1977, Jurney Papers, C3904, Box 1, folder 24.
27. Virgil Fassio to Dorothy Jurney, 28 July 1977, Jurney Papers, C3904, Box 1, folder 24.
28. JoAnne Roslansky to Dorothy Jurney, 21 October 1977, Jurney Papers, C3904, Box 1, folder 24.
29. A March 1977 demonstrates the volume of resumes she regularly received. "Early in February I sent out a letter to 400 women listed in Editor and Publisher as holding administrative or policy making jobs on papers of over 40,000 subscribers. I have received a number of resumes, some from very capable women." Jurney to Harless, 15 March 1977, Jurney Papers, C3904, Box 1, folder 23.
30. Jurney to Gordon Hanna, 4 June 1977, Jurney Papers, C3904, Box 1, folder 23.
31. Jurney to Reg Murphy, 15 March 1977, Jurney Papers, C3904, Box 1, folder 23.
32. Jurney to Reg Murphy, 4 April 1977, Jurney Papers, C3904, Box 1, folder 23.
33. Jurney to John McMullen, 17 March 1977, Jurney Papers, C3904, Box 1, folder 23.
34. Dorothy Jurney to Anthony Insolia, 9 September 1977, Jurney Papers, C3904, Box 1, folder 24.
35. Kurt Luedtke to Dorothy Jurney, 24 June 1977, Jurney Papers, C3904, Box 1, folder 24.
36. Jurney noted in her papers that documents "relating to the Woman's Network which I founded in 1977 as an editorial talent search firm" was disbanded "about two years later after moderate success." See Jurney Papers, C3904, Box 1, folder 22.

37. Linda Busby, "Sex Role Research on the Mass Media," *Journal of Communications* 25, no. 4 (1975), p. 107.

REFERENCES

Primary Sources

Dorothy Misener Jurney Papers. National Women and Media Collection, part of the Western Historical Manuscript Collection, Columbia, MO. C3904.

Fran Harris Papers. National Women and Media Collection, part of the Western Historical Manuscript Collection, Columbia, MO. C1201.

Kasper, Anne S. "Interviews with Marie Anderson, 1989." The Washington Press Club Foundation Oral History Project, National Women and Media Collection, Western Historical Manuscripts Collection, Columbia, MO. C3958, folders 1–3.

———. "Interviews with Dorothy Misener Jurney, 1990." The Washington Press Club Foundation Oral History Project, National Women and Media Collection, Western Historical Manuscripts Collection, Columbia, MO. C3958, folders 115–19.

Marie Anderson Papers. National Women and Media Collection, part of the Western Historical Manuscript Collection, Columbia, MO. WUNP5551.

Ritchie, Anne. "Interviews with Fran Harris, 1990." The Washington Press Club Foundation Oral History Project, National Women and Media Collection, Western Historical Manuscripts Collection, Columbia, MO. C3958, folders 96–101.

Washington Press Club Foundation Women in Journalism Oral History Project Transcripts. National Women and Media Collection, part of the Western Historical Manuscript Collection, Columbia, MO. C3958.

Western Historical Manuscript Collection. Columbia, MO.

Secondary Sources

Anderson, Benedict R. O'G. *Imagined Communities: Reflections on the Origin and Spread of Nationalism.* London: Verso Editions/NLB, 1983.

Ashley, Laura, and Beth Olson. "Constructing Reality: Print Media's Framing of the Women's Movement, 1966 to 1986." *Journalism and Mass Communication Quarterly* 75, no. 2 (1998): 263–77.

Beasley, Maurine. "The Women's National Press Club: Case Study in Professional Aspirations." *Journalism History* 15, no. 4 (1988): 112–20.

Brown, Linda Keller. "Women and Business Management." *Signs* 5, no. 2 (1979): 266–88.

Burt, Elizabeth V. "A Bid for Legitimacy: The Woman's Press Club Movement, 1881–1900." *Journalism History* 23, no. 2 (1997): 72–84.

Busby, Linda. "Sex Role Research on the Mass Media." *Journal of Communications* 25, no. 4 (1975): 107–31.

Calhoun, Craig J. *Habermas and the Public Sphere.* Cambridge, MA: MIT Press, 1992.

Carter, Sue. "'Women Don't Do News'": Fran Harris and Detroit's Radio Station WWJ." *Michigan Historical Review* 24, no. 2 (1998): 77–87.

Everbach, Tracy. "Managing 'Amazonia': A Cultural Case Study of Female Leadership at the *Sarasota Herald-Tribune*." PhD diss., University of Missouri, 2004.

Fuchs, Penny Bender. "Women in Journalism Oral History Collection of the Washington Press Club Foundation." *Journalism History* 28, no. 4 (2003): 191–96.

Gottlieb, Agnes Hooper. "Women Journalists and the Municipal Housekeeping Movement: Case Studies of Jane Cunningham Croly, Helen M. Winslow, and Rheta Childe Dorr." PhD diss., University of Maryland, College Park, 1992.

———. "Grit Your Teeth, Then Learn to Swear: Women in Journalistic Careers, 1850–1926." *American Journalism* 18, no. 1 (2001): 53–72.

Habermas, Jürgen. *The Structural Transformation of the Public Sphere: An Inquiry into a Category of Bourgeois Society*. Translated by Thomas Burger and Frederick Lawrence. Cambridge, MA: The MIT Press, 1989.

Henry, Susan J. "Private Lives: An Added Dimension for Understanding Journalism History." *Journalism History* 6, no. 4 (1979): 98–102.

Marzolf, Marion. "The Woman Journalist: Colonial Printer to City Desk." *Journalism History* 1, no. 4 (1974): 100–46.

Papanek, Hanna. "Men, Women, and Work: Reflections on the Two-Person Career." *The American Journal of Sociology* 78, no. 4 (1973): 852–72.

Rendall, Jane. "Women and the Public Sphere." *Gender and History* 11, no. 3 (1999): 475–88.

Steiner, Linda. "Gender at Work: Early Accounts by Women Journalists." *Journalism History* 23, no. 1 (1997): 2–12.

Stevens, George E. "Discrimination in the Newsroom: Title VII and the Journalist." *Journalism Monographs*, no. 94 (1985): 1–21.

Streitmatter, Rodger. "Transforming the Women's Pages: Strategies That Worked." *Journalism History* 24, no. 2 (1998): 72–81.

Voss, Kimberly Wilmot. "Revising Newspaper History: A Reframing of the Women's Movement." *The Web Journal of Mass Communication Research* 7, no. 3 (2004).

———. "The National Women and Media Collection at the University of Missouri." *Journalism History* 30, no. 4 (2005): 210–14.

———. "Making the Personal Political: Florida Women's Page Journalists Spread News of a Movement." *South Florida History* 34, no. 3 (2006): 22–25.

———. "The Penney-Missouri Awards: Honoring the Best in Women's News." *Journalism History* 32, no. 1 (2006): 43–50.

———. "Resources for Telling the Stories of Contemporary Women's Page Editors: Archives and Oral Herstories." *Journalism History* 32, no. 4 (2007): 240–42.

———. "Vivian Castleberry: An Editor Ahead of Her Time." *Southwestern Historical Quarterly* 110, no. 4 (2007): 514–32.

———. "Dorothy Jurney." *Journalism History* 36, no. 1 (2010): 13–22.

Voss, Kimberly Wilmot, and Lance Speere. "A Women's Page Pioneer: Marie Anderson and Her Influence at the *Miami Herald* and Beyond." *Florida Historical Quarterly* 85, no. 4 (2007): 398–421.

Chapter Eleven

Angela Merkel Has More to Offer

Satirical Images of Germany's First Female Chancellor

Lynn Marie Kutch

Since her 2005 campaign and victory as the first female German chancellor, Angela Merkel has attained international press attention, notably being named *Forbes* magazine's most powerful woman for four consecutive years (Donner, 2009). Despite this seemingly unmistakable record of success, world media have displayed palpable difficulty in characterizing her. In the January 11, 2010, edition of *Time* magazine, when journalist Catherine Mayer places the descriptors "frail" and "kittenish" alongside "trailblazer" and "unchallenged leader" in her article "Merkel's Moment," she unwittingly yet superbly exposes this challenge (32). For American media, part of the uncertainty might stem from the relative novelty of women occupying top government posts. For German media, the problem could originate in the country's somewhat conservative view on the changing status of working women, especially at a time when the Merkel administration advocates strongly for family policy reforms that could redefine motherhood and parenthood (Spieß & Wrohlich, 2007). Regardless of country of origin, however, journalists writing about female politicians often determine how and if they fit into the category of "traditional wife and mother dutifully committed to her family and home" before concentrating on career accomplishments (Montalbano-Phelps, 2005, p. 195). Even for female politicians who seemingly strike the proper balance between home and career, criticism nonetheless keeps pace with, or outpaces, successes. Caricature often emerges as one form of criticism that ruthlessly crosses gender lines; and examples that reference female politicians in general and Merkel in particular appear decidedly gendered in their amplification of typical womanly attributes. As Merkel, her principally female cabinet, and German women steadily undo conventional beliefs about

133

working women, traditionally female markers to depict the chancellor in caricature appear that much more exaggerated and distorted. In this chapter, I will analyze satirical and caricatured renderings of Angela Merkel at the theoretical intersection of German politics, cross-cultural hypotheses on sexist portrayals of women, and rich German and European traditions of satire. By decoding the artistic portrayals at this convergence of perspectives, I address a striking ambiguity that emerges in a country with lingering conservative notions of working women and motherhood, but with relatively radical notions of political satire.

METHOD AND RESEARCH QUESTIONS

In preparation for this chapter, I surveyed hundreds of caricatured images of Angela Merkel that have appeared in German print media, on satirical websites, or blog sites between 2007 and 2010. Not limiting the scope to conventional hand-drawn caricature, I examined additional modes of satire ranging from computer manipulated photographs to German Karneval (Mardi Gras) floats, traditionally shameless in their presentation of critical statement. Of the extensive choice of Merkel caricatures available, I selected those in which the artists center their political comment around the typically female physical attributes of breasts and cleavage, a motif that has come to emblematize Merkel since the publication of a subsequently heavily circulated and criticized April 2008 photograph that shows her at the Oslo opera in a revealing low-cut gown. Caricature artists have since incorporated and expanded on the image to create, to mention the specific example of Götz Wiedenroth, a reappearing cartoon character seemingly weighed down by her chest as much as by executive decisions. With a general definition that specifically encapsulates the antagonism between images of the accomplished politician Merkel and the lampooned Merkel, David Carrier writes that caricature is "the opposite of creating ideal beauty," and instead "involves deformation" (2009, p. 107). While the samples I regard here could readily be dismissed as sexist deformations of the female body when it combines with political power, I propose that the ambiguities of the caricatures epitomize the challenge to reconcile myths of ideal feminine beauty as it relates to expected gender roles with the reality of a powerful woman in charge. In the closer analysis, I will investigate specific methods that the caricaturists use to satirize Merkel, and how they arguably evidence, in unabashed satirical terms, a marked perplexity toward the female "phenomenon of power."

In his article "Political Parody and Public Culture," Robert Hariman describes the potency of parody in terms that could also apply to the effectiveness of the Merkel caricatures: "[Parody] works in great part by exceeding tacit limits on expression—the appropriate, the rational—but it does so to reveal limitations" (2008, p. 251). Caricature artists' heightened attention to Merkel's female attributes in their renderings seem to duplicate the overblown media reaction that the Oslo photograph incited, but they also criticize in part the media-driven implication that Merkel encroached on some predetermined boundaries for female leaders when she appeared publicly with a plunging neckline. Imitating in form and composition the ambiguity and difficulty of describing an accomplished female leader, the caricatures examined in this chapter cleverly merge traditionally typed roles, such as the devoted mother, wife, or sexualized female, and progressive non-stereotypical depictions, such as the successful female leader of a major global economy. Given the collision of the new context of Angela Merkel's chancellorship and the vigorous, often unbridled German tradition of satire, the renderings also could represent a progression of attitudes that confronts previous knowledge and assumptions about female leaders as perpetuated by the media. Indeed, the dominant image of Merkel's cleavage persistently shaped a parallel public consciousness alongside more professional shots of the chancellor shown cooperating with international heads of state or preparing for her second campaign. The present analysis considers whether the renderings criticize women's progress in a sexist way by amplifying biological female qualities, or if the caricatures essentially criticize the backlash against women's advancements by distorting the sources of criticism and controversy, such as Merkel's hair or wardrobe choices.

A BRIEF HISTORY OF MERKEL'S RELATIONSHIP TO GERMAN MEDIA

Although historically the German press has certified its clumsiness in describing Merkel's career trajectory with anything but gender-neutral terms, the ambiguity also typifies Merkel the politician, who has benefited from and criticized provisions for female politicians. In the 1990s, Merkel, whom the press consistently dubbed "Kohls Mädchen" [Kohl's girl], entered the political scene by filling informal internal quotas in Chancellor Helmut Kohl's cabinet. Following a financial scandal in which she publicly spoke out against Kohl, her former mentor, she acquired the gender- and German-specific label of "Trümmerfrau," denoting a post World War II female icon who cleaned up the ruins (Thompson and Lennartz, 2006, p. 106). During her first campaign in 2005, attempting to package this "grey" female candidate for German voters, a majority of journalists gendered the campaign by emphasizing female-oriented terms such as "divorced," "remarried," and "childless." This first campaign also generated the media-driven "Merkel Makeover," with print media often utilizing photographs of the Kohl-era Merkel as grisly "before" photos in a series of before and after shots in her purported quest to become "more feminine" in the public eye. After taking office, Merkel evolved from physically attractive candidate to politically capable world politician or "honorary man," which requires a stereotypically masculine demeanor and wardrobe, or pursuing "policies calculated to make her look tough" (Wiliarty, 2008, p. 82). Through their more recent insistence on publishing and subsequently emphasizing the criticism and importance of Merkel's leisure time photographs, where she does not conceal her womanly traits, the media insinuate that she frustrates common expectations of a more acceptable masculinized female leader. Competition between the undeniably feminine and the professionally masculine Merkel intensifies in ambiguous caricatures that question whether women can assert both power and feminine traits, and that appropriately and grotesquely blend amplified female traits and markers of political power.

WHAT WILL THE NEIGHBORS SAY? MERKEL AS NURSING STEPMOTHER

At the same time that her newly introduced family policy was received optimistically, Merkel was receiving censure for international policy following her visit to Poland in March 2007, when she was criticized for her perhaps condescending treatment of Germany's eastern neighbor (Traynor & Connolly, 2007). In June of that year, predating the Oslo photograph, the Polish weekly magazine *Wprost* featured on its cover a computer manipulated photograph of Merkel breastfeeding the Kaczynski twins with a headline that translates as "Europe's Stepmother." Somewhat surprisingly for Germany, where political satire often borders on the grotesque and obscenely extreme, the cover produced a wave of controversy among stunned German politicians, who labeled the picture tasteless and insulting. Reminding his critics that the illustration resides in the realm of satire, and therefore does not directly malign Merkel, *Wprost* editor Stanislow Janecki explained his editorial board's intentions, but not with particularly non-sexist terms. In his justification, he cites the successful combination of the "sexy stepmother" motif, and the twenty-one-year-old "quite nice body" upon which Merkel's head had been electronically edited (Hawley, 2007). Even if creators also intended the cover to highlight the twins' political neediness, the central and magnified image of Merkel defined by exclusively feminine markers requires a closer analysis that considers why a satire that magnifies and exaggerates the female act of breastfeeding delivers such effective and controversial commentary on women in power.

The cover not so subtly emphasizes that Merkel is a *female* world leader, but its image succeeds as satire because of the potency with which it exceeds limits of expression. Although the photographic image, as opposed to an artist's sketch, arguably imparts some degree of realism, the absurdity of the computer-generated picture and the context in which it places these world leaders relocates it from a photograph, or somehow real record of an event, to a supreme example of political parody. Angela Merkel, who was ironically criticized for not being a mother, has never breastfed any infant, let alone the Polish twins, who are clearly no longer suckling infants. Thus, viewers should see no option but to read this cover as political metaphor. Not intentionally, but nonetheless persuasively, the *Wprost* cover's distorted imagery manipulates a prescribed cross-cultural formula for female politicians that combines power and maternity, and that claims women should "emphasize their 'non-traditional' accomplishments" while balancing these images with "more sedimented ideals of women's perceived 'functions' in society and family" (Montalbano-Phelps, 2005, p. 192). This grotesquely exaggerated distortion of a stereotypical blend of feminine concepts could, according to some feminist interpretations, solidify an already narrow view of female politicians. But in this case, the caricature, which bizarrely merges a private sphere biological act with public worldwide foreign policy, is so fraught with irony that it rewrites, or at least challenges, these principles in a new context. The removal of this realistic photograph from any believable context harks back to entrenched European rules of freedom of expression that accompany satire and that is granted at the "expense of decorum and idealized perfection of the royal body politic," as opposed to the politician's flesh and bones body (Childs, 1997, pp. 149–50). Although this citation refers to male politicians from a different era, the computer-manipulated image of Merkel's head and a model's body parodically separates the female politicians' body from an idealized female body in the same European tradition that Childs describes. Because the magazine relies on female-specific imagery to criticize Merkel's political action, the artificially constructed photograph ironically tears down largely media-determined contradictions between femininity and politics.

A NIGHT AT THE OPERA

The Oslo opera photograph from April 2008 dominated the work of caricaturists and endured even though volumes of photographs had been published at the same time, emphasizing Merkel's career as a capable and competent world leader. In March 2009, artist Samaniego manipulated the photograph and transformed the image into an extreme specimen of political satire by inserting an oversized tattoo of smiling French president Nicolas Sarkozy emerging from Merkel's cleavage. In the form of a wildly out-of-place tattoo, both in terms of physical location and rules of professionalism and decorum for a female leader, the artist imprints an image of world politics onto the figurative German body politic, which for a time marginally defined Merkel's public persona. The caricature achieves irony precisely because it combines realistic or actual images of the European Union's top two leaders, a sexualized rendering of Merkel, and blatant criticism of their cozy political relationship. Official photographs of the two leaders from spring 2008 to spring 2009, when the two had worked very closely on green job creation and financial market regulation, often feature Sarkozy with an arm casually slung around Merkel's shoulders. While the tattooed cleavage does not convey that same sense of a friendly yet professional relationship, it does amplify media criticism of the two leaders working together, sometimes to the perceived exclusion of other European Union leaders. Oddly enough, however, it still seems to give Merkel the upper hand despite initial reactions that might label Samaniego's portrayal sexist.

In much the same way that the Polish magazine cover highlighted expectations for female politicians, the placement of the Sarkozy tattoo interrogates presumptions about women and the construction of their public character. Here, the tattoo, or as interpreted by Phebe Shih Chao, "an emblem of transformation that usually announces the bearer's new identity," combines with the cleavage to become the photograph's central parodic emblem (2006, p. 327). Even though the artist has manipulated the Merkel photograph and thus has arguably appropriated her image through her interpretation, the tattoo's placement implies a degree of feminist assertiveness on Merkel's part. As Michael Hardin affirms, "tattooing, while it is a covering of a body, is also a revealing and affirming of the body and its sexuality" (Hardin, p. 97). Merkel's political record and career attest to her self-assertion as a woman, but this image conveys the new, and for the media, perplexing look of the female politician: powerful but unashamedly female. Western men have traditionally adorned their bodies with sexist tattoos; but now this caricatured Merkel asserts her masculinity by displaying her political sweetheart right where admirers and critics alike will notice. On a deeper level, it signifies a refashioning of the female body that defies elements of a traditional male shaping, or appropriating, of female image. Merkel unwittingly drew attention to her sexuality with her choice of dress; but that caricaturists have emphatically and ambiguously responded to the questions and criticism raised by the original Oslo photograph suggests an enduring irreconcilability of images of female power and images of the female body.

KARNEVAL

Known for its bitingly satirical and unabashed humor, the German version of Mardi Gras (Karneval) still retains some of its age-old characteristics, such as mockery of regal life and those in positions of power (Ribeiro, 1986, pp. 31, 34). In cities throughout Germany, especially Cologne, creators of parade floats preserve the long-held German tradition of satire by allegorizing political issues or ridiculing politicians by way of their three-dimensional caricatures. Early in 2009, as part of Cologne's celebration, parade-goers witnessed a papier-mâché Merkel featuring the chancellor in drab, plain "before" and dazzling, perky "after" stages of several plastic surgery operations, including liposuction (that would, according to the inscription on the float, make all of the new debt disappear), and a tummy tuck and breast lift that would presumably boost national morale, as evidenced by the black eagles covering her nipples. This caricature offers one of the most complicated examples of Merkel criticism because it embeds grotesquely exaggerated female-specific motifs in the robust tradition of German satire that cleverly and intentionally combines the visual, the verbal, and the allegorical (Clark, 2006). Merely "reading" the visual would likely yield a sexist interpretation that criticizes the use of female-specific forms of plastic surgery and the implication that women cannot achieve acceptance until they have completed a series of man-pleasing cosmetic alterations. If we regard the combination of the visual and the verbal within the context of the uninhibited German Karneval humor and within theories of satire that promote equal-opportunity lampooning, then the notion of the float as political allegory, and not necessarily sexism, comes into clearer focus.

As a sublime example of the ambiguity and contradiction that has characterized descriptions of Merkel, as well as of the blurring of lines between the body politic and the politician's body in parody, parade organizers later decided to add a bra with the same eagle motif. While a committee spokeswoman backed the idea for the undergarment, the float's creator, more in tune with the tradition of German Karneval satire and humor, claimed that the celebration came into being and exists today for the purpose of being able, once a year, to boldly make fun of government officials without fear of punishment ("Nackte Angela," 2009). Displaying a sophisticated understanding of political satire and Karneval, Merkel supported the float creator's vision in her response to the Karneval parade float: "We can get past the fact that we won't get away unscathed during the parades. . . . Politicians would probably be sad if nothing happened at all" ("Nackte Angela," 2009). Corresponding to that view, the float attests to the principle of political humor that anyone in power, regardless of gender, is eligible to be a target. Some would even claim that making exceptions, like adding the bra to Merkel's caricatured body, exempts women in power from harsh political satire and criticism that men have had to endure for centuries. For precisely that reason, Haydon Manning, writing about the controversial and purportedly sexist Australian caricaturist Bill Leaks, justifies the equal use of satire that is "quintessentially about cutting down to size those who wield power," writing that cartoonists rely on "easily decipherable emblems," or "visual metaphors," that "should not automatically be construed as mere sexist stereotyping" (Manning, 2005a, p.115). By carefully considering the addition of the words on the float that refer to the country's budget problems, and not really believing that its creators are advocating plastic surgery for Merkel, the viewer can recognize a striking but satirically successful image that serves as the vehicle for the biting political commentary that has typified Karneval since its origins.

A GENEROUS VICTORY

Besides renderings that manipulate and modify the Oslo photograph, some caricaturists have adapted the photo into hand-drawn representations. Cartoonist Tchavdar clearly drew upon the photograph's motif to create a caricature that appeared on September 30, 2009, following Merkel's victory as chancellor for a second term, and the comfortable victory by her party, the Christian Democrats. In the sketched caricature, the viewer can recognize the designer gown that Merkel had worn to the Oslo opera; but unlike in the photograph, the artist has added a ballot box that the caricatured Merkel holds in front of her exaggeratedly large bosom. An anonymous male voter, represented only by an arm adorned with the sleeve of a blue pinstriped suit and a white cuff with cufflink, deposits a ballot in the form of the German flag not into the ballot box, but into Merkel's ample cleavage. Merkel's grotesquely distorted, yet still identifiable, face grimaces with approval. An unofficial blog caption reads "Generous Victory in Last German Election." As opposed to the photograph, which though manipulated could appear as a true-to-life reflection of Merkel, the sketched cartoon asserts itself as an interpretation of the politician as defined by his/her political actions and decisions. Samuel A. Tower, in *Cartoon and Lampoons: The Art of Political Satire*, summarizes this attribute of the caricature limited within a frame: "The cartoon provides a graphic perspective on its times, a kind of time capsule of history" (1982, p. 14). Here, the cartoon depicts the culmination of Merkel's second campaign in which, in contrast to the 2005 campaign with its heavy media focus on her makeover, Merkel was viewed as accomplished, skillful, respected, and above all a victorious woman. The graphic perspective that Tchavdar presents, however, concerns the parallel and popular attention to the Oslo photograph, which provided him the emblem that he exploits in his caricature.

Because the emblem, or central repeated image in this case, is the unmistakable female attribute of breasts and cleavage, those who would read this rendering through a gendered or even feminist lens might find the picture sexist in its suggestion that Merkel's exaggeratedly oversized physical attributes secured her triumph. Vera Lengsfeld, a politician in Merkel's own party, indirectly and unwittingly exposed the irony of such a suggestion by creating a campaign poster that placed her own picture, showing her in a gown very similar to the chancellor's, next to Merkel's Oslo picture with the caption "The CDU has more to offer." Feminists expressed outrage at the centralized cleavage and the implied equation of that physical attribute with political prowess. Lengsfeld herself, adopting the mentality of a caricaturist, lauded the poster as an example of shrewd advertising. It would appear that Tchavdar exaggerates the same emblem in the tradition of German satire and caricature "[that] distorts rather than elevates its subject; [and] works by parodistic and even grotesque exaggeration, hence by deformation of personal traits, habits, ideas, social conditions [. . .] it calls critical attention to what appears as ludicrous" (Knust, p. 218). Along those same lines, it could be argued that this particular cartoonist does not necessarily criticize a victorious female politician, but rather mimics the exaggerated and distorted media attention that drew attention away from Merkel's accomplishment of securing a second term. This particular caricature can thus be read as criticism of the ludicrous, grotesque, largely media-driven representations of female politicians.

CONCLUSION

When feminist critics accuse caricaturists of sexist stereotyping, they often point up an "inability to see the woman that is the politician," claiming that artists perpetuate derogatory female stereotypes rather than analyze the female politician's professional actions (Macklin, 1999). In the examples that I have analyzed here, the artists have undoubtedly distorted distinctly female traits; but in all of the cases the caricaturists have succeeded at deploying the archetype as a satirical metaphor. Although the chosen renderings focus on one often highly sexualized aspect of the female body, the caricatures, like all well-devised satire, cannot be limited to superficial interpretations. Instead, as I have suggested throughout this chapter, the ostensibly sexist photo manipulation, parade floats, and sketches actually underscore the ambiguity toward women in power and the sexist reporting that world media perpetuate.

Although the emblems could superficially be viewed as sexist, the artists present them as part of an evolving political framework that now accommodates highly successful women in power. On this question of sexism in caricature, Bill Leaks, an Australian caricaturist, argues that applying the same rules to both sexes does not automatically equate to stereotyping: "What surprises me is how stereotypical the reactions of a lot of women are. They're the ones who are perpetuating the stereotype by assuming they should somehow be treated differently" (Manning, 2005a, p. 117). Although feminists and fellow politicians have expressed outrage on Merkel's behalf, the chancellor's lack of outraged responses indicates a similar understanding that satirical criticism accompanies public office, whether held by a man or a woman.

Corresponding to codes of political satire and characteristics of traditional German humor, caricature succeeds in part by exposing the vulnerability of the powerful, even if this means exaggerating physical traits to force attention to a political point. In the samples from this chapter, the artists have exploited and thrived on the authenticity or preexistence of images in the popular consciousness, in this case leisure time photographs that visually confirm Merkel's womanhood (Medhurst & Desousa, 1981, p. 202). According to the principles of satire, viewers should not simply get cheap laughs from the exaggerated bosom or the surgically enhanced Merkel, although those images certainly strike an immediate chord and garner attention. Instead, the artist uses potentially shocking images as an invitation to investigate which genuinely shocking political issue, whether the domestic budget, or foreign relations, has instigated the satire. Moreover, by employing the satiric method of removing the highly recognizable visual concept from any believable natural context through "surreal imagery," the caricatures work to "highlight the artificiality of media reality" (El Rafaie, 2004, p. 333–34). As the renderings evidence, the robust tradition of satire in Germany and Europe continues to yield bold yet ambiguous artistic criticism of the media's often failed attempts to avoid sexist terms when describing character and achievements. Given the unprecedented success of Germany's first female chancellor, these images of media criticism reasonably take on typically feminine contours as well.

REFERENCES

Carrier, D. (2000). *The aesthetics of comics*. University Park: Pennsylvania State University Press.

Chao, P. (2006). Tattoo and piercing: Reflections on mortification. In L. Prelli (Ed.), *Rhetorics of display* (327–43). Columbia, SC: University of South Carolina Press.

Childs, E. (1997). The body impolitic: Censorship and the caricature of Honoré Daumier. In E. Childs (Ed,), *Suspended license: Censorship and the visual arts* (pp. 148–84). Seattle: University of Washington Press.

Clark, F. (2006). *Zeitgeist und zerrbild: Word image and idea in German satire, 1800–1848.* Oxford: Peter Lang.

Donner, F. (2009, August 19). German chancellor Angela Merkel is "Forbes" most powerful woman. *USA Today Online.* Retrieved July 15, 2010, from www.usatoday.com/money/companies/ management/2009- 08-19-forbes-most-powerful-women_N.htm.

El Refaie, E. (2004). Dramatist with a talent for dramatisation: Elfriede Jelinek's manipulation of the media. *German Life and Letters, 57*(3), 327–41.

Gaschke, S. (2005, August 25). Was Merkel so anders macht. *Zeit Online Politik.* Retrieved August 5, 2010, from www.zeit.de/2005/35/Ministerin_Merkel.

Hardin, M. (1999). Ma(r)king the objected body. *Fashion Theory, 3*(1), 81–108.

Hariman, R. (2008). Political parody and public culture. *Quarterly Journal of Speech, 94*(3), 247–72.

Hawley, C. (2005, September 7). Letter from Berlin: Angela Merkel realizes she's a woman. *Spiegel Online International.* Retrieved September 30, 2010, from www.spiegel.de/international/0,1518,373540,00.html.

Hawley, C. (2007, June 26). Mother's milk for the Kaczynskis. *Spiegel Online International.* Retrieved July 2, 2010, from www.spiegel.de/international/europe/0,1518,490795,00.html.

Knust, H. (1975). George Grosz: Literature and caricature. *Comparative Literature Studies, 12*, 218–41.

Macklin, J. (1999, June 9). Are political cartoonists sexist? The evidence is the naked truth. The Australian, p. 13.

Manning, H. (2005a). Political arts: Haydon Manning talks to Bill Leak about cartooning, sexual politics and the relationships between caricature and portraiture. *Meanjin*, 114–21.

Manning, H. (2005b). Sexism and the cartoonists' licence . *Ejournalist, 4*(2), 1–23.

Medhurst, M., & Desousa, M. (1981). Political cartoons as rhetorical form: A taxonomy of graphic discourse. *Communication Monographs, 48*(3), 197–236.

Mayer, C. (2010, January). Merkel's moment. *Time*, 32.

Merkel surprised by attention to low-cut dress. (2008, April 15). *Spiegel Online.* Retrieved August 5, 2010 from www.spiegel.de/international/germany/ 0,1518,547512,00.html.

Meyer, B. (2009). Nachts, wenn der Generalsekretär weint—Politikerinnen in der Press. *Aus Politik und Zeitgeschichte, 50*, 9–15.

Montalbano-Phelps, L. (2005). Performing politics: media aesthetics for women in political campaigns. In T. Carilli and J. Campbell (Eds.), *Women and the media: Diverse perspectives* (pp. 184–202). Lanham, MD: University Press of America.

Nackte Angela Merkel in der Problemzone Karneval. (2009, February 12). *Welt Online.* Retrieved August 12, 2010, from www.welt.de/vermischtes/article3229430/Nackte-Angela-Merkel-in-der-Problemzone-Karneval.html.

Nackte Kanzlerin im Rosenmontagszug tabu. (2009, February 18). *n24.de.* Retrieved August 6, 2010 from www.n24.de/news/newsitem_4836688.html.

Pinl, C. (2003). Uralt, aber immer noch rüstig: Der deutsche Ernährer. *Aus Politik und Zeitgeschichte, 44*, 6–8.

Ribeiro, A. (1986). The old and new worlds of Mardi Gras. *History Today, 36*(2), 30–35.

Samaniego. (2009, March 23). Sarkozy tattoo. Retrieved September 30, 2010, from www.toonpool.com/cartoons/Angela%20Merkel_41480.

Spieß, K. and Wrohlich, K. (2007, February 26). Streit um Familienpolitik *Bundeszentrale für politische Bildung.* Retrieved July 2, 2010, from www.bpb.de/themen/MKJOCX,0,0,Streit_um_Familienpolitik.html.

Stylists battle to claim Merkel makeover. (2005, September 30). *DW-WORLD.DE Deutsche Welle.* Retrieved August 5, 2010, from www.dw-world.de/dw/article/0,,1726676,00.html.

Tchavdar. (2009, September 30). Generous victory. Retrieved September 30, 2010, from www.toonpool.com/cartoons/Angela%20Merkel_65024.

Thompson, M. R., and Lennartz, L. (2006). The making of Chancellor Merkel. *German Politics, 15*(1), 99–110.

Tower, S. (1982). *Cartoons and lampoons: The art of political satire*. New York: Julian Messner.

Traynor, I., & Connolly, K. (2007, June 27). Poland riles Germany with a lewd take on the motherland. *The Guardian Online*. Retrieved July 2, 2010, from www.guardian.co.ukworld/2007/jun/27/germany.poland.

Wiliarty, S. E. (2008). Angela Merkel's path to power: The role of internal party dynamics and leadership. *German Politics, 17*(1), 81–96.

Chapter Twelve

All Hail the Queen

The Metamorphosis or Selling Out of Queen Latifah

Elizabeth Johnson

For Queen Latifah, the message and image of self-empowerment, self-worth, and black pride began in 1989 with her first album, "All Hail the Queen." On the front cover, Latifah, (Dana Elaine Owens) is posed as African royalty with a silhouette of the continent of Africa in the background. Since then, Latifah has given up her Afrocentric style and focuses solely on her appearance. Entertainers like Queen Latifah reinforce the stereotypical Mammy, endorsing internalized and institutionalized racism. The popular images of black women reinscribe negative stereotypes that keep black women trapped in limited roles in the entertainment field and society.

This chapter takes an interdisciplinary approach to critique how Latifah's characters are read through film and cultural studies. The objective of using film and cultural studies is to analyze media content by deciding what message is produced and its connection to race and representation. Thus, the critique of Queen Latifah will not be simplified into just positive and negative because in doing so, this entertainer is measured only by dominant cultural standards, excluding any sense of blackness (authentic or inauthentic); instead, the ideological framework of race, representation, and identity are included. Stuart Hall and bell hooks have written extensively on the connections between race, representation, and identity in films, and I will discuss how these theorists explain stereotypical roles reinforcing legitimacy to the audience about what is "real" and "true" (Evans & Hall, 1999). Specifically, I examine three films identifying Queen Latifah's character as a Mammy (*Living Out Loud, Chicago, and Bringing Down the House*), and two more recent films about which I argue that Queen Latifah casts aside this stereotype: *Mad Money* and *Life Support*.

When trying to make meaning out of Queen Latifah playing "Mammy" roles, one must understand the signified concept of stereotypical black women. For example, one may see a sign representing a female restroom. While the words "female restroom" may not be on the door, one can conclude that it is a female restroom if there is a symbol or picture of a female on the door. The sign for Mammy is something one recognizes as an ethnic signifier, which conveys meaning through learned messages. Signifiers are both visual and auditory in films. A Mammy is often signified as an overweight, asexual black woman who is more concerned about the safety and happiness of whites in her life than about her own contentment (Anderson, 1997; West, 1995; Yarbrough & Bennett, 2000). This stereotypical character fails to acknowledge the politics of its own representation (Migraine-George, 2008, pp. 207–8). The idea is complicated because the Mammy stereotype is based on a history that allows no space for potential change and reinforces negativity. During slavery, black women were forced to nurse plantation owners' children and to cater to the white family's every need, thus the term "Mammy." Ever since, literature and film have exploited this history through stereotypical Mammy characters. Tina Harris notes that the aforementioned stereotypes and others have adapted to the changing times, but they have only evolved into "sophisticated ghettoized" images of black female identity (Harris, 2004). This becomes harmful when black women with African features, dark skin, and kinky hair, which are typically associated with the Mammy image, internalize the message of unattractiveness and shame (West, 1995, p. 460).

STEREOTYPICAL ROLES

The Mammy image, for the spectator, evokes an expectation of not only a hard worker, but a mentally colonized robot. This passive robot, as explained by bell hooks, seeks to serve the will of whites, without expecting anything in return except their "love" (hooks, 1981, pp. 84–85). Many films portray the Mammy as a full-figured and unattractive character, giving support and guidance to whites above her own interests. The full-figure stereotype in some way makes her more nurturing and less a sexual being with needs and wants. In *Living Out Loud* (1998) Queen Latifah plays the full-figured jazz singer Liz Bailey, who befriends a white woman, Judith Moore (Holly Hunter). Judith divorces her cheating husband and gains solace in Liz's singing by resting her head on Liz's ample bosom. Each time Judith goes to the jazz club to hear Liz perform, Judith becomes more powerful in regaining her identity. Through the friendship with Liz, Judith understands her role as a "free" white woman. Though Liz Bailey does not automatically fit the asexual Mammy category, she denies her boyfriend's sexual motivation for staying in the relationship. Just when one hopes that maybe Liz is not a Mammy, she steps off the stage, having belted out a beautiful jazz tune, cloaked in a beautiful evening gown, with abundant breasts protruding, only to console, yet again, the slight and delicate Judith.

So how can audiences understand the image of Liz Bailey? According to Stuart Hall, movie viewers should interrogate the roles presented on the screen rather than just accept them. As the audience probes the image of Liz Bailey, the Mammy character becomes transparent. The Mammy represents negative notions through the signage of her physical appearance, her colonized mind, and her nurturing values above self-interest. Hall argues that the audience is given stereotypical images of a Mammy normalized through recurring scripts and made possible by the filmmaker's power (Jhally, 1997). Then, each time the audience sees an ample-breasted woman with all the aforementioned characteristics and ideology bestowed upon her by the filmmaker, the stereotype becomes an expectation. Our perceptions of others can be based on either beliefs taught by and held in society, or on beliefs taught by the media. Negative portrayals reinforce implicit racial attitudes (Gerbner, Gross, Morgan, Signorielli, & Shanahan, 2002). Michele Wallace (1990) goes one step further in her claim that "The negative/positive images conception is unable to contend with the important question of how Afro-American culture, which is a product of 'internal colonization,' constitutes an important variation of postcolonial discourse" (p. 2). The audience receives reinforcement that the Mammy image is true and natural.

The Liz Bailey character was early in Latifah's career (1998) before her breast reduction (2003) and Jenny Craig promotions (2008). One may question whether Queen Latifah became a Jenny Craig spokesperson as an attempt to shed the Mammy image. She was seen on commercials getting to a "healthy weight" with the assistance of Jenny Craig, but it was made clear that this "healthy weight" would be inconsistent with dominant cultural standards. Carolyn West (1995) argues that, "For black women, issues around weight and body image may be intensified because the image of thinness has historically been based on a white, middle-class standard of beauty" (p. 459). The important point here is not the desire to get to a healthy weight, but rather that she, yet another celebrity, advertised Jenny Craig as a way to gain insider status.

Somewhat similar to *Living Out Loud* is *Chicago* (2002), where Queen Latifah plays Matron "Mama" Morton—a role that landed her a nomination for an Academy Award. *Chicago* is a musical comedy about two white women, Roxie Hart (Renée Zellweger) and Velma Kelly (Catherine Zeta-Jones), on death row for murder. Mama, the warden for the Cook County female prison in the 1920s, is a big-breasted Mammy figure, catering to the white women convicted of murderous crimes. Roxie and Velma seek fame and fortune by fighting for media and courtroom attention. Mama comes to Velma's aid by hiring the best lawyer in Chicago. bell hooks (1992) explains that when we view films with an oppositional gaze, we can clearly see that the purpose of black females in movies is only to enhance white femininity (pp. 122–23). A traditional Mammy served in a white home, but in *Chicago* a prison substitutes for the home. How can audiences interrogate the image of Mama Morton? Black women assisting white women is a familiar image in American culture. Mama Morton is scripted in accordance with the Mammy stereotypes of being unable to define herself as she pleases (because she is powerless outside the jail) and lacking a dignified sense of self (Jackson, 2006, p. 41). There is nothing new in the identity of Mama Morton connected to race, but as bell hooks (1992) observes, there is a necessity to "transform the image of blackness, of black people, our ways of looking and our ways of being seen," and this involves unlearning Mammy stereotypes (p. 7).

Another Mammy role that has given Queen Latifah a lot of attention is in *Bringing Down the House* (2003), where she plays Charlene. Charlene meets Peter (Steve Martin), in an Internet chat. Peter, a tax attorney who has taken a fancy to Charlene online, believes that Charlene is an attractive, blond, white female attorney. Charlene, an escaped convict, is trying to clear her name from a robbery where she was framed. When Charlene appears at Peter's house for their first face-to-face meeting, Peter frantically tries to get rid of her. Because of Charlene's threats Peter reluctantly allows her refuge in his home where she instantly becomes the Mammy/maid to Peter's two children Sarah (Kimberly J. Brown), a rebellious teenager, and Gregory (Angus T. Jones), a middle-school child who struggles with reading.

While trying to clear Charlene of charges, Peter tries to reunite with his estranged wife, Kate (Jean Smart). Peter's friend Howie (Eugene Levy) becomes infatuated with Charlene and is constantly attempting to be "hip" by noting his love for dark meat and a "Congo Goddess," a code for black women. This attraction, based on the power structure of enslaver and enslaved, results in Charlene encouraging the gaze by calling Howie her "Freakboy."

The movie is filled with stereotypes of whites being wealthy and standoffish and blacks being poor and loud. Charlene nurtures the children, helps Peter, and cares for the home as a domestic. This stereotype disallows any alternative textual reading. The images in *Bringing Down the House* mandate that the viewer read Charlene as oppositional: loud, lower class, criminal, deviant, negative, and uncontrollable. Not only a Mammy, then, Charlene portrays additional stereotypes of black women.

NON-STEREOTYPICAL ROLES

Queen Latifah's character Nina in *Mad Money* (2008) does not fit the traditional stereotype of a Mammy but is still problematic because the character exists to complement the white character as the authority figure (Diawara, 2009, p.771). The movie focuses on three women employed at the Federal Reserve who need each other's assistance to pull off heisting dollar bills that are being sent to the shredder. Nina, a struggling single mother, views stealing money from the bank as a means to fund private education for her two sons and give them a more stable future. Jackie (Katie Holmes), the other coworker at the Federal Reserve, is presented as an absentminded, trailer-residing white female. Bridget (Diane Keaton) is a fifty-something married white woman whose husband has lost his job. In desperation, Bridget accepts a janitorial position at the Federal Reserve where she concocts a plan of smuggling the money out of the bank.

After the smuggling incident, Nina sets limits for Bridget, stating that she cannot spend a large sum of money on a purchase for fear that it will draw attention to their scheme. Bridget does not comply with Nina's instructions and buys an expensive ring. When Nina find out what Bridget has done, Nina flushes the ring down the toilet in Bridget's presence and reminds her of the instructions. Even though Nina claims she will not participate in any more heists because the rule was broken, she later rescinds her threat and participates in many more robberies. Eventually, the women have so much money that they can no longer find places to hide it until Bridget's husband Don (Ted Danson) steps in and saves the day.

From a filmic and cultural studies perspective, Nina has a role that needs to be contested because she is presented as intellectually inferior. Moreover, Bridget and Don, while currently economically strapped, still have a superior class status compared to Nina and Jackie. This class structure marginalizes working class people and people of color. The characters' images are closed and fixed. Visually the text transmits that blacks and the underclass, regardless of race, are subservient to those in power (Jhally, 1997).

Unique to all the other characters examined thus far, Queen Latifah as Ana Wallace makes the greatest departure from the Mammy with the role of an HIV-positive black woman in Brooklyn, New York, based on a true story. In *Life Support* (2007), Queen Latifah portrays a former drug addict. Ana Wallace (fictional name) works with an AIDS outreach group (Life Force) consisting mainly of women of color. She passes out condoms and educates them about the HIV virus and AIDS. This outreach group provides not only education but solace for the women who are at all different stages of the illness. Although the film refers to medical conflicts the group members go through, greater emphasis is placed on Ana's family conflicts and struggles to gain/regain her dignity. Throughout the film, Ana seeks to reconnect with her teenage daughter Kelly (Rachel Nicks) who has little forgiveness or empathy for her mother's previous life choices because Ana gave up Kelly eleven years ago. The plot revolves around the search for Kelly's friend, Amare (Evan Ross), a homeless HIV-positive teenager whose addiction has led him to prostitution. When Kelly unites Ana with her friend Amare, a breakthrough occurs that mends the mother-daughter relationship. While Ana is looking for Amare, she is seeking forgiveness from Kelly.

In *Life Support,* Queen Latifah is an activist. Her activism demonstrates that the black woman does not have to follow the proscribed role of Mammy. A more recent film, *Life Support* serves as a harbinger of future change and balance, encouraging a message of non-conformity and independence for black female actors. The film allows for a greater opportunity to expose and educate audiences to the in-group daily challenges of black women struggling with HIV/AIDS while debunking some of the myths. This film may even encourage some viewers to get an AIDS test and/or encourage others around them to be tested. Ever since *Life Support* was first released in 2007, viewings of the film have been offered across the nation on HIV/AIDS Awareness Day.

CONCLUSION

The initial questions that I asked about Queen Latifah were: what made her give up her Afrocentric style and focus—not only in her music, but also in her appearance and acting agenda; is she a mere pawn in Hollywood's arena of reinforcing the stereotypical Mammy, endorsing internalized and institutionalized racism; and have her decisions to take on roles as an actress, model, or singer kept up with the mission of black feminism? In attempting to answer these questions, I came to understand that actors make choices to be involved in a movie not only for financial gain, but also to fine-tune their craft, remain in the limelight, and/or meet new challenges. I do applaud Latifah for taking her role in *Life Support,* but I find her earlier choices to reinforce negative images of racism for black female characters.

Is it possible that Academy Awards will begin to be issued for roles devoid of stereotypes? Such a change will come about when racial and ethnic stereotypes are contested, and viewers begin the practice of deconstruction to allow for new knowledge and new identities (Jhally, 1997). When viewers analyze discriminatory roles and reject popular stereotypical beliefs about black women, a debunking of the harmful hegemonic perceptions of black women will occur. And such has been the purpose of this critique of Queen Latifah's roles.

While the fact that there are black actresses in more films can be viewed positively, future roles should debunk and dissolve stereotypes. I argue, in agreement with Stuart Hall (1997), that there is a need for more cultural awareness by the audience, and this can be undertaken with resistance, a constant contestation (p. 130). Stereotypical roles reinforce white patriarchal institutions such as the film industry. On the other hand, the refusal of black actresses to remain silenced constitutes a core theme of black feminism (Collins, 2000, pp. 100–101). By investigating the growth of Queen Latifah's characters between 1998 and 2008, we see that she is as complex as the roles she plays on the screen. All hail the Queen!

REFERENCES

Anderson, L. M. (1997). *Mammies no more: The changing image of black women on stage and screen*. Lanham, MD: Rowman & Littlefield Press.

Collins, P. H. (2000). *Black feminist thought: Knowledge, consciousness, and the politics of empowerment* (2nd ed.). New York: Routledge.

Diawara, M. (2009). Black spectatorship: Problems of identification and resistance. In L. Brady & M. Cohen (Eds.), *Film theory and criticism: Introductory readings* (7th ed., pp. 767–76). New York: Oxford Press.

Evans, J., & Hall, S. (Eds.). (1999). *Visual culture: The reader*. Thousand Oaks, CA: Sage Publications.

Gerbner, G., Gross, L., Morgan, M., Signorielli, N., & Shanahan, J. (2002). Growing up with television: Cultivation processes. In J. Bryant & D. Zillmann (Eds.), *Media effects: Advances in theory and research* (2nd ed., pp. 43–67). Mahwah, NJ: Lawrence Erlbaum.

Hall, S. (1997). What is this "black" in black popular culture? In V. Smith (Ed.), *Representing Blackness: Issues in film and video* (pp. 123–33). New Brunswick, NJ: Rutgers University Press.

Harris, T. M. (2004). Interrogating the representation of African American female identity in the films *Waiting to Exhale* and *Set It Off*. In R. L. Jackson II (Ed.), *African American communication and identities: Essential Readings* (pp. 189–96). Thousand Oaks, CA: Sage Publicatiosn.

hooks, bell. (1981). *Ain't I a woman?* Boston: South End Press.

hooks, bell. (1992). *Black looks: Race and representation*. Boston: South End Press.

hooks, bell. (2000). *Feminism is for everybody: Passionate politics*. Cambridge, MA: South End Press.

Jackson II, R. L. (2006). *Scripting the black masculine body: Identity, discourse, and racial politics in popular media*. New York: State University of New York Press.

Jhally, S. (Director). Hall, S. (Narrator). (1997). *Representation and the media* [Video]. Northampton: Media Education Foundation.

Migraine-George, Therese. (2008). *African women and representation: From performance to politics*. Trenton, NJ: Africa World Press.

Monahan, J. L., Shtrulis, I., & Brown Givens, S. (Aug. 2005). Priming welfare queens and other stereotypes: The transference of media images into interpersonal contexts. *Communication Research Reports*, 22(3), 199–205.

Tan, M. (2007, November 5). Making it big. *People*. Retrieved September 13, 2010, from www.people.com/people/ archive/article/0,,20160777,00.html.

U.S. Department of Health and Human Services. (2010, May 18). *Minority Women's Health: HIV/AIDS*. Retrieved September 18, 2010, from www.womenshealth.gov/minority/african-american/hiv.cfm.

Wallace, Michele. (1990). *Invisibility blues: From pop to theory*. New York: Verso.
Wallace, Michele. (2004). *Dark designs and visual culture*. Durham, NC: Duke University Press.
West, C. M. (1995). Mammy, Sapphire, and Jezebel: Historical images of black women and their implications of psychotherapy. *Psychotherapy, 32*(3), 458–66.
Wilson, C. C., Gutierrez, F., & Chao, L. M. (2003). *Racism, sexism, and the media: The rise of class communication in multicultural America*. Thousand Oaks, CA: Sage Publications.
Yarbrough, M., & Bennett, C. (2000). Cassandra and the sistehs: The Peculiar treatment of African-American women in the myth of women as liars. *Journal of Gender, Race, and Justice.* (*Spring*). Pp. 626–57.

Chapter Thirteen

18,000,000 Cracks or How Hillary Almost Became President

Lori L. Montalbano

The 2008 presidential campaign represented a new era in American politics. For the first time in U.S. history, two of the major players in the national election were not the traditional middle-aged white males driven by generational privilege and political power, but instead, a white woman and an African American man. With two terms under the Bush *regime*, two divisive wars, and economic failure, American voters were ready for change. For the years immediately preceding the campaign, speculation grew to certainty that Hillary Clinton would take the main stage and become a star player in the political contest. Years spent as an atypical First Lady, a national icon, and a United States senator positioned Hillary Clinton as a media-seizing force who would shake up the mundane candidacy of her aged Republican counterpart, Senator John McCain, war hero, patriot, and "good ole boy" of the GOP. Meanwhile, Americans were looking to breathe fresh air into party politics that were outmoded by decades past. Young voters entered the political scene *en masse*, looking for a leader to promote their future, their objectives. They sought to identify with a new leader who promised to work toward *their* agenda. Their candidate? Barack Obama. What resulted was a split down the middle of the Democratic Party that threatened an earlier-perceived Clinton win as a given, into a fight to the finish for the top spot. While Hillary Clinton's bid for the Democratic ticket was unsuccessful, she launched a campaign that would change the history of American national politics.

Identification with an audience is a necessary component of any political campaign. The successful candidate must find multiple paths of connection with constituents. She or he must build community identification, facilitated by rhetorical themes embedded in the mediated discourse, and embody a political persona that constituents trust and believe in and with whom they identify. Constructing a persona of identification relies to a great extent on the ability of the candidate to demonstrate alliances with their constituents, emphasizing shared visions and goals, similarities in their struggles, and an allegiance to national pride. The successful candidate relies on a constructed identity that shapes perceptions and creates solidarity. Hillary Clinton's 2008 bid for president is a primary example of a transformation of the traditional construct of the presidential character as specifically male into an expanded national view of the boundaries and possibilities of that office.

Of course, no candidate can succeed without championing the influence of media. As Trent and Friedenberg (2004) remark, "The contemporary candidate needs the mass media, in part because voters have expectations regarding the media's role in providing information about the candidate and the campaign . . . media have tremendous power in determining which news events, which candidates, and which issues are to be covered in a given day" (p. 141).

This chapter examines the evolution of Hillary Rodham Clinton as a national political icon into a credible candidate for president, exploring how this evolution was propelled through the construction of a persona of identification with her constituents. Additionally, the performative elements that constrained and promoted her candidacy as displayed by media coverage are discussed. Finally, the evolution of the candidate after concession, or what I like to call the "what do her followers do now?" or "is this really all there is?" is offered up for consideration as we ponder the impact of the Clinton campaign on long-term advances of women in national politics.

BUILDING A PERSONA OF IDENTIFICATION

Hillary Rodham Clinton has been a formidable political presence in the United States for approximately forty years. During the past four decades, Clinton has captured media attention in numerous roles and in various circumstances. It was in the 1980s that some of the more memorable media frenzy began as she took the role of First Lady of Arkansas and made her infamous utterance that she could have "stayed at home and baked cookies," when criticized about continuing to practice law during her husband Bill Clinton's tenure as governor of Arkansas. While she was no stranger to the political scene at this point, her statement became a recurring media blunder of sorts that would shape perceptions of later presences within national politics. Later, we witnessed a vibrant and vocal campaigner for Bill Clinton's successful race for the presidency in 1992. Not to anyone's surprise, as First Lady

Hillary Clinton rocked the White House with role variations and participation in decision and policy making during the Clinton (*that is, Bill Clinton*) administration. "In November of 2000, Hillary Rodham Clinton was elected to the U.S. Senate from New York. Not only was she the sole First Lady to serve in an elected office, she was also the first woman to win a state-wide election in New York" (Mattina, 2005, p. 232). In 2008, Hillary Rodham Clinton ran a campaign for the presidency of the United States. Eventually, she became secretary of state. Whatever opinion the public holds, it is undeniable that Hillary Clinton has made an impression on American politics. Mattina (2005) explains that "Rodham Clinton's public image remains a contested site among scholars, the press, and the American public. Admired and loathed with equal passion" (p. 217).

Defining a public persona with whom the public can identify is crucial to any successful rhetor/candidate or political character. In his discussion of identification, Burke (1950) claims that we persuade others by talking their "language by speech, gesture, tonality, order, image, attitude, idea," and by "identifying" our ways with theirs. Hillary Clinton's attempt to identify with her audience is considered in the pages that follow. Foss, Foss, and Trapp (1991) explain that rhetorical acts are often best understood as performance events: "To study rhetoric as performance is to examine any of the enabling and emerging forms of action through which humans and cultures constitute and reconstitute themselves. Performance is the act of bringing to completion the sense of reality—of bringing the significance or meaning of some cultural form" (p. 329). The performance of gender expectations, that is "performing feminisms" (Butler, 1990; Case, 1990), is also an operating factor within the performance event that is explored in this chapter. The analyses and discussions that unfold are done through a performative lens. Excerpts from five speeches will demonstrate that at many points during her campaign and beyond, Clinton used the process of identification when creating her public persona. There are many facets of the Clinton persona. These include, but are not limited to, her credibility as a sustained political presence, her role as an agent of change, her commitment to the "American Dream," and her status as a woman making a difference.

CLINTON IDENTIFIES WITH HER AUDIENCE AS A SUSTAINED POLITICAL PRESENCE

Throughout her campaign, Clinton referenced past successes of the Democratic Party and launched accolades hailing the accomplishments of the Clinton administration specifically. She emphasized her long-term commitment to Democratic themes, including ending the war, providing health care for all

Americans, and revitalizing an economy in recession. She attempted to position herself as a powerful and sustainable candidate who would take her party to victory against the Republican frontrunner. What she and her camp did not count on was the swift rise of Barack Obama. Young, attractive, and a natural in front of the camera, Obama possessed a communicative savvy difficult to surpass. To counter Obama's media appeal, Clinton emphasized her own experience and attempted to cast doubt on his ability to stand as a commander in chief, claiming his inexperience would hinder his ability to lead. After a victory at the Ohio primary, Clinton stated:

> This is a great night, but we all know that these are challenging times. We have two wars abroad. We have a recession looming here at home. Voters face a critical question—who is tested and ready to be commander-in-chief on day one? . . . Protecting America is the first and most urgent duty of the president. When there's a crisis and that phone rings at 3:00 a.m. in the White House, there's no time for speeches or on-the-job training. You have to be ready to make a decision.

This speech became a major theme in her rhetoric, as Obama gained in popularity and her own candidacy was at risk. Clinton tried to demonstrate that her many years of public service put her at a distinct advantage over her counterpart, who was a relative newcomer to the political arena. Despite Clinton's early successes in the primary elections, Obama hit the political scene with great strength, quickly diminishing her speculated victory. Walker (2008) describes the shift in Democratic support:

> For most of the political year, from Senator Barack Obama's crucial victory in the Iowa caucuses in January until the two parties held their nominating conventions almost nine months later, the presidential election process seemed to be in the grip of an insurgency. A little-known freshman senator from Illinois, rallying unprecedented numbers of young voters and African Americans, laid siege to the well-funded campaign of the establishment candidate, the Democratic Party's frontrunner, Senator Hillary Clinton. . . . When the campaign began, Clinton commanded the largest war chest in campaign history and the overwhelming support of party officials, known as the super-delegates since they were entitled to vote *ex officio* at the party convention. (p. 1095)

Despite Obama's success, Clinton had clearly established herself as a credible party candidate and continued to campaign on that theme. Another factor that surged the Obama agenda was the skilled use of the Internet as a persuasive tool. These strategies targeted many of the young voters and gave them resources and opportunities to participate in the political process on their own terms. This management of the Internet generation propelled the Obama campaign:

The manner in which Obama defeated Clinton also appeared to be revolutionary, a grass-roots movement surging from below to humble and defeat the Democratic establishment that Hillary and her husband dominated. . . . Obama prevailed in the primaries because his second revolution was to understand the new politics made possible by the social networking of the Internet through systems like Facebook and MySpace. His campaign organized over 8,000 web-based affinity groups and 750,000 active volunteers, and recruited over 1.6 million voters. . . . In February alone Obama raised $55 million—almost $2 million a day—almost all of it in small donations over the Internet. This was a month in which Obama himself attended not a single fundraising event, while Clinton pursued her grueling schedule of fundraising cocktails, receptions, and dinners. (Walker, 2008, pp. 1096 & 1098)

As a major party leader, during her concession speech Clinton reemphasizes her commitment to the party and the American people:

You know, I've been in politics and public life in one way or another for four decades. And during those—during those 40 years, our country has voted ten times for president. Democrats won only three of those times, and the man who won two of those elections is with us today. We made tremendous progress during the 90s under a Democratic president, with a flourishing economy and our leadership for peace and security respected around the world. Just think how much more progress we could have made over the past 40 years if we'd had a Democratic president. . . . We cannot let this moment slip away. We have come too far and accomplished too much.

In the above quote, Clinton takes an opportunity to stress her strength as a sustained political presence and shifts her support to the party and to Obama. While she ends her campaign for president with this speech, she also fulfills an important role within the Democratic Party, a sustainable voice that leaves inroads for future cooperation with party leaders.

CLINTON POSITIONS HERSELF AS AN AGENT OF CHANGE

Throughout her political career, as evidenced in the 2008 campaign, Clinton used media moments to exalt her role as an agent of change on the political stage. In her primary speeches, Clinton identified several strategies of change, including health care reform, and an end to war and energy independence:

We're ready for health care, not for just some people or most people, but for every American . . . we're ready to declare energy independence and create millions of green collar jobs. We're ready to reach out to our allies and confront our shared challenges. We're ready to end the war in Afghanistan. And we're past ready to serve our veterans with the same devotion that they served us.

Typically, critiquing the incumbent becomes a powerful method for challenging candidates to boost their own credibility and articulate their own plans for change. Clinton took this opportunity early in the campaign, by aligning herself with the major themes of the anti-Bush, anti-Republican movement that was sweeping the nation. In many ways, her rhetoric was not decisively different from that of Obama's. Nevertheless, this positioning was not only a plan, but an expectation of her constituency. Later, during her concession speech, Clinton threw her support to Obama, and reiterates her earlier ideology:

> The way to continue our fight now, to accomplish the goals for which we stand, is to take our energy, our passion, our strength, and do all we can to help elect Barack Obama . . . it's time to restore the ties that bind us together and come together around the ideals we share, the values we cherish, and the country we love . . . we all want a health care system that is universal . . . we all want an America defined by deep and meaningful equality . . . and we all want to restore America's standing in the world.

In this quote and many others in subsequent speeches, Clinton reiterates her commitment to change of the status quo; further, she invites her supporters to facilitate change by shifting their support to Senator Obama. In her keynote speech at the Democratic National Convention, she states, "My friends, it's time to take back the country we love. And whether you voted for me or you voted for Barack, the time is now to unite as a single party with a single purpose." This quote typifies the notion of Clinton as a continued agent of change, a premise that would eventually result in her appointment to secretary of state in the Obama administration.

CLINTON POSITIONS HERSELF AS A PROPONENT OF THE "AMERICAN DREAM"

References to the "American Dream" are common in political speeches and campaigns. Candidates often take opportunities to align their political "visions" around the ideal of the American Dream. This ideal resonates across constituencies and has become an expectation in political rhetorical strategies. Throughout the campaign, Clinton reiterated this theme time and again. In Ohio, she stated, "I think we're ready for an economy that works for everyone, not just at the top, but every single hard-working American who deserves a shot at the American Dream." Later, during her concession speech, she said:

> We all want an economy that sustains the American Dream, the opportunity to work hard and have that work rewarded, to save for college, a home and retirement, to afford that gas and those groceries, and still have a little left over at the end of the month, an economy that lifts all of our people and ensures that our prosperity is broadly distributed and shared.

While less explicit, the theme is embedded in strategies that arouse the constituents' patriotism. Many times at the Democratic National Convention (DNC), she tied themes of the "American Dream" to symbols of American patriotism:

> We need leaders once again who can tap into that special blend of American confidence and optimism that has enabled generations before us to meet our toughest challenges—leaders who can help us show ourselves and the world that with our ingenuity, creativity, and innovative spirit there are no limits to what is possible in America. . . . You know, America is still around after 232 years because we have risen to the challenge and every new time, changing to be faithful to our values of equal opportunity for all the common good. . . . I've seen it. I have seen it in our teachers and our firefighters, our police officers, our nurses, our small business owners, and our union workers. I've seen it in the men and women of our military. In America, you always keep going. We're Americans. We're not big on quitting.

This quote reaffirms her commitment to the party, her patriotism, and her leadership role in the party. She offers her supporters a reason to shift their support to Obama, implying that even though she conceded the election, she is an American and a Democrat. She is not a quitter and will not give up on the "American Dream."

CLINTON POSITIONS HERSELF AS A WOMAN WHO HAS MADE A DIFFERENCE

Examining the campaign of Hillary Clinton is incomplete without a discussion of the role she played as the first American woman to create a powerful voter base that made her a genuine potential candidate for the lead spot on the Democratic ticket. Many authors conclude that campaign coverage by the media included a barrage of sexist remarks and insults propelled against

Clinton in an attempt to discredit her character. For example, Carlin and Winfrey (2009) discuss the sexism that was prevalent in both Hillary Clinton's and Sarah Palin's campaigns:

> The 2008 U.S. presidential election was historic on many levels. The country elected its first African American president, who narrowly defeated a female candidate in the Democratic primary race. The Republicans nominated their first woman as a vice presidential candidate. Hillary Clinton and Sarah Palin demonstrated that women politicians have come a long way; however, an analysis of media coverage reveals that lingering sexism toward women candidates is still alive and well. . . . The analysis indicates that there was a considerable amount of negative coverage of both candidates and that such coverage has potential to cast doubt on a woman's suitability to be commander-in-chief or in the wings. (p. 326)

Their analysis covers a vast array of print media representations, televised reports, and humor in television programming directed at the candidates of the 2008 campaign, uncovering a plethora of examples of sexism against the women running in the national election. Stansell (2008) reinforces our understanding of the magnitude of the sexist coverage:

> By now the "sexism" charge is an old chestnut in the annals of this campaign. What is the substance, and what exactly happened? Sexism trailed Clinton's campaign from the start in the form of objections voiced, observations made, jokes cracked, and gossip circulated—the sorts of things that have never been said about a man running for president. From her cleavage to her feminine handwriting (silly) to nepotism and dynastic privilege (never seriously raised during the younger Bush's campaign), Clinton was fair game. She was detail-oriented, not masterful; narrow, not commanding; experienced, maybe, but not charismatic. To feminist-minded women, the chatter was irritatingly familiar. (p. 35)

The author above carefully pointed out that many, including liberal feminists, ignored the blatant misogyny that eventually developed against Clinton. This is a disturbing situation, as Simon and Hoyt (2008) found that "research on political ideologies suggests than those who identify themselves as liberal will be more likely to support a female candidate than those who identify themselves as conservatives" (p. 161). Her supporters were mute and failed to demand a fair assessment of Clinton as a credible candidate. Stansell (2008) charges:

> The Ohio win set off a misogynist frenzy. The dreadful election detritus already in circulation proliferated: the Hillary nutcrackers popped up in airport gift shops, bumper stickers sported slogans such as, HILLARY CLINTON— JUST LIKE YOUR EX-WIFE BUT BITCHIER. . . . But it wasn't only the right-wing hoi polloi. A chorus of naysayers screeched and brayed from major

newspapers, networks, liberal journals, and cable shows calling for her to drop out of the race. Yet neither Obama, his aides, his supporters, nor the Democratic National Committee condemned the misogyny. (p. 38)

Despite sexism in media coverage and stereotypes plaguing the campaign stops, Clinton established a truly presidential character. Clinton's rhetoric took the "high road," by introducing rhetoric that lifted women up, by offering the Clinton persona as the women's representative, a champion to move America forward in the quest for equal rights and equal representation in the nation. For example, in the following quote, Clinton discusses the historical significance of her campaign, by tying it into the American Dream:

> I want to end by sharing with you a message that I got late last month from someone who didn't have much money to spare but sent me $10 for my campaign and sent an e-mail in which she wrote: "My two daughters are two and four, and we chant and cheer for you at every speech we see. I want them to know anything is possible." Tonight I say to them, keep on watching. Together, we're going to make history. To those little girls, I say this is America, and we do believe you can be anything you want to be, and we want our sons and our daughters to dream big. I have big dreams for America's future. The question is not whether we can fulfill those dreams; it's whether we will. And here's our answer: yes, we will. (Clinton, Ohio, 2008)

In this story and others of similar content, Clinton embraced the historic element of her candidacy. At the DNC, she claimed, "I am a United States Senator because in 1848 a group of courageous women and a few brave men gathered in Seneca Falls, New York, many traveling for days and nights, to participate in the first convention on women's rights in our history." Strategically, this speech was given on the eighty-eighth anniversary of the day when the Nineteenth Amendment became part of the Constitution. She stated, "My mother was born before women could vote. My daughter got to vote for her mother for president. This is the story of America, of women and men who defy odds and never give up." For many, this statement demonstrated the significance of the moment. It gave her supporters a certain optimism, or at least, a sense of accomplishment about her candidacy and somewhat appeased their disappointment.

In an earlier writing, I described media performance aesthetics that severely constrain women in politics, by judging them in terms of a presidential character that is a male model of behavior and presentation (Montalbano-Phelps, 2005). While the sexism that plagues women in politics by the media and other voices remains significant, it is the response of the candidate to these types of media that can have an important impact on the residual perception of the candidate. In an analysis of the rhetoric of Clinton's 2008 campaign, I found a candidate that exhibited confidence in displaying herself as a woman, without demonstrating a need to defend her credentials, but instead embraced the fact that she was a woman who was making a difference. This notion is well expressed in the following quote from Clinton's concession speech:

> I want to start today by saying how grateful I am to all of you, to everyone who poured your hearts and your hopes into this campaign, who drove for miles and lined the streets waving homemade signs, who scrimped and saved to raise money, who knocked on doors and made calls, who talked, sometimes argued, with your friends and neighbors, who e-mailed and contributed online, who invested so much in our common enterprise, to the moms and dads who came to our events, who lifted their little girls and little boys on their shoulders and whispered in their ears, "See, you can be anything you want to be."

PERFORMATIVE ELEMENTS THAT CHANGED A NATION

> In storytelling . . . embodiment constitutes a system of relations among storyteller, narrator, character, and audience. That is, these embodied relations are extensions of an incarnate subject capable of moving reciprocally between participation and expression. The storyteller lives as both narrator and character in performing narrative for an audience. . . . Performing narrative is radically contextualized: in the bodies and voices of participants, in its situated and material conditions, in the discursive regularities that shape language, experiences, and identity. (Langellier & Peterson, 2004, pp. 9, 30)

It is through embodiment that narrators create a character and a relationship with their audiences. They become cocreators in the unfolding stories that they contextualize and make present at any given time, in any given situation. Frank (2000) states, "Storytelling is the recursive collaboration of the relationship between those sharing the story. Shared memories are made present, and shared failures are projected. . . . Stories reaffirm what people mean to each other and who they are with respect to each other" (p. 355). These meanings were quite present in the relationships Clinton built with her supporters.

In addition to the formation of a political persona of identification, Hillary Clinton used an important strategy of storytelling in her campaign rhetoric. She "gave voice" to her followers and shared personal experiences of her own to create an embodied relation with her constituents. Clinton has noted, "Sometimes stories make the point much better . . . one single story can pierce through and make clear that we are all in the same story, we all face the same challenges" (Clinton, UN Speech, 1999). Storytelling became one of Clinton's most effective rhetorical strategies. The stories typified the discourse of Clinton: as she told her supporters at the DNC, "You allowed me to become part of your lives, and you became part of mine." This affinity-gaining strategy formed a bond between Clinton and those who identified with the stories she told. During the campaign, she spoke of her political background, experiences, and successes. Additionally, she shared the memoirs of her campaign, as she traveled across America, collecting stories of everyday Americans, making extraordinary commentary on the political status of the United States in troubled times. By telling these stories, she invoked a meta-narrative event in which her constituents' persuasive voices were cast in her rhetorical scenes. In the pages that follow, two sites of narrative performances are examined. These narrative paths include the story of her political journey and the stories of her constituency.

STORIES OF CLINTON'S POLITICAL JOURNEY

Stories of Clinton's political journey were ongoing and evolving throughout the campaign. Upon winning the Ohio primary, for example, she credited Ohio as a state of voters who have had great impact on her campaign as well as national politics, positioning herself and the voters in a partnership within her campaign:

> For everyone here in Ohio and across America who has ever been counted out but refused to be knocked out, and for everyone who has stumbled but stood right back, and for everyone who works hard and never gives up, this one is for you. You know what they say, as Ohio goes, so goes the nation. Well, this nation's coming back, and so is this campaign.

In the above quote, Clinton casts herself as a candidate/character who can sustain and overcome, despite her declining support. Later, in her concession speech, she characterizes this candidate as an ongoing, important part of the Democratic Party and mission. While she uses the opportunity to endorse Barack Obama, she also takes the opportunity to position herself in the party:

> I entered this race because I have an old-fashioned conviction that public service is about helping people solve their problems and live in their dreams. I've had every opportunity and blessing in my own life, and I want the same for all Americans. And until that day comes, you'll always find me on the front lines of democracy, fighting for the future . . . understand that we all know this has been a tough fight, but the Democratic party is a family. And now it's time to restore the ties that bind us together and come together around the ideals we share, the values we cherish, and the country we love.

At the DNC, Clinton uses her story to convince Democrats to unite to defeat the Republican Party:

> I haven't spent the past 35 years in the trenches advocating for children, campaigning for universal healthcare, helping parents balance work and family, and fighting for women's rights here at home and around the world to see another Republican in the White House squander our promise of a country that really fulfills the hopes of our people. And you haven't worked so hard over the last 18 months or endured the last eight years to suffer through more failed leadership.

In this quote, Clinton defers to her persona of identification through sustainability once again. She draws attention to her many years of public service not only to increase the credibility of her claims, but to pave the way for the future of the party and her role within the party as a major political player. Her comments clearly set the stage for unity between party factions, linking her work with that of her listeners as she petitions them to take active roles of alliance against their shared antagonists, the Republican players. This is also closely tied to her role as an agent of change. In this dialogue, she casts her audience as connected agents of change in the fight to win back the White House for the Democratic Party.

STORIES FROM HER CONSTITUENCY

In her campaign speeches, as well as speeches delivered after her concession speech, Clinton told the stories of others, and she discussed the life struggles that voters she met shared with her during the course of her campaign. Clinton often discussed the stories in a meta-narrative style that alluded to her discovery of American "characters." She often referred to those who "want their voices to count," claiming that "they should be heard." In Ohio, she said:

> For more than a year, I've been listening to the voices of people across our country. The single mom who told me she works two jobs; neither provides healthcare for her kids. She just can't work any harder. The little girl who asked how I helped people without homes—turns out her family was about to lose their own. The young man in a Marine Corps shirt who said he waited for months for medical care. He said to me, "Take care of my buddies. A lot of them are still over there. And then, will you please take care of me?"

In the above story, Clinton implies that the needs of the individuals she names are not experiencing the rights associated with the American Dream, as we have envisioned them. Clinton attempts to create a level of discomfort regarding their disadvantages in the minds of her audience, to prompt them to take action.

The stories Clinton spoke of during her campaign journey became familiar ones to those who followed her speech-making process. She often expounded on the stories on different occasions, sometimes providing more detail. In the following quote, she thanks her supporters for believing in her campaign:

> To all those women in their 80s and 90s born before women could vote, who cast their votes for our campaign. I've told you before about Florence Stein of South Dakota who was 88 years old and insisted that her daughter bring an absentee ballot to her hospice bedside. Her daughter and a friend put an American flag behind her bed and helped her fill out the ballot. She passed away soon after, and under state law her ballot didn't count, but her daughter later told a reporter, "My dad's an ornery old cowboy, and he didn't like it when he heard Mom's vote wouldn't be counted. I don't think he had voted in 20 years, but he voted in place of my mom."

With this quote, she reinforces the commitment to change that has taken place throughout America's history, and more recently, in the acts of individuals who participate in this historic voting process.

At the DNC, Clinton acknowledged the power of storytelling as a process of bonding and discovery:

> For me, it's been a privilege to meet you in your homes, your workplaces, and your communities. Your stories reminded me that everyday Americans' greatness is bound up in the lives of the American people. Your hard work, your devotion to duty, your love for your children, and your determination to keep going—often in the face of enormous obstacles—you taught me so much. And you made me laugh, and yes, you even made me cry. You allowed me to become part of your lives; you became part of mine.

Through the use of personal storytelling, as well as the meta-narrative described above, Clinton formed a bond with her supporters that manifested (or is that *womanifested*?) itself into alliances for Barack Obama and a positioning of her political character as an ongoing and important part of the Democratic Party's story. This story made perhaps the greatest impact leaving a permanent footprint on the road of the future for women in American politics.

POLITICAL AFTERLIFE: THE IMPLICATIONS OF THE CLINTON
PERSONA ON THE FUTURE OF WOMEN IN AMERICAN
POLITICS

To examine the role Clinton's persona has had on the future of American
politics, we must revisit for a moment the major roles that Clinton has played
in the mediated political scene. Anderson (2005) explains that any woman
playing the role of First Lady influences the public's perception of what
constitutes "American Womanhood":

> First Ladies also influence conceptions of "American Womanhood," and how
> they do that has broad implications for all women. Indeed, by virtue of their
> husband's elections, First Ladies become "sites" for the symbolic negotiation
> of female identity. Discourses by and about First Ladies function culturally to
> shape notions of femininity, and so both foster and constrain women's agency.
> Thus, the study of First Ladies is important not only for a historical apprecia-
> tion of some of the "great women" who have contributed to that institution but
> also a critique of how "American Womanhood" has been and continues to be
> inscribed, negotiated, and contested in the United States. (p. 2)

As First Lady, Hillary Clinton was a confident and determined political
player. Clinton's persona was typified by agency rather than femininity, risk
taking rather than complacency. Despite the significant amount of sexism
embedded in and often blatant within the media coverage of her as presidential candidate, Clinton emerged a stronger, more powerful voice in the campaign by accentuating her credentials. In her examination of Clinton a decade
prior to the 2008 campaign, Campbell (1998) suggests that Clinton's rhetorical style was more characteristically masculine than feminine. She claims,
"Hillary Rodham Clinton's style of public advocacy typically omits all of the
discursive markers which publicly enact their femininity" (p. 6). Further, she
adds, "Clinton plays the roles for which she has been professionally trained,
the roles of lawyer, advocate, and expert" (1998, p. 6). These types of behaviors do seem to resonate as characteristically appropriate for a "presidential
character." Yet, Clinton's use of storytelling was often positioned from a
more characteristically maternal perspective, as an advocate of women and
children. Her rhetoric often seemed to align her with what many researchers
label as women's communication, as we find that women's speech often
centers upon the power of storytelling (Aptheker, 1989; Baldwin, 1985; Bucholtz, Liang, & Sutton, 1999; Cameron, 1992; Langellier & Hall, 1989;
Langellier & Peterson, 2004; Montalbano-Phelps, 2004; Presnell, 1989; Spitzack & Carter, 1989).

Often, while taking risks against the normative behavioral constraints of the role of First Lady, and in the other very public roles she has played, Clinton has opened widespread conversations and heated debates about appropriateness, boundaries, significance, and support. Her relationship with her husband, former President Bill Clinton, is still debated across her constituency, within her party, as well as in the Republican camp. Clinton's political life has historically been and remains a site of political contestation. As discussed earlier in this chapter, she is a character that members of the public either love or hate. There is little in-between. But, despite the love/hate relationship, Clinton is undeniably a force to contend with. Mattina (2005) writes:

> While political pundits and media sages have debated her "place" as a First Lady, and her image has undergone numerous revisions in the press, Rodham-Clinton's message has remained unchanged. She has committed her life, her intellect, and her considerable rhetorical skill to empowering women and improving the lives of children. (p. 217)

Clinton carries with her an impressive resume of accomplishments, political causes, and personal victories that demonstrate the multiple contributions one woman can make to her country and her world. Pollitt (2008) wrote that because Clinton "normalized the concept of a woman running for president, she made it easier for women to run for every office, including the White House." She added, "That is one reason women and men of every party and every candidate preference, and every ethnicity too, owe Hillary Clinton a standing ovation, even if they can't stand her" (In Sklar, 2008, p. 316).

Simon and Hoyt (2008) summarize the current state of women in politics in this way:

> While Senator Clinton did not receive the Democratic nomination, her emergence as the first woman to be considered as a serious frontrunner in a US presidential election illustrates how today more women are reaching higher-level leadership positions in the political sphere than ever before in US history. Women now hold 16 percent of the seats in both the House of Representatives and the Senate in the US Congress (Center for American Women and Politics, 2008). In 2005, Condoleezza Rice became the second woman to hold the powerful position of Secretary of State, and in 2007, Nancy Pelosi became the first woman to hold the top leadership position of Speaker of the House of Representatives. Nonetheless, these women still represent exceptions to the rule, and attainment of such high power leadership positions remain a rarity for women. (p. 159)

What *does* the future hold for women in American politics? Sklar (2008) offers a counterpoint when she writes, "Clinton's candidacy built on the gradual change that took place over two generations since 1930; she consolidated those changes into a permanent base for women presidential candidates in the future" (p. 315).

Whatever the individual's preferences or perceptions, one must contend that Clinton's political persona has made a significant impact on the future of women in American politics.

In her concession speech, Clinton speaks at great length about the significance of her role as a woman running for president of the United States:

> When I was asked what it means to be a woman running for president, I always gave the same answer, that I was proud to be running as a woman. . . . I ran as a daughter who benefited from opportunities my mother never dreamed of. I ran as a mother who worries about my daughter's future and a mother who wants to leave all children brighter tomorrows. . . . There are no acceptable prejudices in the twenty-first century in our country. You can be so proud that, from now on, it will be unremarkable for a woman to win primary state victories; unremarkable to have a woman in a close race to be our nominee; unremarkable to think that a woman can be president of the United States— and that is truly remarkable, my friends. Although we weren't able to shatter that highest glass ceiling this time, thanks to you, it's got about 18 million cracks in it, and the light is shining through like never before, filling us all with the hope and the sure knowledge that the path will be a little easier next time.

These words typify the residual messages from the 2008 campaign. How they will come to pass remains to be seen. In this excerpt from Clinton's speech on the Obama administration's human rights agenda for the twenty-first century, she identifies the purpose as she speaks from her new role of secretary of state, an important role for the continued evolution of the Clinton persona:

> The potential within every person to learn, discover, embrace the world around them, the potential to join freely with others to shape their communities and their societies so that every person can find fulfillment and self-sufficiency, the potential to share life's beauties and tragedies, laughter and tears with the people we love—that potential is sacred. That, however, is a dangerous belief to many who hold power and who construct their position against the "other"—another tribe or religion or race or gender or political party. Standing up against that false sense of identity and expanding circle of rights and opportunities to all people—advancing their freedoms and possibilities—is why we do what we do.

The profundity of the situation of women in American politics remains. What is indeed remarkable is that we *haven't* seen a woman in the office of president. Perhaps such a notion has become less shocking and more plausible for the upcoming generation of voters. For my children, particularly my two young daughters, I feel a debt of gratitude to all of the American women who have given their energy and strength, sacrificed their privacy, and endured great criticism to advance the movement of women in American politics. I can say with some degree of confidence that after the 2008 presidential race, my children and their generation will no longer see the participation of women and people of all diversities as unusual, but a normative example of the possibilities for us all.

REFERENCES

Anderson, K., Vasby. (2005). The First Lady: A site of "American womanhood." In M. Meijer Wertheimer (Ed.), *Leading ladies of the White House* (1–15). Lanham, MD: Rowman and Littlefield Publishers.

Aptheker, B. (1989). *Tapestries of life: Women's work, women's consciousness, and the meaning of daily experience.* Amherst: The University of Massachusetts Press.

Baldwin, K. (1985). "Woof!" A word on women's roles in family storytelling. In R.A. Jordon and S. J. Kalcik (Eds.), *Women's folklore, women's culture* (pp. 149–62). Philadelphia, PA: University of Pennsylvania Press.

Bucholtz, M., Liang, A. C., & Sutton, L.A. (Eds.). (1999). *Reinventing identities: The gendered self in discourse.* New York: Oxford University Press.

Burke, K. (1950). *A rhetoric of motives.* New York, NY: Prentice Hall.

Butler, J. (1990). Performative acts and gender constitution: An essay on phenomenology and feminist theory. In S. Case (Ed.), *Performing feminisms: Feminist critical theory and theatre* (270–82). Baltimore, MD: Johns Hopkins University Press.

Cameron, D. (1992). *Feminism and linguistic theory* (2nd ed.). New York, NY: St. Martin's Press.

Campbell, K. Kohrs. (1998). The discursive performance of femininity: Hating Hillary. *Rhetoric and Public Affairs, 1*(1), 1–19.

Carlin, D. B., & Winfrey, K. L. (2009). Have you come a long way baby? Hillary Clinton, Sarah Palin, and sexism in 2008 campaign coverage. *Communication Studies, 60*(4), 326–43.

Case, S. (Ed.). (1990). *Performing feminisms: Feminist critical theory and theatre* (270–82). Baltimore, MD: Johns Hopkins University Press.

Clinton, H. (2008, June 7). *Announcing suspension of presidential campaign and Obama support.* Speech given at the National Building Museum, Washington, DC. Retrieved from www.americanrhetoric.com/speeches/hillaryclintoncampaignsuspensionspeech.htm.

Clinton, H. (2008, August 28). *Democratic National Convention keynote address.* Speech delivered at INVESCO Field at Mile High Stadium, Denver, Colorado. Retrieved from www.americanrhetoric.com/speeches/convention2008/hillaryclinton2008dnc.htm.

Clinton, H. (2008, March 4). *Ohio primary victory speech.* Speech delivered in Columbus, Ohio. Retrieved from www.realclearpolitics.com/articles/2008/03/hillary_clintons_ohio_primary.html.

Clinton, H. (2009, December 14). *Speech on human rights agenda for the twenty-first century.* Speech delivered at Georgetown University, Washington, DC. Retrieved from www.americanrhetoric.com/speeches/hillaryclintonhumanrightsagenda.htm.

Clinton, H. Rodham. (1999, March 4). *United Nations International Women's Day speech on women's rights.* Speech given in New York City, NY. Retrieved from www.whitehouse.gov/wh/eop/first-lady/html/generalspeeches, accessed 14 March 1999.

Foss, S. K., Foss, K. A., & Trapp, R. (1991). *Contemporary perspectives on rhetoric* (2nd ed.). Prospect Heights, IL: Waveland Press.

Frank, A. W. (2000). The standpoint of the storyteller. *Quality Health Research, 10*(3), 354–66.

Langellier, K., & Hall, D. (1989). A phenomenological approach to feminist communication and research. In C. Spitzack & K. Carter (Eds.), *Doing research in women's communication: Perspectives on theory and research* (pp. 193–220). Norwood, NJ: Ablex.

Langellier, K., & Peterson, E. E. (2004). *Storytelling in daily life: Performing narrative.* Philadelphia, PA: Temple University Press.

Mattina, A. F. (2005). Hillary Rodham Clinton: Using her vital voice. In, M. Meijer Wertheimer (Ed.), *Leading ladies of the White House* (pp. 217–34). Lanham, MD: Rowman and Littlefield Publishers.

Montalbano-Phelps, L. (2004). *Taking narrative risk: The empowerment of abuse survivors.* Lanham, MD: University Press of America.

Montalbano-Phelps, L. (2005). Performing politics: Media aesthetics for women in political campaigns. In T. Carilli & J. Campbell (Eds.), *Women and the media: Diverse perspectives.* Lanham, MD: University Press of America.

Pollitt, K. (2008, June) Iron my skirt. *The Nation.*

Presnell, M. (1989). Narrative gender differences: Orality and literacy. In C. Spitzack & K. Carter (Eds.), *Doing research on women's communication: Perspectives on theory and research* (pp. 221–24). Norwood, NJ: Ablex.

Simon, S., & Hoyt, C.L. (2008). Exploring the gender gap in support for a woman for president. *Analysis of Social Issues and Public Policy, 8*(1), 151–81.

Sklar, K. Kush. (2008). A woman's history report card on Hillary Rodham Clinton's presidential primary campaign, 2008. *Feminist Studies, 34*(1), 315–22.

Spitzack, C., & Carter, K. (Eds.). (1989). *Doing research on women's communication: Perspectives on theory and research.* Norwood, NJ: Ablex.

Stansell, C. (2008). All fired up: Women, feminism, and misogyny in the Democratic primaries. *Dissent, 55*(4), 34–39.

Trent, J., & Friedenberg, R. (2004). *Presidential campaign communications: Principles and practices* (5th ed.). Lanham, MD: Rowman and Littlefield Publishers.

Walker, M. (2008). The year of the insurgents: The 2008 US presidential campaign. *International Affairs, 84*(6), 1095–1107.

V

Reflective Essays

Chapter Fourteen

Big, Black, Boisterous Badasses

Why Queen-Sized African American Women Are Never Really Royalty

Deatra Sullivan-Morgan

Three predominant stereotypes rule mainstream media depictions of full-figured black women. African American women of size fall into three categories: the "loud and proud Big Mama," the "Beast," and the "WoMan" (the representation of a large black female portrayed by a black male). Diverse audiences have not only embraced these stereotypes, but cling to them as reality. This fantasy turned reality has resulted in distorted self-concepts in terms of African American women, in turn making the entire label of "Queen Sized" a cruel joke. Queens are typically thought of as regal rulers who are larger than life in every way. In contrast, reality finds African American women who weigh much more than the norm to be anything but regal. These women are labeled loud, lazy, crazy, and lewd, along with a host of other less than royal descriptions. I will examine the effects of these stereotypes on full-figured African American women's self-concept, identity management, and rhetorical coping strategies by addressing the disparity between the depicted stereotypes and reality.

SELF-CONCEPT, IDENTITY MANAGEMENT, AND RHETORICAL COPING STRATEGIES

The African American woman's world is one unable to provide an adequate environment for self-conceptualization. Because of this inability and her constant quest to define herself using constructs present in her world, she uses rhetoric to re-create her own self-perception as well as how others perceive her. This rhetoric is steeped in stereotypical Hollywood/media depictions of African American women who are larger than most. These women adapt to the confines of the stereotype and actually "live down" to cultural norms established for obese individuals. Their rhetorical coping strategies include the neck swiveling, eye rolling, gum popping behaviors of a two-tons-of-fun, large and in charge *Sistah*. Unfortunately for her, this Sistah is an example of reaction formation at its worst. Her behavior is in direct contradiction to her true feelings. While her exterior attitude and posturing may say "I'm a queen and loving it!" her self-esteem is damaged by the real knowledge that no amount of posturing can overshadow her stark reality: when you are black, fat, and a woman, royalty is the least likely label to be linked to you. These woman work to re-language negative word associations such as "fat," "obese," or "overweight" with fresh and funny new references to their XL bodies. Terms such as "thick," "big boned," and "queen sized" are tossed around with a wink and a knowing smile. The keen need to survive while appearing to thrive kicks in, and then this Sistah suddenly embodies one of the culturally mediated stereotypes with whom we are all familiar.

THE LOUD AND PROUD BIG MAMA

Tyler Perry's *House of Payne* television comedy serves viewers a huge helping of big, black mother love in the character Ella Payne. Ella is the family matriarch, full of sass, spunk, and a fierce determination to love God, her man, and her family—in that order. The audience is often pleasantly shocked at how limber Ella is in spite of her extra pounds. She meets all of the requirements for a Big Mama. She has the requisite heart of gold, her family loves her and offers complete devotion, and she can take a fat joke with the best of them. The self-deprecating humor Perry weaves throughout the show further impedes any real self-actualization. Ella remains the ever loyal devoted wife, mother, and sisterfriend. After all she is the queen of her household. A closer look by the viewer reveals this sovereign's domain to be far less than fit for a queen; however, her reality is that she is constantly ribbed or depicted in awkward positions because of her weight. Of course, she has thought that losing a few pounds would be good. She has even made a valiant attempt. She did not lose the weight, but she gained loads of laughter as the audience watched her struggle with an exercise video and a personal trainer.

Big Mama finds her validation in the old black saying, "No one wants a bone but a dog." This saying has been around for decades in the African American community, and once affirmed the traditional approval of plus-sized women by black men. According to the National Sexuality Resource

Center, these attitudes are changing, as African American men, products of the middle class, are inclined to adopt more mainstream values, including a preference for thinner women. A January 2004 study (McGee, 2004) published in *The Journal of Black Studies* reported that African American men between the ages of eighteen and thirty-five found smaller women more attractive than women with larger body types. The reality of big, black, and beautiful once reflected and largely accepted in media is now being now rejected by an entire group that finds old norms no longer valid or acceptable. At the same time, the love for Big Mama grows. Why? Perry's theory about the process is interesting and worthy of examination.

Perry maintains that his characters are so loveable and believable because of their authenticity. He claims that all black people know somebody who matches each of his characters. The question becomes, according to Dill (2010), how does the principle of the availability heuristic come into play? Since this principle states that whatever image the media constantly feeds us is the one we readily evoke, it stands to reason that we automatically and subconsciously attribute Big Mama's characteristics to every large African American woman. Thus, Big Mama is with us, always and forever a reminder that while she is not really a queen, or even worthy of our sexual attention, she sure is nice to have around.

THE BEAST

The movie *Precious*, based on the novel by Sapphire, directed by Lee Daniels, and produced by Oprah Winfrey, Tyler Perry, and Lisa Cortes, presents the viewer with two contrasting stereotypes of the Beast. The main character, Clareece "Precious" Jones, is a morbidly obese, illiterate African American teen living in Harlem about to give birth to her second child fathered by her biological father. She is depicted as hopeless and helpless, locked in a mediated fantasy world where she is the star of her own show and "beautiful" like the girls and women she watches on television. Her massive girth results in her awkward gait that really isn't walking but rather a hulking form of lumbering. Her bleak circumstances are significantly worsened by her relationship with the film's other Beast: her mother, Mary Jones.

The fact that Mary is played by actress/comedian Mo'Nique, a celebrated role model for plus-sized women (especially African American women), is quite ironic. Mo'Nique's comic persona is loud, uncouth, and foul mouthed. Despite the fact that she juggles her identity as an African American plus-sized role model and spokeswoman, the media still labels her as a Beast because the negative traits outweigh the positive ones. While real life finds the actress constructing a social image and public identity as an African

American woman who is large, luscious, and lovely, the film casts her as a child-molesting monster whose soul's existence is doubtful . . . in other words, a Beast of epic proportions. She perpetuates her daughter's sexual, physical, verbal, and emotional abuse, all while being complicit with the abuse the girl's father is heaping on his daughter. Mary's monster–like qualities are the stuff of nightmares, and she is definitely her daughter's worst one. The Beast stereotype is brutal, dark, animalistic, and ugly. African American women cast in this light are hardly regarded as even human, much less gendered. Mary's status as Beast casts her in a role that is demoralizing to African American women. Her rhetorical coping strategies are socially unacceptable, and the sickness and shame viewers feel while watching her horrible actions solidify her place as being a "thing" that needs to be exterminated.

THE WO-MAN

A man is the new WoMan in twenty-first-century film. Tyler Perry has joined the growing ranks of men who don "fat" suits and play the roles of large African American women. Perry's character Madea is a staple in both his television series *House of Payne* and *Meet the Browns*, as well as in many of his films. Again Perry states that this character is one all black folks relate to, because they know her all too well. Since mediated communication constantly blurs the line between fantasy and reality, what is really being depicted in this scenario? African American women are being stripped of all that makes them uniquely female and turned into a non-gendered being whose size is its most striking feature. Because the WoMan's true gender is male, she always appears disproportionately large in comparison to all other depicted characters. She is never sexualized, only commodified as a laughable box office draw. Since all of this is done to get laughs and build community with the audience, the serious ramifications are often ignored. To have this image appreciated by the masses is to mock African American women and their essential female nature. The characterization is manipulated and used to get a desired effect with a definite agenda. The WoMan erases and replaces realistic images of African American women with a caricature that borders on vaudeville and minstrel shows.

The fact that this particular stereotype is widely accepted points to the notion of the victim believing the hype. Why would a black woman buy tickets for a movie where the main character is a man engaging in a game of ultimate charades? The answer must lie in that woman's self-concept. She is internalizing the stereotype, and in that internalization lies acceptance.

The 2011 BET Music Awards featured famed singer Patti LaBelle receiving the coveted Lifetime Achievement Award, the evening's highest honor. Patti LaBelle is a *Diva* in every sense of the word. She is viewed as a role model in the African American community: elaborate and elegant, yet a true Sistah—one who can listen to your troubles and solve them, all the while whipping up a delicious soul food meal. Various current chart-topping artists honored Diva Patti by performing her most recognizable hits. Longtime Patti fans smiled and rocked along to her greatest hits when out of the blue it happened: famed singer Cee Lo sang and danced *his* way to center stage rocking a definite "Patti" ensemble complete with diva hair! Cee Lo sang Patti's hit *Somebody Loves You* while the Diva herself laughed, smiled, and sang along. I could not help wondering if Patti in her crowning moment felt as let down and embarrassed as I did.

CONCLUSION

Because the competent media consumer knows that it is *never* "just" a movie or a TV show, the stage is set for individuals, especially African American women, to question the stereotypes and then reject them. Self-actualization of stereotypes needs to be eradicated, starting with the one about being "fat and jolly." African American women of size are being traumatized by the drama these persistent stereotypes portray. The need to clearly redraw the line between fantasy and reality has come. African American women must without delay pick up the chalk.

REFERENCES

Dill, K. E. (2010). *How fantasy becomes reality.* New York: Oxford University Press.
Foss et al. (1991). *Contemporary perspectives on rhetoric.* Prospect Heights, IL: Waveland Press.
hooks, b. (1992). *Black looks: Race and representation.* Boston: South End Press.
McGee, R. (2004). Can a big girl get some love? *Journal of Black Studies,* 226–29.
Norville-Perez, L. C. (2002). Speaking out: Why so many black women are overweight. *Ebony,* 76–79.
Orr, C. (1978). How shall we say: Reality is socially constructed through communication? *Central States Speech Journal, 29,* 263–64.

Chapter Fifteen

Lesbian Comics

Negotiating Queer Visibility

Theresa Carilli

Over the past decade, three prominent lesbian comediennes have ruptured the master narrative by achieving mainstream media fame and celebrity. Rosie O'Donnell, Ellen DeGeneres, and Jane Lynch, against all odds, have received considerable celebrity for their work as comediennes, in both television and film. Does their success signify a cultural shift, an acceptance of lesbians that goes beyond the stereotypical images of the bull dyke or the "girls gone wild" male fantasy?

For lesbians like me who came out in the late 1970s when words such as "gay" or "lesbian" were whispered either with vehement hatred or behind the scenes in unnamed bars located in places known only to others with the same proclivities, watching these three lesbians publicly come out and revel in their identities has been shocking. Back then, such a revelation, in spite of the 1973 American Psychological Association ruling that homosexuality was not aberrant or psychotic behavior, meant losing your family, job, and future. Many of us learned to live in silence, starved for media images of ourselves even if they seemed remote. Shows like *Laverne and Shirley* were a potential oasis. Even though the characters might not be lesbians, many of us sought subtle cues, experiencing Laverne as butch and Shirley as femme.

Now, we have real images, real women who are openly lesbian, in relationships with lesbian partners. While making people laugh, they have contributed to normalizing lesbian relationships because they are likeable and seemingly authentic. For O'Donnell, DeGeneres, and Lynch, the timing was right, and the media world opened the door, helping the general public acknowledge that lesbians can and should be taken seriously.

In 1996, Rosie O'Donnell was dubbed "The Queen of Nice," for inaugurating a new type of talk show where guests were praised for their success. Prior to this, she had appeared in several blockbuster movies like *Sleepless in Seattle* and *A League of Their Own*, always portraying a brash, outspoken woman, with a disarming sense of humor. After *The Rosie O'Donnell Show* ended, O'Donnell came out as a lesbian in 2002, as a result of Florida's ban against gay adoption. In 2006, O'Donnell became a daily host of *The View* until a political argument about the Iraq war with perfectly coifed heterosexist working mother Elisabeth Hasselbeck ended O'Donnell's term. While the argument appeared to be about politics, on some level it was about upholding mainstream heterosexist views and values. During the argument, O'Donnell remarked, "Big fat lesbian loud Rosie attacks innocent pure Christian Elisabeth," echoing her belief that the argument would be characterized in a heterosexist context. *Advertising Age* followed with an article entitled, "Mouth Wide Open: Rosie O'Donnell's very busy week," alluding to her sexuality and the threat it imposed on the American public (Ives, 2007). The network insisted that Rosie was not fired but ended her term at *The View* because of a contract dispute, perhaps corroborated by the fact that the argument took place during the May sweeps—a way that O'Donnell could garner support from her audience and justify her departure. This incident sparked a firestorm of media commentary, demonstrating heterosexual privilege and lesbian marginalization, and as such, promoting an awareness of struggles faced by the LGBT community. Since that time, O'Donnell has been a spokesperson for gay parenting, overseeing numerous children's charities and hosting cable shows directed toward gay parents.

In spite of the non-controversial, a political stance which Ellen DeGeneres adopted after coming out in her 1997 show *Ellen*, DeGeneres has put a likeable, accessible face on the LGBT community, transforming us from secretive weirdos to good, caring American citizens.

Her bold move to come out during an episode of *Ellen* might have resulted in the failure of that show, but this bold move has allowed Ellen to build an empire with her daily talk show. DeGeneres, the tame talk show host of *The Ellen DeGeneres Show*, begins each show with a dance that demystifies her lesbian body. The affection she displays to her male colleagues and guests erodes the stereotype that lesbians hate men. She purposefully tones down her queerness so it is not overtly visible. While DeGeneres's daily dance might seem like a routine part of her show, she allows the audience to view a lesbian body in motion, thus encouraging her heterosexual viewers to make peace with a body that sleeps and engages in sexual activity with women. When DeGeneres married Portia DeRossi, she spoke openly about the event, showing photos to her audience, thus normalizing gay marriage.

Lynch, meanwhile, has struck it big as Sue Sylvester on the television show *Glee*. As Sylvester, the closeted gym teacher bully, Lynch taunts both teachers and students. At times, the taunting becomes mean, and the jokes invoke the stereotype of the butch bulldagger.

Lynch, whether performing comedy club venues or as the sarcastic lawyer and love interest of a college president played by Cybil Shepherd on *The L Word*, has a deadpan comedic manner, accessible to an audience. Tromping around in a sweat suit that marks her closeted status, Lynch's only vulnerability on *Glee* is having a sister with Down's Syndrome. Lynch's character Sue Sylvester was created as a lonely, unlikeable, and difficult individual for whom others feel empathy. As an out lesbian and political activist, Lynch's character collides with that of Sue Sylvester. While stories surface about Lynch as being a wonderful role model to the young cast members of *Glee* and a mother herself, Sue Sylvester has moments of reinscribing the lesbian as a tough, mean, uncaring individual. This rendering might be intended to dispel and humanize lesbian stereotypes, but the depiction is premature, since images of lesbians are still so few. In spite of her sexual identity, Lynch's fame forecasts increased lesbian visibility in the media, and with that visibility will come acceptance.

In the introduction to his book *Media Queered*, Kevin Barnhurst (2007) cautions against the media dichotomy of the LGBT community, caught between being exoticized and being normalized. He writes, "A simple acknowledgement that difference is inescapable is the first step toward understanding what is at stake in queer visibility." O'Donnell, DeGeneres, and Lynch have successfully avoided the pitfall and created rich media identities that will change the landscape of homophobic perception. By calling attention to lesbian identity and increasing media visibility, these three comics contribute to a feminist revolution which values difference, one of the key tenets of the feminist movement. As they maneuver through new terrain, these women become guides for a new feminist frontier.

REFERENCES

Barnhurst, K. (Ed.). (2007). *Media queered: Visibility and its discontents*. New York, NY: Peter Lang Publishing, Inc.

Brennan, I., Kousakis, J. P., Murphy, R., & Falchuk, B. (2009). *Glee*. United States: Fox Broadcasting.

Chaiken, I. (2004–2009). *The L word*. United States: MGM Worldwide Television.

Gabel, J., & Dimich, M. (2001–current) *The Ellen DeGeneres show*. United States: Telepictures.

Geddie, B., & Gentile, M. (2006). *The view*. United States: ABC Productions.

Ives, N. (2007, April). Mouth wide open: Rosie O'Donnell's very busy week. *Advertising Age*, *78*(18), 45.

Kaplan, V., & Trainor, D.O. (1994–1998). *Ellen*. United States: Black-Marlens Co.

Marshall, G. (1976–1983). *Laverne and Shirley*. United States: Paramount Television.
Marshall, P. (1992). *A League of their own*. United States: Columbian Pictures Corp.
Obst, L., & Ephon, N. (1993). *Sleepless in Seattle*. United States: Tristar Pictures.
O'Donnell, R., & Cabeca, A., (1996–2002). *The Rosie O'Donnell show*. United States: KidRo
    Productions.

Selected Bibliography

Alat, Z. (2006). News coverage of violence against women. *Feminist Media Studies*, *6*(3), 295–314.

Al-Mahadin, S. (2011). Arab feminist media studies. *Feminist Media Studies*, *11*(1), 7–12.

Ammu, J., & Kalpana, S. (2006). *Whose news? The media and women's issues*. Thousand Oaks, CA: Sage Publications Inc.

Ayish, Muhammad I. (2010). Understanding Arab women's role in media industries: An empowerment-based perspective. *Journal of Arab and Muslim Media Research*, *3*(3), 191–206.

Barker-Plummer, B. (2010). News and feminism: A historic dialog. *Journalism and Communication Monographs*, *12*(3/4), 145–203.

Bollinger, L., & O'Neill, C. (2008). *Women in media careers: Success despite the odds*. Lanham, MD: University Press of America.

Bronstein, C. (2005). Representing the third wave: Mainstream print media framing of a new feminist movement. *Journalism and Mass Communication Quarterly*, *82*(4), 783–803.

Byerly, C. M., & Ross, K. (2006). *Women and media: A critical introduction*. Indianapolis, IN: Wiley-Blackwell.

Carilli, T., & Campbell, J. (2005). *Women and the media: Diverse perspectives*. Lanham, MD: University Press of America.

Chen, Y. (2009). Negotiating fragmented women's news: State, market, and feminism in contemporary Chinese media. *Asian Journal of Communication*, *19*(1), 97–115.

Cole, E., Henderson, J. D., & Daniel, J. H. (2005). *Featuring females: Feminist analyses of media*. New York, NY: American Psychological Association.

Creedon, P. J., & Cramer, J. (2006). *Women in mass communication* (3rd ed.). Thousand Oaks, CA: Sage Publications Inc.

Cuklanz, L. M. (2006). Television's "new" feminism: Prime-time representations of women and victimization. *Critical Studies in Mass Communication*, *23*(4), 302–21.

Davis, A. M. (2005). The "dark prince" and dream women: Walt Disney and mid-twentieth century American feminism. *Historical Journal of Film, Radio, and Television*, *25*(2), 213–30.

D'Enbeau, S. (2011). Sex, feminism, and advertising: The politics of advertising feminism in a competitive marketplace. *Journal of Communication Inquiry*, *35*(1), 53–69.

Ford, C. (2007). Women in the media can't have it all. *Media*, *13*(1), 16–17.

Friedman, B., Kitch C., Lueck T., Winfield B., & Roessner A.(2009). Stirred, not yet shaken: Integrating women's history into media history. *American Journalism*, *26*(1), 160–74.

Geertsema, M. (2009). Women and news. *Feminist Media Studies*, *9*(2), 149–72.

Gill, R. (2007). *Gender and the media*. Cambridge, England: Polity Press.

Hamilton, C. (2009). Feminist testimony in the Internet age: Sex work, blogging and the politics of witnessing. *Journal of Romance Studies*, *9*(3), 86–101.

Helford, E. R. (2006). The Stepford wives and the gaze. *Feminist Media Studies*, *6*(2), 145–56.

Hua, J. (2009). "Gucci geishas" and post-feminism. *Women's Studies in Communication*, *32*(1), 63–88.

Kim, S. (2008). Feminist discourse and the hegemonic role of mass media. *Feminist Media Studies*, *8*(4), 391–406.

Lewis, N. P. (2008). From cheesecake to chief: Newspaper editors' slow acceptance of women. *American Journalism*, *25*(2), 33–55.

McRobbie, A. (2008). Young women and consumer culture. *Cultural Studies*, *22*(5), 531–50.

Minic, D. (2008). What makes an issue a woman's hour issue? *Feminist Media Studies*, *8*(3), 301–15.

North, L. (2009). Rejecting the "f-word": How "feminism" and "feminists" are understood in the newsroom. *Journalism*, *10*(6), 739–57.

Pozner, J. L. (2005). Reclaiming the media for a progressive feminist future. *Media Development*, *52*(3), 12–17.

Press, A. L. (2011). Feminism and media in the post-feminist era. *Feminist Media Studies*, *11*(1), 107–13.

Radovic, M. (2005). Images of women in Serbian media. *Media Development*, *52*(3), 45–49.

Robinson, G. J. (2008). Feminist approaches to journalism studies: Canadian perspectives. *Global Media Journal: Canadian Edition*, *1*(1), 123–36.

Ross, K. (2011). *The handbook of gender, sex, and media.* Indianapolis, IN: Wiley-Blackwell.

———. (2009). *Women, men, and identity politics.* Lanham, MD: Rowman and Littlefield Publications, Inc.

Stephenson, S. (2007). The changing face of women's magazines in Russia. *Journalism Studies*, *8*(4), 613–20.

Thornham, S. (2007). *Women, feminism and the media.* Edinburgh, Scotland: Edinburgh University Press.

Selected Websites

About-face, www.about-face.org
Alliance for Women in Media, www.allwomeninmedia.org
Girls, Women and Media Project, www.mediaandwomen.org
Guerilla Girls, www.guerillagirls.com
International Women's Media Foundation, www.iwmf.org
Media Awareness Network, www.media-awareness.ca
Media Report to Women, www.mediareporttowomen.com
Women in Media and News, www.wimnonline.org
The Women's Media Center, www.womensmediacenter.com

Index

About the Contributors

ABOUT THE EDITORS

Theresa Carilli, PhD (Southern Illinois University), is a professor of communication at Purdue University Calumet. Her two areas of concentration include media studies and playwriting. She has published two anthologies which delve into media depictions of women and ethnicity (*Women and the Media: Diverse Perspectives*, 2005, coedited with Jane Campbell; and *Cultural Diversity and the U.S. Media*, 1998, coedited with Yahya Kamalipour). She coedited a special issue of women and the media for the online *Global Media Journal* with Jane Campbell. As a playwright, Carilli has published two books of plays (*Familial Circles*, 2000; and *Women as Lovers*, 1996). She edited a special theater issue of the journal, *Voices in Italian Americana*. Her plays have been produced in San Francisco, San Diego, Victoria, B.C., Melbourne, Australia, Athens, Greece, and most recently, New York City. Her book, *Scripting Identity: Writing Cultural Experience*, features student scripts. Carilli has published numerous performance articles and creative scripts. She is currently working on an anthology of articles which explores media depictions of the LGBT community with her partner and colleague, Jane Campbell.

Jane Campbell, professor of English at Purdue University Calumet, received her BA from the University of Arkansas and her MA and PhD from Northern Illinois University. She is the author of *Mythic Black Fiction: The Transformation of History* (1986). Her literary criticism has appeared in *Callaloo: A Journal of African and African American Arts and Letters*, *Obsidian*, *Black Women in America*, *The Oxford Companion to Women's Writing in the U. S.*, the *Dictionary of Literary Biography*, the *Heath Anthology* *of American Literature, Belles Lettres,* and *U.S. Media and the Middle East: Image and Perception.* She coedited, with Theresa Carilli, *Women and the Media: Diverse Perspectives* (2005). In 2006 she coedited a special issue on women and the media for the *Global Media Journal* with Theresa Carilli. Currently, with her partner and colleague Theresa Carilli, she is editing a new anthology of articles about depictions of the LGBT community.

ABOUT THE CONTRIBUTORS

Rukhsana Ahmed, PhD (University of Ohio), is an assistant professor in the Department of Communication at the University of Ottawa. Her research interests lie at the intersections of health, interpersonal, intercultural, gender development, religious diversity, and ethnic media. Her scholarship has been published in mainstream communication journals, health studies outlets, nursing journals, and in journals at the intersections of health, communication, and culture, and in several book chapters. She has presented numerous papers at regional, national, and international conferences and conventions.

Kimiko Akita, PhD, associate professor in the School of Communication at the University of Central Florida in Orlando, teaches international and intercultural communication and a cultural studies honors seminar in *manga* and *anime*. Her more than two dozen research articles on gender and cross-cultural issues have appeared in books and journals including *Global Media Journal, Women and the Media: Diverse Perspectives*, and the *Journal of Mass Media Ethics*.

Saayan Chattopadhyay is an assistant professor and head of the Department of Journalism and Mass Communication at Baruipur College, affiliated with the Calcutta University. He has published articles and book chapters in *Studies in South Asian Film and Media, South Asia Research, Journal of Contemporary Literature, Sarai Reader*, and *Journal of Boyhood Proteus: A Journal of Ideas*. His research interests include masculinity studies, performative theory, postcolonial journalism, sexuality, and the body in Bengal.

Nicole Defenbaugh, PhD (Bloomsburg University), uses rhetorical, critical, and interpretive approaches to researching the construction of illness identity. She recently published a book on hidden chronic illness entitled, *Dirty Tale: A Narrative Journey of the IBD Body*. Dr. Defenbaugh has been awarded multiple grants to improve provider-patient communication and has won several awards (e.g., Ellis-Bochner and Norman K. Denzin). She has published in journals such as the *International Review of Qualitative Research*, *Qualitative Inquiry*, and *Journal of Health Communication* and has forthcoming articles in *Health Communication* and *Women & Language*.

Lisa French is an associate professor of cinema studies, media, and communication at RMIT University where she is the head of cinema studies. She is the coauthor of the books, *Shining a Light: 50 Years of the Australian Film Institute* (2009) and *Womenvision: Women and the Moving Image in Australia* (2003). She has published widely on the cinema and the Australian film industry, particularly in relation to gender.

Barbara Friedman is an associate professor at the University of North Carolina of Journalism and Mass Communication. Her teaching and research areas include historical and contemporary mass media representations of gender and race. She is a former newspaper editor and reporter, whose work has appeared in the *Chicago Tribune* and the *New York Times*.

Elza Ibroscheva, PhD (Southern Illinois University), is an associate professor and director of graduate studies in the Department of Mass Communications, Southern Illinois University, Edwardsville. She has authored several book chapters on Eastern European media, including research on Bulgarian women in politics. Her work has been published in the *Howard Journal of Communication*, *International Journal of Communication*, and *Sex Roles: Journal of Research*. Her research interests include gender representations in the media as well as the effects of globalization on culture.

Zara Idrees holds an MPhil degree in communication and media studies (Beaconhouse National University, Lahore, Pakistan). She has a forthcoming publication in the *Journal of Human Rights*.

Elizabeth Johnson is an assistant professor of history and social sciences at Governors State University in University Park, Illinois. Dr. Johnson's research and speaking interests are grounded in group identity and critical race theory including hair aesthetics, body image, nineteenth-century U.S. history, and media representations of ethnicity and gender.

Anne Johnston is a professor in the School of Journalism and Mass Communication at the University of North Carolina in Chapel Hill. Her research interests include political communication, political advertising, women political bloggers, diversity issues in the media, and media's framing of sex trafficking. She is codirector of The Irina Project (TIP), which provides resources for the responsible and accurate reporting of sex trafficking.

Kimberly N. Kline, PhD (University of Georgia), is an associate professor at the University of Texas at San Antonio. Her research focuses on the social construction of health, illness, and medicine, especially with regard to women's health issues. Her publications address topics including the theoretical and methodological issues in the study of health and popular media, and the use of textual analysis to evaluate the persuasive potential of health education materials.

Lynn Marie Kutch is an assistant professor at Kutztown University of Pennsylvania. She has published on the German playwright Ilse Langner, and on using drama pedagogy to teach Ruth Klinger's *weiter leben* (Still Alive) Holocaust memoir. She has forthcoming articles in Veit Muller's regional crime fiction, and is currently conducting research on the utility of German graphic novels for the language classroom. She devotes much of her professional time and efforts to advocacy and program-building.

Wei Luo, PhD, is an assistant professor of communication at Indiana University/Purdue University Fort Wayne. Luo's current research explores the intersecting issues of gender, ethnicity, and class in Chinese consumer culture. Luo would like to thank the two editors for their insights, suggestions, and editorial assistance.

Lori L. Montalbano, PhD (Southern Illinois University), is an associate professor of communication, chair of the Department of Performing Arts at Indiana University Northwest, and artistic director of *Theatre Northwest*. Montalbano has published a book entitled *Taking Narrative Risk: The Empowerment of Abuse Survivors* along with several articles and book chapters. She has recently coauthored a textbook, *Public Speaking and Responsibility in a Changing World*, with Dr. Dorothy W. Ige.

Vanessa Reimer is a PhD student in York University's Women's Studies Programme in Toronto, Canada. Her research examines sexual purity discourses in Evangelical Christian devotional literature through a religious feminist methodological framework. She is currently coediting an anthology for Demeter Press entitled *Mother of Invention: How Our Mothers Influenced Us as Feminist Academics and Activists*, to be published in 2014.

Autumn Shafer, PhD (University of North Carolina), is an assistant professor in the College of Mass Communications at Texas Tech University. Her research investigates the effects of exposure to mass media on health-related beliefs, attitudes, and behaviors. Her principal topical focus is sexual health among adolescents. She approaches research questions from an interdisciplinary perspective that draws from communication, public health, social psychology, and consumer behavior.

Steven Carl Smith is a PhD candidate in history at the University of Missouri. Named the 2012 Malkin New Scholar by the Bibliographical Society of America, he has received fellowships from the American Antiquarian Society, the Library Company of Philadelphia, the Gilder Lehrman Institute of American History, the New York Public Library, and the New York State Library.

Deatra Sullivan-Morgan, PhD, is an associate professor of communication at Elmhurst College. Her research focuses on the rhetoric and rhetorical coping strategies of marginalized communities. She teaches a variety of communication classes including Intercultural Communication, Interpersonal Communication, and Media Influences and Cultural Identity.

Saman Talib, PhD (Rutgers University), focuses her research on the nexus of new media and social change. She studies the various conceptualizations of "new media" and how technological innovations impact social conventions. Talib has published work on the media portrayal of minorities and dissenting voices. She has taught and conducted research in the United States and Pakistan.